The Ghost in the Machine Reconsidered
Metacognitive Compatibilism and Human Agency

Joshua Robertson

THE GHOST IN THE MACHINE RECONSIDERED, Metacognitive Compatibilism and Human Agency

First edition. October 13, 2025.

Copyright © 2025 Joshua Robertson.

All rights reserved. No part of this publication may be reproduced, distributed, or transmitted in any form or by any means, including photocopying, recording, or other electronic or mechanical methods, without the prior written permission of the publisher, except in the case of brief quotations embodied in critical reviews and certain other noncommercial uses permitted by copyright law.

Printed in the United States of America

Table of Contents

The Exhausted Binary 1

The Ghost of the Past 63

The Mind Observing Mind 90

The Architecture of Becoming 124

The Metacognitive Hierarchy 173

An Expressivist Foundation 203

Graduated Responsibility in Practice 248

Collective Cognitive Evolution 293

Natural Self-Creation 327

Further Reading and Selected Bibliography 369

Index 376

About the Author 382

The Ghost in the Machine Reconsidered

Metacognitive Compatibilism and Human Agency

Joshua Robertson

The Exhausted Binary

"What if freedom were not the absence of chains, but the forging of better ones?"

PHILOSOPHY HAS LONG BEEN haunted by a ghost we call freedom. The question of its nature has tormented thinkers since its inception, often trapping them in a false dichotomy that obscures more nuanced possibilities. From Aristotle's musings on voluntary action to contemporary debates between determinists and libertarians, our discourse tends to swing between extremes. Either we are ghosts in the machine, exercising uncaused agency that exempts us from the natural order, or we are sophisticated automata whose choices are no more than the universe's inevitable self-expression through neural machinery. The longer this debate persists, the more it seems to revolve around its own axis, producing more heat than light. What continues to escape notice is not simply which side is right, but whether the very structure of the debate has led us away from the phenomenon we hope to understand.

This enduring binary has blinded us to the quiet, almost imperceptible ways human behavior develops, persists, and evolves over a lifetime.

We are like those early astronomers who, in their desire for a tidy cosmos, insisted the stars must move in perfect circles. By imposing such rigid categories, they obscured the true complexity of the universe, rendering their models not merely wrong but absurd. Yet, like them, we insist on seeking simplicity, perhaps because the real mechanisms of human freedom are messier, slower, and far less predictable than any tidy god-or-machines trap allows. Perhaps because acknowledging this complexity would force us to abandon the comfortable illusion that human agency can be reduced to a simple either-or proposition.

Before us lies a choice that isn't really a choice: a real ghost or a mere machine, exemption or subjection, miraculous transcendence or mechanical reduction.

Yet what if this forced march between impossible alternatives conceals the very territory where genuine human agency dwells? What if there exists a capacity that traditional philosophical categories cannot capture, one that operates neither through supernatural intervention nor mechanical determinism, but through something more subtle and more powerful?

Consider the person who recognizes destructive patterns in their relationships and begins the slow work of change. They cannot simply will different behavior into existence through some miraculous act of choice. Neither do they remain helplessly trapped by their conditioning. Instead, they engage in what I call temporal scaffolding, the systematic use of present cognitive resources to construct the decision environments that will shape future behavior. They seek therapy to understand their patterns, cultivate friendships that model healthier dynamics, establish practices that strengthen their capacity for reflection and restraint, and gradually architect the conditions under which their future selves will choose differently. This surpasses the false dichotomy altogether. It is the deliberate arrangement of causal conditions so that determination works in the service of chosen ends rather than against them.

Such capacity emerges from what I term metacognitive compatibilism, or the recognition that while all mental events occur within deterministic systems, the hierarchical structure of human cognition creates possibilities for systematic self-modification that are both causally grounded and practically significant.

This represents no return to traditional compatibilism, which typically focuses on reconciling determinism with moral responsibility by showing how they might peacefully coexist. Instead, metacognitive compatibilism investigates how determined cognitive systems can engage in sophisticated forms of causal architecture, deliberately structuring the conditions under which future choices will emerge. Like architects who cannot violate the laws of physics but can use them to create structures that would not arise spontaneously, conscious agents cannot escape causation, but they can deploy causal understanding to build behavioral patterns that express their deepest values and most considered judgments.

Human freedom is not merely a theoretical problem. Consider the courtroom where a judge must sentence a teenager whose still-developing brain made choices no adult would make. Consider the classroom where educators must motivate students whose attention has been fractured by a digital world that evolves faster than pedagogical theory. Consider the therapist's office where a person seeks help with behaviors they understand intellectually but cannot seem to modify. Our legal systems, educational institutions, and therapeutic practices all depend on a coherent account of human agency, yet they are built upon what amounts to metaphysical quicksand. We construct our most crucial social institutions without adequate understanding of the very capacity they presuppose, then wonder why they sink beneath the weight of genuine human complexity.

Contemporary neuroscience and psychology reveal the complex, layered mechanisms that drive human thought and behavior, unsettling our traditional notions of agency. Human action appears less a product of absolute, uncaused freedom and more an emergent response, the result of a dynamic interplay between neural processes and environmental conditions.

We are left to confront an uneasy tension between the dignity promised by metaphysical ideals and the mechanistic reality science appears to uncover. Yet this tension dissolves when we recognize that the hierarchical organization of human cognition creates genuine possibilities for self-modification that operate through deterministic processes rather than despite them.

The root of our philosophical paralysis lies in shared assumptions that constrain all sides of the traditional debate. All positions assume that genuine freedom requires ultimate origination, meaning we must be the absolute source of our actions, or we lack real agency. They treat causation as a purely mechanical force that either completely determines outcomes or allows for random intervention. And crucially, all assume that moral responsibility hinges on backward-looking notions of what an agent inherently deserves, rooted in the metaphysical fabric of their being.

These assumptions create a false choice that has fuddled philosophical progress for centuries, preventing recognition of how human agency truly operates through temporal scaffolding and metacognitive architecture. Rather than existing as a sudden spark of uncaused freedom or as the mechanical output of impersonal forces, agency takes shape across time, built gradually through habits, reflection, and the environments that sustain or erode them. To miss this is to mischaracterize the very phenomenon under investigation, mistaking its scaffolding for a prison or its architecture for an illusion. Only by shifting our perspective from impossible absolutes to lived processes can we begin to see how freedom emerges within human life.

The Libertarian Sanctuary

Libertarian free will asks us to believe that human choices are not only real but also capable of producing genuine effects in the world without being bound by the same natural laws that govern every other event. It envisions a form of causation set apart, as though the mind could reach into the stream of physical reality while never being carried along by its current.

In this view, a thought is not just a byproduct of the brain but something that rises above it, able to move the body and shape events while remaining untouched itself. The mind appears as a kind of sovereign power, suspended above the machinery of nature, exercising a form of agency that transcends the causal web that binds everything else in existence.

At the heart of libertarianism lies the claim that genuine human choice requires exemption from the causal chains that govern everything else in nature. When we deliberate about whether to help a stranger in need, alternative futures genuinely hang in the balance until our choice actualizes one possibility and forecloses others. Decisions emerge from us as agents rather than from prior events that made the decision inevitable. When someone chooses to donate money to charity, that choice must be neither random nor the inevitable result of character, circumstance, or reasoning. It must emerge from agency in a way that transcends both chance and necessity. A compassionate character provides context for choice without determining it. Reasoning about the charity's effectiveness informs the choice without compelling it. The choice itself represents a genuine creative act that brings something new into existence, something that was not contained in the prior state of the world.

This view has a powerful appeal because it preserves moral responsibility in its strongest form.

It allows individuals to be the ultimate source of their actions. Praise or blame can be deserved because choices truly flow from essential agency rather than external determinants. The view aligns with our immediate experience of deliberation, where we feel that alternatives genuinely compete for actualization rather than a predetermined outcome merely playing itself out. If someone hesitates before deciding whether to intervene when a stranger falls in the street, we sense that the decision itself shapes what happens next and that our moral attention matters in a way that makes a real difference. The libertarian preserves this intuitive sense that our choices matter not just as links in a causal chain but as genuine expressions of agency that could have been otherwise.

Yet libertarian freedom faces decisive challenges, particularly from modern neuroscience.

If choices are uncaused by prior events, they appear random rather than free. A truly uncaused choice would bear no connection to the agent's character, values, or reasoning. It would be arbitrary, happening to coincide with the agent rather than expressing rational agency. The choice would be no more "mine" than a coin flip that happens to occur in my brain.

Experiments consistently show that brain activity predicts decisions hundreds of milliseconds before individuals report awareness of having made a choice. What feels like a conscious choice is often the brain's after-the-fact interpretation of processes that have largely already occurred unconsciously. The experience of choosing appears to be consciousness catching up with decisions that neural processes have already made, like a narrator explaining events that have already unfolded rather than a director shaping events as they occur.

These findings extend beyond simple motor actions to complex moral and practical decisions. Brain imaging reveals activity in reward-processing regions during charitable giving, suggesting that generous behavior reflects automatic evaluation of social rewards rather than purely altruistic choice. Economic decisions show neural patterns that anticipate choices before conscious awareness, indicating that even careful deliberation operates largely outside conscious control.

As neuroscience continues to map the brain, the less room there appears to be for a hidden agent pulling the strings. What once seemed like a miracle now appears as a mechanism, and what once seemed inexplicable becomes familiar cause and effect. To hold onto libertarian freedom, one must retreat into the shadows where our knowledge remains incomplete, but those shadows are shrinking with each advance in neuroscience, leaving the ghost in the machine with fewer places to hide.

In response to these challenges, libertarian theorists have developed increasingly sophisticated models that attempt to preserve genuine agency within naturalistic constraints.

Robert Kane introduces the concept of self-forming actions, arguing that certain critical moments of moral conflict allow indeterminacy in the brain to influence macro-level choices. When someone faces a difficult decision between honesty and personal advantage, quantum indeterminacy in neural processes might enable a choice that is neither determined by prior character nor completely random. These self-forming actions occur at pivotal junctures in moral development, shaping future character in ways that preserve responsibility. Choosing honesty over personal gain in a decisive moment can make future honest choices more likely, even if the original choice remains undetermined by prior events. Kane emphasizes that such moments preserve moral responsibility because they are anchored in the agent's effortful deliberation rather than mere chance, creating islands of genuine agency in an otherwise determined world.

Timothy O'Connor develops agent-causal theories, treating agents as substances with special causal powers that differ fundamentally from ordinary event causation. In his view, agents can cause events without those events being fully determined by prior neural or physical events. When someone chooses to comfort a grieving colleague or to help a friend move, the decision emerges from rational consideration of reasons rather than being compelled by prior events. The agent as substance exercises a form of causation that transcends the mechanical processes operating in their brain, reaching into the physical world to shape events while remaining partially exempt from the causal closure that governs everything else. O'Connor's account allows moral responsibility to remain robust because the agent, rather than chance or physical processes alone, is the true source of action.

Even these sophisticated approaches face persistent challenges that reveal the depth of the libertarian's predicament.

Kane's reliance on quantum indeterminacy risks making moral choices partly random, which threatens the rational grounding that responsibility requires. If the difference between choosing honesty and choosing deception depends partly on quantum events in the brain, how can the agent be credited with the choice rather than simply lucky in their neural lottery?

O'Connor's agent causation must explain how immaterial agency interacts with the physical brain without violating causal closure or collapsing into ordinary event causation. As neuroscience advances, experiments increasingly extend the time window between detectable neural activity and reported conscious choice. Techniques such as transcranial magnetic stimulation can influence decision-making by manipulating brain activity, suggesting that choices depend on physical states rather than immaterial intervention. Libertarian theories must therefore explain how conscious choice intervenes in neural processes in ways that current neuroscience cannot detect, at locations and timescales that appear increasingly implausible as our knowledge of the brain advances.

Libertarian theories remain compelling in principle because they honor our experience of deliberation and our sense of being genuine sources of action. At the same time, they confront a growing tension between the philosophical ideal of undetermined moral agency and the empirical reality of decision-making as a process rooted in neural activity that unfolds according to discoverable patterns and mechanisms. This tension highlights the central problem for libertarian freedom: it must explain how agents can remain genuinely free in a world where the brain appears to account for both ordinary and morally significant choices.

The libertarian seeks to preserve human dignity by exempting agents from the causal order; however, this exemption threatens to render agency mysterious rather than meaningful, random rather than rational. Any further defense will need to grapple with the narrowing space for such agency, clarifying exactly where and how it could operate without being either arbitrary or reducible to brain processes that operate according to natural laws.

The Determinist Capitulation

Hard determinism offers an alternative that is brutally consistent but emotionally costly. This opposing position accepts the implications of naturalistic science by denying that humans possess genuine agency or deserve moral responsibility in any ultimate sense.

In this view, human beings are natural objects subject to the same causal laws as everything else. If every human action follows inevitably from the conditions that came before it, then the story of our lives is no different from the path of a comet or the motion of a tide. What we call choice becomes nothing more than the conscious registration of deterministic processes, no different in principle from the "choice" a river makes when flowing downhill toward the sea.

What feels like choice becomes nothing more than the working out of necessity through neural mechanisms that create an illusion of alternatives. Whether it is a parent who thinks they are shaping a child's character, the friend who believes their words can change another's path, or the individual who struggles against their own destructive impulses, each is caught in a drama whose ending was fixed long before the curtain ever rose. On this view, the first spark that ignited the stars already contained every heartbreak, every triumph, and every quiet decision we mistakenly thought was our own.

Human consciousness becomes a passive observer of events it cannot influence, a narrator of stories it did not write, forever telling itself that it is the author of actions that were inevitable from the moment the universe began.

When someone helps a person in need, this action inevitably flows from compassionate character traits that result from fortunate genetics and nurturing experiences over which they had no control. When someone commits a crime, this action stems from antisocial character traits that result from unfortunate genetics and traumatic experiences that shaped their development in ways they could not choose or resist. In neither case does the individual deserve praise or blame for outcomes that were determined by their causal history.

The logic appears airtight and ruthlessly consistent. To be truly responsible for an action, you would need to be accountable for the mental states and character traits that produced it. However, those mental states and character traits were shaped by genetics, upbringing, social environment, and formative experiences that were entirely beyond your control. Since you are not responsible for the factors that shaped your character, you cannot be responsible for actions that flow from that character. The chain of responsibility leads backward through causes you did not create until it disappears entirely into factors that preceded your existence. Your parents shaped your character, but they were shaped by their own parents and the circumstances of their upbringing. Your genes influence your behavior, but you did not choose your genes. Your social environment significantly affects your development, but you did not choose it.

At no point in this causal chain do we find the ultimate self-creation that responsibility would seem to require.

Consider a specific case that illuminates this logic with uncomfortable clarity. Someone grows up in poverty with parents who struggle with addiction and mental illness. They receive inadequate education, experience trauma and neglect, and lack positive role models or opportunities for legitimate advancement. When they later commit crimes, the determinist argues, they are not truly blameworthy because their criminal behavior emerged from circumstances they did not choose and could have been predicted by anyone who understood their history. Their actions, however harmful, represent the inevitable unfolding of causal processes that were set in motion before they possessed the capacity for moral reflection or choice.

To blame them for crimes that resulted from such circumstances seems as senseless as blaming a tree for falling in the direction the wind was already blowing.

This analysis extends equally to positive actions, eliminating not only blame but also praise from our moral vocabulary.

Someone who grows up in a stable, loving family with good educational opportunities and positive role models may develop into a generous, law-abiding citizen who makes meaningful contributions to their community. However, they deserve no special credit for this outcome, as their virtuous character was largely the result of fortunate circumstances beyond their control. Their generosity reflects the working out of favorable conditioning rather than genuine moral achievement. The determinist strips away not only guilt but also pride, not only condemnation but also celebration, leaving only the recognition that all human action unfolds according to forces that operate through us rather than from us.

Contemporary philosophers have developed this foundational logic with systematic precision. Derk Pereboom, for instance, extends the regress argument to challenge not just deterministic views but libertarian ones as well, describing his view as hard incompatibilism. His reasoning sharpens the determinist conclusion through analysis of the conditions moral responsibility appears to require.

If determinism is true, our choices are the inevitable outcome of prior causes beyond our control. If determinism is false and our actions contain elements of indeterminism, this introduces chance into the system, which in turn undermines responsibility by rendering actions random rather than rational. Even in the libertarian picture, agents act from character traits and motives they did not ultimately create. Since ultimate self-creation is impossible, which is to say we cannot create ourselves ex nihilo, the kind of moral responsibility we ordinarily ascribe to people cannot exist in any coherent form.

Pereboom argues that eliminating moral responsibility would not unravel morality or social cooperation, contrary to the fears of those who view responsibility as essential to human community. The practices most essential to human life can survive without the fiction of ultimate desert. Parents may still cultivate virtues in their children, not because the child will one day deserve praise or blame for their character, but because such formation helps shape healthier individuals and communities. Societies may still protect themselves from those who pose dangers, not as retribution against culpable agents, but as a means of safeguarding the vulnerable and discouraging destructive behavior through behavioral modification. Even in personal relationships, people may still seek repair after betrayal or harm, not because the wrongdoer deserves blame in some ultimate metaphysical sense, but because reconciliation restores the bonds necessary for shared life and mutual flourishing.

From this perspective, the loss of ultimate responsibility does not mean the loss of morality, but rather a reorientation of morality toward forward-looking aims that remain coherent even in a determined world.

Bruce Waller focuses the critique specifically on the psychological capacities that moral responsibility itself requires, arguing that these foundational abilities are themselves products of factors beyond individual control.

To be morally responsible, an individual must possess capacities for rational reflection, impulse control, and understanding of moral requirements. However, these capacities themselves result from genetic endowments, developmental experiences, and social influences that are entirely beyond individual control. Someone who lacks empathy due to genetic factors or childhood trauma cannot be blamed for antisocial behavior that flows from this psychological limitation, as they never possessed the emotional foundation that moral behavior requires. Again, however, someone who possesses strong empathy due to fortunate genetics and nurturing experiences cannot be credited solely for prosocial behavior that stems from this psychological advantage, as they did not create the emotional capacities that enable their moral success.

The psychological foundations of moral agency are themselves matters of luck rather than personal achievement, making moral responsibility impossible regardless of the metaphysical status of free will.

Decades of research in social psychology provide empirical support for this determinist position, revealing how powerfully situations influence behavior in ways that override individual moral character. In one famous experiment, seminary students preparing to give a presentation about the Good Samaritan parable—which explicitly teaches the importance of helping those in need—were sent to a nearby building. Some were told they were running late; others had time to spare. On their way, they encountered a person slumped in a doorway, appearing to need help. The results proved striking: students told to hurry were far less likely to stop and help than those with time, demonstrating that situational factors (being in a hurry) had greater influence on helping behavior than individual factors (being religious students literally thinking about compassion). Classic experiments by Milgram (obedience to authority), Asch (conformity to group pressure), and Zimbardo (adoption of assigned roles) reveal similar patterns: situational pressures consistently override individual moral convictions. Even basic moral judgments can be influenced by irrelevant environmental factors, such as whether people are in clean or messy surroundings when making moral evaluations. If moral behavior depends more on situational factors than individual character, and those situational factors remain largely beyond personal control, then moral responsibility appears to dissolve entirely.

Yet this determinist position faces serious problems that undermine its philosophical viability and practical coherence.

Most obviously, it undermines itself by making all beliefs, including belief in determinism, products of causal forces rather than rational evaluation of evidence. If determinists believe in determinism only because their brains were caused to believe it by prior neural states and environmental influences, why should anyone take their arguments seriously rather than dismissing them as the inevitable outputs of particular causal histories? The determinist cannot appeal to the rational force of their arguments while simultaneously maintaining that rationality itself is an illusion created by deterministic processes.

The position becomes self-refuting by eliminating the rational agency required to evaluate its own truth claims or to distinguish good arguments from bad ones.

More practically, hard determinism eliminates the moral emotions and practices that appear essential to human social cooperation and individual psychological health. When someone harms us, we naturally feel resentment and anger. When someone helps us, we feel gratitude and appreciation. These emotional responses appear built into human psychology rather than optional attitudes that could be eliminated through philosophical arguments. Hard determinism provides no satisfactory account of how these moral emotions could be eliminated from human life or why they should be eliminated, given that they serve important social functions in maintaining cooperation and relationship bonds.

The reactive attitudes that P.F. Strawson identified as central to moral responsibility practices appear to be fundamental features of human psychology that enable social cooperation and relationship maintenance. These are not mere philosophical errors that could be corrected through a better understanding of causation.

Hard determinism also fails to provide adequate frameworks for understanding how behavioral change occurs or can be promoted. If all behavior flows inevitably from prior causes, there is no basis for preferring some behaviors over others or for developing strategies to encourage beneficial change. The view becomes practically self-defeating by eliminating the very agency required to act on its insights into human psychology. When hard determinists argue that we should eliminate moral responsibility practices and adopt alternative approaches to behavioral modification, they presuppose the agency and rational choice-making that their theory denies.

If people cannot choose to accept or reject philosophical arguments, then there is no point in making such arguments. If behavior change is simply the inevitable result of prior causes, then there is no basis for preferring one kind of cause over another or for deliberately creating conditions that promote desired changes.

Yet recent developments in cognitive science and neuroscience suggest an escape from this either-or prison that has trapped philosophical thinking about human agency. Rather than treating determinism as a monolithic force that either does or does not apply to human action, we can recognize that different types of causal processes possess different properties and potentials for human agency.

Some forms of behavioral determination operate through immediate stimulus-response mechanisms with minimal cognitive mediation, such as the startle response that jerks your body away from sudden sounds, the emotional contagion that spreads panic through crowds, or the many habitual behaviors that are triggered automatically by environmental cues. Others involve complex recursive processes where cognitive systems monitor, evaluate, and modify their own operations across extended temporal horizons. For instance, deliberative reasoning that weighs competing values against long-term consequences, systematic planning that sacrifices present gratification for future goals, or metacognitive processes that use present insight to reconstruct future choice architectures.

The difference between these types of causal processes is not that one is determined while the other is free, but that they operate through different mechanisms with different potentials for conscious participation and systematic modification.

There is something uniquely human about our capacity to take today's limitations and transform them into tomorrow's possibilities. History shows us again and again that we do not simply endure constraints but learn to turn them into instruments of progress and growth. Perhaps this capacity for temporal scaffolding, more than any metaphysical gamble about ultimate origination, is what makes us most distinctively human and provides the foundation for a coherent account of human agency within naturalistic frameworks.

The Compatibilist Compromise

Traditional attempts to preserve moral responsibility within a deterministic world do not reject causation but instead reconsider what freedom means in light of it. The claim is that a person can be free even when every event has a cause, so long as the way an action comes about reflects the right kind of process. What matters is not whether someone escapes determination, but whether the determination runs through them in a manner that expresses who they are.

From this standpoint, an act counts as free when it grows out of an agent's desires, values, and character, even if those very traits were themselves shaped by genetic inheritance, upbringing, and circumstance. The absence of ultimate self-creation does not, for the compatibilist, strip the act of freedom. What matters is that it arises through the agent's own motivational states rather than through another person's force or manipulation.

Freedom, then, becomes not the absence of causation but the presence of a particular structure of causation. It is the difference between being moved by reasons or by threats, between being guided by character or being constrained by compulsion.

This can be seen in two cases of charitable giving. In the first scenario, someone donates to an organization after researching where their contribution will be most effective, motivated by a genuine concern for others. In the second, someone donates the same amount only because a criminal has threatened their family with harm. Both actions have prior causes, and both are determined by circumstances beyond the agent's control. Yet one is recognized as a free and praiseworthy act, the other as coerced and undeserving of moral credit.

Compatibilists emphasize that this distinction does not depend on the donor's character being entirely self-created or their choice standing outside the chain of causation. The decisive point is that the act of giving in the first case belongs to the person who gives. It reflects their evaluative standpoint, their reasons, and their care. In the second case, the act belongs to the threat, not to the agent.

In this way, moral responsibility attaches to the source and structure of action rather than to its ultimate causal origins. Human freedom is found in the psychological mechanisms that give rise to what we do, not in some imagined exemption from the forces that shaped those mechanisms.

The analogy of a river illustrates this. A river does not carve its own channel, yet once the channel exists, the river moves through it in a way that belongs to the river itself. The course was set by geology, but the flow is its own. Human beings, compatibilists suggest, are similar. We do not design the conditions that shape our character, but our actions still count as free when they arise from the character and reasoning that make us who we are.

Harry Frankfurt developed influential compatibilist arguments that focused on identification with desires rather than on the availability of alternative possibilities. In what he calls a hierarchical model of the will, people act freely when their actions flow from first-order desires they themselves endorse at a higher level rather than from desires they wish they did not have. A person who acts from first-order desires they disown or reject acts unfreely, even if they could have done otherwise, while a person who acts from desires they identify with acts freely, even if they could not have done otherwise.

Frankfurt illustrates this distinction with cases of drug addiction that reveal the complexity hidden within our ordinary concept of freedom. An unwilling addict who wishes they did not desire drugs acts unfreely when they use them, even if abstaining were physically possible, because their action flows from desires they reject and would eliminate if they could. A willing addict who endorses their drug use and has no desire to quit acts freely when they use drugs, even if brain changes have made it impossible to abstain, because their action flows from desires with which they identify and which express their actual values rather than impulses they wish to resist.

This approach shifts the ground of moral responsibility away from ultimate origination toward harmony between different levels of the self. Responsibility does not require that agents be the ultimate creators of their desires or that their actions emerge from some causal void, but rather that there be appropriate integration between their first-order motivations and their higher-order values and commitments. Someone who acts from desires they identify with acts freely and can be held responsible, even if their desires themselves trace back to causes beyond their control.

The willing addict who endorses their addiction may be acting freely even if they are powerless to change, while the unwilling addict who despises their addiction acts unfreely even if they retain the physical ability to abstain. Freedom becomes a matter of internal psychological integration rather than exemption from causal determination.

Susan Wolf offers a different compatibilist approach that shifts attention from identification with desires to the capacity for rational agency. For Wolf, responsibility depends on whether a person can recognize and respond appropriately to moral reasons rather than on whether they possess alternative possibilities or ultimate origination. Someone who possesses this capacity acts as a moral agent even if they did not ultimately create these capacities for themselves, just as someone with the ability to see acts as a visual agent even if they did not create their own eyes.

Responsibility arises not from ultimate origination but from the presence of rational agency that can perceive moral requirements and guide behavior accordingly. The person who helps others because they recognize moral reasons for helping acts responsibly, even if their capacity for moral recognition resulted from a fortunate upbringing and education rather than self-creation.

This distinction helps explain why we naturally treat some individuals as less than fully responsible without appealing to mysterious forms of agency. Children, for example, may lack the cognitive maturity to grasp moral reasons in all their complexity and force, making them less than fully responsible even when they possess the physical ability to act otherwise. Psychopaths may understand moral reasons intellectually but lack the emotional and motivational capacity to be moved by them in ways that guide behavior, creating a different kind of impairment to responsibility. In both cases, the absence or impairment of responsibility stems not from the absence of free will in some metaphysical sense but from the absence of psychological capacities that moral responsibility presupposes.

By contrast, an adult who clearly perceives reasons against harming others yet chooses to inflict harm anyway reveals themselves as a responsible agent whose action deserves moral condemnation because it flows from rational capacities operating properly but directed toward inappropriate ends.

P. F. Strawson's famous essay *Freedom and Resentment* carries the compatibilist argument further by shifting attention from metaphysical puzzles to the reactive attitudes that shape human life. In his view, responsibility is not secured by some ultimate power of self-creation but by attitudes such as resentment, gratitude, and indignation. These responses arise naturally in relationships and play a central role in sustaining cooperation and accountability.

Blame and praise, on this account, are not discoveries of some hidden truth about who ultimately "deserves" them. They are practices that express these attitudes and, in doing so, preserve the bonds of social life. When someone wrongs us, resentment creates distance and pushes for acknowledgment and change. When someone helps us, gratitude draws us closer and encourages us to reciprocate. These reactions are not choices we make after weighing philosophical theories. They are basic features of human psychology that help maintain relationships and hold communities together, regardless of whether people are truly free in any ultimate sense.

Strawson stresses that such attitudes cannot be eradicated by argument. Resentment and gratitude no more vanish under philosophical scrutiny than love or friendship vanish when traced to their biological origins. Even if metaphysical freedom were shown to be impossible, the practice of holding one another responsible would remain. Like rituals that continue to carry meaning long after their religious foundations have faded, these attitudes would still provide structure to human life. In this light, responsibility is not a discovery of metaphysics but an achievement of human interaction.

Compatibilism has clear strengths that explain its enduring appeal to philosophers seeking to preserve moral responsibility without abandoning naturalistic frameworks. It explains why we naturally treat addiction, mental illness, or overwhelming emotion as impairments to freedom while still holding ordinary choices open to moral evaluation. The framework allows moral responsibility to coexist with scientific understanding of human behavior without requiring us to imagine human beings standing mysteriously outside the natural order.

Instead of demanding impossible exemptions from causation, compatibilism roots responsibility in psychological mechanisms that are integral to human social life and can be studied scientifically. In this way, compatibilism preserves much of what we care about in moral practice without appealing to mysterious forms of agency that conflict with empirical knowledge of how human behavior actually works.

But the compatibilist picture is not without serious cracks that threaten its foundations.

A deeper concern arises when we observe that compatibilist criteria for freedom and responsibility can apparently be satisfied even in cases where freedom appears to be entirely absent. The so-called manipulation arguments bring this problem into sharp focus by inviting us to imagine an agent whose desires and reasoning capacities have been engineered by external forces, yet who nevertheless acts in perfect accord with them while meeting every standard condition that compatibilists propose for free action. The manipulated agent acts from their own desires rather than external compulsion, their actions express their values rather than alien impositions, and their behavior flows from their character rather than foreign constraints.

Yet our moral intuitions recoil at the thought that such a life could be genuinely free or that such actions could deserve praise or blame. If responsibility can survive in cases that resemble sophisticated programming more than genuine agency, then perhaps compatibilism has failed to capture what we truly mean by freedom and has succeeded only in defining the problem away rather than solving it.

Alfred Mele sharpens this manipulation problem with cases of gradual manipulation that more closely resemble the ordinary processes through which all human character develops. Imagine a professor who wishes to cultivate a student with violent tendencies for some experimental purpose. Instead of direct control or coercive threats, he slowly arranges the student's environment over many years so that certain desires and dispositions are strengthened while others are weakened through carefully orchestrated experiences and influences. By the time the student reaches adulthood, he has developed a stable character that includes strong inclinations toward violence and sophisticated rationalizations for aggressive behavior. When he eventually commits murder, the act flows from his own deep desires and careful rational reflection about what he considers justified responses to perceived slights.

By compatibilist standards, the action appears free because it expresses the agent's character and values rather than external compulsion, emerges from his rational deliberation rather than impulsive reaction, and flows from psychological sources he identifies with rather than alien impositions he resists.

And yet the murder does not feel free in any meaningful sense. The student's violent character was never chosen or consented to; it was engineered through manipulation so subtle that he remains unaware of its operation. His rational deliberation operates within parameters that were established without his knowledge or consent, like a computer program that processes inputs according to code it did not write. What makes the case deeply unsettling is that the mechanism of manipulation appears indistinguishable from the ordinary processes that shape all human character development.

Genetics, upbringing, social influences, and formative experiences also shape our dispositions and values without our recognition or explicit consent. If compatibilism insists that the manipulated student acts freely, then it struggles to explain why the rest of us should be considered any different. The distinction between engineered and ordinary character formation becomes increasingly thin under scrutiny, and with it, the compatibilist account of freedom begins to fray at its conceptual edges.

Derk Pereboom develops four-case arguments that systematically challenge compatibilist theories by presenting scenarios where manipulation gradually approaches ordinary causation while intuitions about freedom and responsibility remain constant across all the cases. In his scenarios, an agent's character and actions are first influenced by direct neural manipulation from neuroscientists, then by psychological conditioning from behavioral scientists, and subsequently by social and environmental influences deliberately arranged by social planners. Finally, they are shaped by ordinary genetic and environmental factors operating through normal developmental processes.

What emerges is a striking pattern. Even as the form of manipulation becomes harder to distinguish from normal causation, our judgment remains unchanged. The agent seems unfree in every case. This suggests that ordinary causal determination is no less threatening to freedom than overt manipulation, and that the compatibilist's attempt to draw a line between internal and external causation does not capture what we truly care about when we speak of human agency.

The source incompatibilist argument maintains that ultimate origination remains necessary for moral responsibility, even if alternative possibilities are not required, as the Frankfurt cases might suggest.

Michael McKenna argues that even if our actions flow through sophisticated rational capacities and express our deepest values, those capacities and values ultimately trace back to genetic and environmental factors we did not choose and could not control. How can we be truly responsible for actions that ultimately trace back to factors beyond our control, no matter how sophisticated the psychological mechanisms through which those factors operate? The causal chain that produces our actions leads backward through character traits we did not create, cognitive capacities we did not develop, and formative experiences we did not choose, until it terminates in factors that preceded our existence entirely.

Neil Levy develops this source incompatibilist argument by contending that moral responsibility requires not just rational agency but responsibility for the psychological capacities that make responsible action possible. Since we are not responsible for our cognitive abilities, emotional regulation capacities, or fundamental motivational structures, we cannot be responsible for actions that depend on these psychological foundations, any more than we can be credited for athletic achievements that depend on physical talents we did not create. The person who acts generously because they possess strong empathy cannot be credited for their generosity if their empathy resulted from genetic luck and fortunate developmental experiences. The person who controls aggressive impulses because they possess effective self-regulation cannot be praised for their restraint if their self-regulatory capacities resulted from neurological advantages and cultural training they did not choose.

At every level, responsible action appears to depend on psychological resources that agents did not create for themselves.

These arguments suggest that compatibilism faces a dilemma that may prove inescapable regardless of how sophisticated its psychological accounts become.

Either it sets the bar for responsibility so high that few, if any, human actions satisfy the requirements, making moral responsibility as rare and mysterious as libertarians claim free will to be, or it accepts conditions so lenient that manipulated and coerced actions count as free, making responsibility as universal and meaningless as hard determinists claim it to be. Neither horn of this dilemma provides a satisfactory foundation for the moral responsibility practices that both preserve meaningful accountability and remain psychologically realistic about how human behavior actually develops and changes over time.

Yet compatibilist responses to these challenges reveal that the manipulation arguments may not be as decisive as they initially appear. Some compatibilists argue that our intuitions about manipulation cases reflect not deep insights into the requirements of freedom but culturally conditioned responses that may not track the features of agency we should care about. Historical compatibilists note that people in different societies with different practices of moral responsibility often have different intuitions about which factors excuse or diminish responsibility, suggesting that these intuitions reflect social conventions rather than universal truths about the nature of agency.

If responsibility practices serve functions such as maintaining cooperation, encouraging beneficial behavior, and expressing important values, then what matters may not be whether agents satisfy abstract metaphysical conditions, but whether responsibility attributions serve these practical functions effectively.

Other compatibilists develop more sophisticated accounts of the conditions under which character formation undermines rather than supports responsible agency. John Martin Fischer and Mark Ravizza argue that responsibility requires not just rational agency but agency that develops through the right kind of history, where the agent has opportunities for moral reflection and self-evaluation that allow them to take ownership of their values and commitments over time. In this view, manipulation cases involve the wrong kind of history because they bypass the agent's rational capacities and prevent the kind of reflective endorsement that responsible agency requires. Ordinary character formation, by contrast, typically involves extensive opportunities for moral reflection, value clarification, and self-modification, allowing agents to participate consciously in their own development, even if they do not control all the factors that shape them.

This suggestion points toward what may be the most promising direction for defending compatibilist approaches to human agency, although it requires moving beyond traditional compatibilist frameworks toward a more sophisticated and naturalistic approach. Rather than treating all causal determination as equally compatible or incompatible with freedom, we might recognize that different types of causal processes create different possibilities for conscious participation in character development and behavioral modification.

The capacity for such metacognitive self-modification represents neither a libertarian exemption from causation nor a simple mechanical determination, but something more complex that traditional philosophical categories struggle to capture. When agents engage in systematic reflection on their values, deliberate cultivation of character traits, and conscious construction of decision environments that support their long-term goals, they participate in causal processes that shape their future behavior without exempting themselves from natural law. This capacity for temporal scaffolding through metacognitive architecture may provide the foundation for a more adequate understanding of human agency that preserves moral responsibility without requiring impossible metaphysical commitments.

The Experimental Philosophy Challenge

Recent research in experimental philosophy suggests that ordinary people's intuitions about free will and moral responsibility are more complex and context-dependent than traditional philosophical categories often assume. These findings suggest that folk concepts of freedom and responsibility encompass multiple dimensions, vary across cultures, and are shaped by situational factors. This complexity complicates attempts to draw universal philosophical conclusions from everyday judgments.

Joshua Knobe and Shaun Nichols, for example, have shown that people's attributions of free will often depend on the moral character of actions in the scenarios they evaluate. Participants are presented with hypothetical situations in which agents perform actions that are either harmful, helpful, or neutral. Some scenarios specify that the agents' behavior is determined by neuroscientists or other deterministic factors.

Participants are then asked whether the agents acted freely and whether they deserve moral blame.

The results reveal that people sometimes attribute more free will and blame to agents who perform harmful actions than to those who perform helpful or neutral actions, even when the actions are determined in the same way. This pattern suggests that moral considerations shape judgments about freedom, rather than freedom judgments determining moral evaluations. It also highlights that responsibility attributions may reflect social and emotional motivations, such as justifying condemnation or punishment, rather than purely assessing metaphysical facts about agency.

These findings do not settle philosophical debates about free will. They show that common-sense intuitions are more context-dependent than often assumed. Understanding how ordinary people make judgments about freedom and responsibility requires attention to psychological, social, and cultural factors as well as philosophical reasoning.

Cross-cultural studies reveal significant variation in concepts of agency and responsibility across different societies, further undermining claims about universal human insights into the nature of free will. Shaun Nichols finds that individuals from cultures that emphasize individual agency and personal achievement show stronger commitments to free will beliefs than those from cultures that emphasize collective context and environmental influences on behavior. Western participants are more likely to attribute responsibility to individual agents for both positive and negative outcomes, while East Asian participants are more likely to consider situational factors, social relationships, and environmental conditions when making responsibility judgments.

These cultural differences suggest that responsibility practices reflect historical and social developments rather than universal human insights about the nature of agency, making philosophical theories based on analysis of folk concepts culturally parochial rather than universally valid.

Studies of indigenous cultures reveal even more dramatic variations in concepts of agency that challenge Western assumptions about individual responsibility. Some cultures attribute agency primarily to collective entities rather than individual people, making decisions through group processes that distribute responsibility across communities rather than locating it in particular agents. Other cultures emphasize environmental and spiritual influences on behavior in ways that would seem to undermine individual responsibility from Western perspectives yet maintain robust practices of accountability and behavioral modification that serve similar social functions.

These variations suggest that responsibility is a social construction that can take many different forms while serving similar functions, rather than a natural kind that philosophical analysis might discover.

Eddy Nahmias and colleagues find that people's intuitions about free will and moral responsibility often conflict with their beliefs about causal determination when both are explicitly examined in the same contexts. When presented with scenarios involving complete causal determination of behavior by prior causes, many people simultaneously affirm that agents' actions are completely determined and that the agents remain morally responsible for those actions. This pattern suggests that folk concepts may be genuinely inconsistent rather than revealing deep truths about the compatibility of freedom and determinism, or that people use different concepts of causation and responsibility in different contexts without recognizing the tensions between them.

Either possibility undermines attempts to resolve philosophical debates by appealing to what ordinary people believe about responsibility and freedom.

Studies examining the impact of neuroscientific information on moral responsibility judgments reveal complex patterns that do not clearly support either compatibilist or incompatibilist positions. Learning about neural correlates of decision-making sometimes reduces responsibility attributions, but the effects are often small, temporary, and dependent on how neuroscientific information is presented to participants. People seem to maintain responsibility attributions despite accepting scientific accounts of behavior that should undermine these attributions according to many philosophical theories. This suggests either that folk concepts of responsibility are more sophisticated and nuanced than philosophers assume, or that people maintain inconsistent beliefs without recognizing the tensions, or that responsibility attributions serve emotional and social functions that override purely cognitive considerations about the causal determinants of behavior.

Experimental studies of people's responses to different types of factors that influence behavior reveal that not all causal influences are treated equally when making responsibility judgments. People are more likely to excuse behavior that results from obvious external constraints like physical coercion or direct threats than behavior that results from internal factors like character traits, emotional states, or mental illness, even when the internal factors are equally beyond the agent's control.

This pattern suggests that folk concepts of responsibility track something more complex than simple presence or absence of causal determination, possibly involving distinctions between different types of causal processes or different levels of identification between agents and the factors that influence their behavior.

These experimental findings support reconceptualizing moral responsibility as a complex social practice that serves multiple psychological and social functions rather than tracking objective metaphysical facts about agents and their relationship to causation.

The research suggests that responsibility practices emerge from evolved psychological mechanisms designed to promote social cooperation, maintain relationships, and coordinate group behavior rather than from philosophical insights about the ultimate nature of agency. This makes responsibility attributions functional rather than factual, pragmatic rather than metaphysical, serving important roles in human social life regardless of their accuracy as descriptions of some deeper reality about human nature.

Yet experimental philosophy faces significant methodological and interpretive challenges that limit its philosophical significance and raise questions about what conclusions can legitimately be drawn from empirical studies of folk concepts. Studies typically examine participants' immediate responses to simplified scenarios rather than their reflective judgments about complex cases after sustained consideration, measuring fast thinking rather than slow thinking, intuitive responses rather than considered judgments developed through careful analysis. The experimental scenarios often omit crucial details that might influence philosophical evaluation, testing responses to philosophical caricatures rather than careful analysis of realistic cases that capture the full complexity of human agency and moral evaluation.

More fundamentally, the fact that folk concepts are complex, culturally variable, or potentially inconsistent does not determine which philosophical theory is correct about the nature of free will and moral responsibility. Folk concepts might reflect important truths about agency and responsibility that philosophical theories should accommodate and explain, or they might reflect cognitive biases, cultural conditioning, and evolved psychological mechanisms that systematically distort our understanding of agency and obscure philosophical truth about human nature.

The relationship between descriptive facts about how people actually think about responsibility and normative claims about how people should think about responsibility remains philosophically complex and empirically underdetermined.

The diversity of folk concepts across cultures might indicate that responsibility is indeed a social construction without objective foundations, but it might alternatively indicate that different cultures have developed different aspects of a complex objective reality about human agency that no single cultural perspective captures completely. The inconsistencies in folk judgments might reveal genuine paradoxes in human agency that philosophical theories must somehow accommodate, or they might reflect conceptual confusions that philosophical analysis should resolve rather than simply describe. Experimental philosophy provides valuable data about how people actually think about agency and responsibility, but translating these empirical findings into philosophical conclusions requires theoretical frameworks that experimental studies alone cannot provide.

The Hard Problem of Mental Causation

Any credible theory of human agency must confront a fundamental paradox that threatens its very foundation: the problem of mental causation. This challenge strikes at the heart of our capacity for self-modification, questioning whether our conscious thoughts and intentions have any real power in a world governed by physical laws.

The problem can be stated as follows: If mental events, such as the conscious recognition of anxiety, depend on physical brain events, and if these brain events unfold according to the deterministic laws of nature, how can our minds genuinely influence our brains and bodies? This question creates a dilemma that seems to leave no room for conscious control. If a physical event in the brain already has a complete physical cause, what work is left for a mental event to do?

This threatens to reduce consciousness to a mere byproduct akin to an impotent spectator watching a neural drama it cannot influence. Concepts central to this book, like metacognitive control and temporal scaffolding, risk becoming elaborate illusions. The feeling of "self-modification" could be nothing more than the brain modifying itself through purely physical processes, with consciousness simply creating a story about it after the fact.

When you notice your mind wandering and consciously redirect it, does your *awareness* actually cause the change? Or does it merely witness a change that was already predetermined by underlying neural mechanics? Unless this paradox can be resolved, any account of human agency remains vulnerable to the charge that the "ghost in the machine" is not a pilot but a passenger, narrating a journey whose course was set long before.

Jaegwon Kim's causal exclusion argument poses this challenge with systematic precision that reveals its depth and generality. If every physical event has sufficient physical causes operating according to natural laws that fully account for its occurrence, there appears to be no genuine causal work left for mental events to perform in bringing about behavioral outcomes. Either mental events are identical to physical events, in which case they are not genuinely mental but simply physical events described in mental language, or they are genuinely mental but causally impotent, floating above the physical processes that actually determine behavior like shadows that accompany but do not influence the objects that cast them.

The dilemma appears to eliminate genuine mental causation regardless of which argument we choose, reducing consciousness to either an eliminable description or a powerless accompaniment.

The problem becomes particularly acute when considering the metacognitive processes that theories of self-modification and temporal scaffolding centrally require. If both the monitoring processes and the cognitive processes they purport to regulate are implemented in neural mechanisms that operate according to physical causation, how can the monitoring processes exert genuine causal influence over the regulated processes rather than merely correlating with changes that would occur anyway through purely physical mechanisms operating at the neural level? The metacognitive supervisor would be no more causally efficacious than the supervised processes, both dancing to the tune of physical laws that determine their every move according to prior neural states and environmental inputs.

The appearance of control becomes an illusion created by the correlation between monitoring and regulated processes, both of which are controlled by deeper neural mechanisms that operate independently of conscious awareness or intention.

Consciousness becomes akin to a newspaper reporting on events that have already been predetermined by deeper processes, rather than a government directing events as they unfold through its decisions and policies.

The causal exclusion problem threatens to undermine any theory of human agency that depends on genuine mental causation for its plausibility. If conscious mental events cannot genuinely influence behavior through causal mechanisms that operate independently of physical processes, then apparent self-modification reduces to the brain modifying itself through purely physical processes, while consciousness provides an illusory narrative interpretation after the fact, much like a commentator describing a game while mistakenly believing they are playing it.

The sense of agency becomes a systematic illusion created by the temporal proximity of conscious states to behavioral outcomes, combined with the brain's tendency to construct causal narratives that place consciousness at the center of behavioral control even when it operates primarily as a passive monitor of processes it does not genuinely influence.

Several philosophical responses attempt to preserve genuine mental causation while remaining consistent with naturalistic frameworks and empirical knowledge about brain function, though each faces significant challenges that reveal the depth and persistence of the mental causation problem.

Emergentism argues that mental properties emerge from, but are not reducible to, physical properties, acquiring genuine causal powers that operate through, but cannot be fully explained by, underlying physical processes. Higher-order neural patterns constrain and influence lower-order processes through top-down causal relationships that operate within natural laws while exhibiting emergent properties that transcend their physical substrate in ways that create new causal powers.

This approach resembles how hurricanes emerge from atmospheric processes yet possess genuine causal efficacy in influencing weather patterns in ways that cannot be predicted from knowledge of molecular behavior alone. The hurricane's large-scale organization constrains and directs the behavior of air molecules in ways that cannot be predicted solely from knowledge of individual molecular properties and interactions, creating genuine downward causation from higher-level weather patterns to lower-level atmospheric components. Similarly, metacognitive patterns might constrain and direct neural activity in ways that cannot be predicted from knowledge of individual neural mechanisms alone, enabling the mind to influence the brain through organizational properties that transcend physical reductionism while remaining entirely natural in their operation.

Yet emergentism faces the fundamental challenge of explaining how higher-level properties acquire genuine causal powers without violating physical laws or creating mysterious forms of downward causation that conflict with our scientific understanding of how natural systems operate.

Strong emergence involving truly novel causal powers appears to conflict with physical causal closure by allowing mental events to influence physical events through mechanisms that transcend physical explanation and cannot be captured by any extension of physical theory. Weak emergence involving only novel patterns of organization among existing properties struggles to explain genuine top-down causal influence that goes beyond mere correlation or systemic description of bottom-up processes, threatening to collapse back into reductive physicalism that eliminates genuine mental causation.

Recent work in complexity science and systems theory suggests that emergent properties can possess genuine causal efficacy through the setting of constraints and boundary conditions, rather than through the application of novel forces that violate physical laws. Higher-order patterns create organizational contexts that channel lower-order processes in specific directions without adding energy to the system or violating conservation laws, like riverbanks that shape water flow without contributing additional force to the current. Metacognitive awareness may constrain neural processing by establishing attentional priorities, goal hierarchies, and regulatory contexts that influence how neural networks process information and interact with each other, creating genuine top-down causation through organizational constraint rather than mysterious intervention in physical processes that would require violating natural laws.

Non-reductive physicalism maintains a related but more modest position. While emergentism posits that higher-level properties possess genuinely novel causal powers that cannot be predicted from lower-level physical properties, non-reductive physicalism makes a different claim: mental events are physical events described at higher levels of organization, and these higher-level descriptions capture real causal patterns that remain invisible when the same events are described at lower levels of physical analysis. The crucial distinction lies in what the higher level adds. Strong emergentism suggests the existence of new causal powers that transcend physical explanation. Non-reductive physicalism suggests only new patterns within physical causation—real patterns that matter for explanation but don't involve mysterious additional forces.

Just as biological explanations of organism behavior remain valid and explanatorily powerful even though biological events are ultimately physical events, psychological explanations capture genuine causal relationships even though psychological events are ultimately implemented in neural events that operate according to physical laws. The crucial insight is that the same events can participate in causal relationships described at different levels of analysis, each of which captures real patterns that may not be visible or tractable at other levels.

The key insight underlying non-reductive physicalism is that higher-level patterns can have genuine causal efficacy even when they emerge from and depend entirely on lower-level processes for their existence and operation. Metacognitive control represents a real causal organization that operates through neural mechanisms, possessing emergent properties that cannot be captured by purely neural descriptions, much like musical patterns that emerge from but cannot be reduced to the physics of sound waves. The conductor influences the orchestra through entirely physical mechanisms involving sound waves and neural processes; yet, the musical patterns that emerge from this interaction transcend any description that focuses solely on individual instruments or the acoustic properties of sound waves.

Biological systems provide compelling examples of such multilevel causation that demonstrate how higher-level patterns can possess genuine causal efficacy without violating physical laws. Genetic regulatory networks control protein synthesis through entirely chemical mechanisms yet exhibit emergent properties, including robustness, modularity, and evolvability, that cannot be predicted from knowledge of individual chemical reactions and that have genuine causal influence on organismal development and evolutionary dynamics. These emergent properties create feedback loops between different levels of biological organization, enabling sophisticated forms of biological regulation and adaptation that transcend what could be achieved through simple chemical mechanisms alone.

Yet non-reductive physicalism faces persistent challenges in specifying exactly how higher-level properties relate to lower-level properties and how higher-level causation relates to lower-level causation without creating problematic causal overdetermination. The view risks collapsing into either reductive physicalism, which eliminates genuine higher-level causation, or property dualism, which conflicts with naturalistic frameworks by positing non-physical properties with causal powers.

Non-reductive physicalism must walk a narrow conceptual path between the Scylla of reductionism and the Charybdis of dualism, maintaining that higher-level properties are nothing over and above physical properties while somehow possessing causal powers that cannot be captured by physical descriptions alone.

Interventionist approaches to causation offer a different strategy for preserving mental causation by grounding causal relationships in counterfactual dependencies rather than in underlying mechanisms or metaphysical connections between cause and effect. In this view, mental events count as genuine causes if manipulating them would make a systematic difference to their alleged effects under appropriate conditions, regardless of the mechanisms through which this causal influence operates.

Cognitive interventions that successfully modify behavior demonstrate genuine psychological causation regardless of their neural implementation, just as biological interventions demonstrate genuine biological causation regardless of their implementation in chemical and physical processes.

This interventionist approach aligns naturally with experimental methodology in cognitive science and psychology, where researchers routinely manipulate attention, memory, emotional states, and other psychological variables and observe systematic changes in behavior that confirm causal relationships at the psychological level of description. When researchers use meditation training to enhance attention regulation, cognitive therapy to modify emotional responses, or environmental restructuring to change behavioral patterns, they demonstrate genuine psychological causation even when these interventions operate through neural mechanisms that can be described in purely physical terms. The causal relationship exists at the psychological level of description, regardless of its neural implementation, much like software causation that operates through hardware mechanisms without being reduced to a purely hardware-based description.

Meditation training provides particularly compelling evidence for genuine mental causation that cannot be dismissed as mere correlation or post-hoc narrative construction.

Systematic cultivation of metacognitive awareness through contemplative practices produces measurable changes in brain structure and function, including increased cortical thickness in attention-related regions, enhanced connectivity between control networks and emotional processing areas, and reduced activity in mind-wandering networks associated with self-referential thinking. These neural changes correlate with improved attention regulation, enhanced emotional stability, reduced stress reactivity, and increased psychological well-being, suggesting that mental training produces physical changes that support enhanced psychological functioning through mechanisms that operate from mind to brain rather than simply from brain to mind.

Yet, interventionist approaches face their own challenges in distinguishing genuine causation from mere correlation and in explaining how mental causation relates to physical causation without creating causal overdetermination or violating physical causal closure. If mental events are genuine causes that make systematic differences to behavioral outcomes, how do they interface with physical causal processes without either violating physical laws or becoming reducible to physical descriptions?

The relationship between different levels of causal description remains conceptually problematic even when the effectiveness of higher-level interventions is clearly established through experimental research and practical application.

The mental causation problem remains one of the most serious challenges facing any naturalistic theory of human agency that depends on the genuine causal efficacy of conscious mental processes. Yet, the overwhelming evidence from cognitive science, neuroscience, and practical psychology for genuine mental causation suggests that a solution must be possible, even if current philosophical theories remain inadequate to capture its nature. The mind clearly does influence itself and behavioral outcomes through mechanisms we do not fully understand, but the reality of this influence cannot be denied without denying the evidence of science itself and abandoning the practical approaches to human development that depend on the efficacy of conscious reflection and deliberate behavioral modification.

Beyond the Traditional Framework

The persistence of free will debates despite centuries of increasingly sophisticated philosophical analysis suggests that the binary framework dominating these discussions may be fundamentally malformed, akin to a mathematical equation containing a basic conceptual error that no amount of algebraic manipulation can resolve. Perhaps human agency operates through mechanisms that neither fit the libertarian exemption from causation nor the hard determinist reduction to mechanical forces but rather exist in a conceptual territory that our traditional philosophical categories cannot adequately map or comprehend.

Why do these exhausted categories persist with such tenacity? The answer reveals itself when we examine the historical inheritance that shapes even secular discussions of human freedom. Christianity bequeathed to philosophy the demand for ultimate moral responsibility, the conviction that agents must be ultimately praiseworthy or blameworthy based on their essential character. When secular thought inherited this framework, it retained the impossible standards while removing the metaphysical apparatus that made them coherent. The soul that could stand partially outside the natural order vanished, but the demand for ultimate moral worthiness remained, creating a conceptual vacuum that generates endless debate without resolution.

Contemporary psychology reveals systematic cognitive biases that reinforce this binary thinking. The fundamental attribution error leads people to attribute behavior to internal dispositions rather than situational factors, while the illusion of conscious will creates subjective experiences of agency that feel more robust than neuroscience suggests they are. These cognitive tendencies create intuitive support for libertarian positions that philosophical argument alone cannot dislodge, while simultaneously generating the sense of contradiction that drives people toward hard determinist conclusions when confronted with scientific evidence about the causes of behavior.

Perhaps most significantly, neuroscientific findings about decision-making have been systematically misinterpreted by both sides of the traditional debate. Libertarians view evidence for neural determinism as a threat to human dignity that must be resisted or explained away. At the same time, determinists regard the same evidence as vindication of mechanistic reductionism, which eliminates genuine agency. Both responses reflect the shared assumption that genuine agency requires exemption from natural causation, preventing recognition of how sophisticated natural processes might create genuine possibilities for self-modification and conscious behavioral architecture.

The result is a philosophical tradition that oscillates between impossible metaphysical commitments rather than investigating the actual mechanisms through which human behavioral sophistication emerges from entirely natural processes. We remain trapped in conceptual prisons of our own making, like those early astronomers who insisted the stars must move in perfect circles and created increasingly complex epicycles to preserve their geometric assumptions rather than questioning whether the circles themselves might be the problem.

Breaking free requires recognizing that agency and causation are not mutually exclusive alternatives but complementary aspects of sophisticated natural processes. The question becomes not whether human beings are exempt from causation or subject to it, but rather what kinds of causal processes generate the remarkable behavioral flexibility that characterizes human agency at its most developed and effective.

Toward a Third Path

The framework of temporal scaffolding and metacognitive compatibilism introduced earlier must now address a crucial question that previous attempts to transcend the traditional debate have failed to answer adequately: how does sophisticated agency actually develop and operate in the world as we find it?

Unlike emergentism, which remains vague about the mechanisms through which higher-level properties acquire causal powers, or non-reductive physicalism, which struggles to explain how higher-level causation relates to lower-level causation, the approach developed here focuses on empirically tractable processes through which conscious agents participate in their own development. Agency reveals itself not as a fixed property that agents either possess or lack, but as a capacity that develops through systematic cultivation and can be enhanced or impaired depending on how individuals engage with the causal processes that shape their behavior.

Consider how this operates in transforming destructive patterns that seem most resistant to change. The person caught in cycles of violence cannot simply choose to become peaceful through an act of will, nor are they condemned to remain forever trapped by their conditioning. They can learn to identify the environmental triggers and emotional states that precede destructive episodes, not to excuse them but to create systematic interventions that modify their future choice architecture. They establish routines that remove them from triggering situations during vulnerable periods, develop relationships with those who can provide perspective during emotional escalation, and cultivate practices that enhance their capacity for emotional regulation and moral reflection.

This represents neither libertarian free choice nor determinist rehabilitation. Instead, they become architects of their own conditioning, using present cognitive resources to construct the causal conditions that will shape their future behavior. Their agency develops through this process rather than making change possible from the beginning. What emerges is genuine behavioral transformation through mechanisms that are entirely naturalistic while enabling authentic self-modification that transcends what could be achieved through unconscious conditioning alone.

The same principles extend to the cultivation of intellectual and creative capacities. The student struggling with patterns of procrastination and academic underperformance cannot escape these patterns through sheer willpower alone. They must understand how procrastination emerges from specific patterns of emotional avoidance, perfectionist anxiety, and environmental cues that trigger distraction. They learn to construct systematic interventions: creating physical environments that reduce distraction and support focus, establishing social accountability structures that provide gentle pressure and encouragement, and developing emotional regulation techniques that allow them to approach challenging tasks without being overwhelmed by anxiety.

Most significantly, they develop the capacity to observe and modify these interventions based on their effectiveness, creating feedback loops that enhance their agency over time. They learn to treat their own psychology as a system that can be understood and modified rather than as a fixed set of traits that determine their fate. This represents genuine skill development in the art of conscious behavioral architecture, learning to work with natural psychological processes rather than against them, creating conditions under which determination operates in service of chosen ends.

The objection arises that this approach still fails to address the fundamental problem of ultimate responsibility. If the capacity for such temporal scaffolding depends on cognitive abilities and environmental supports that the agent did not create, how can they be truly responsible for their behavioral changes? This objection reveals the persistence of impossible standards that traditional frameworks impose on human agency.

Ultimate self-creation is not required for genuine agency, any more than ultimate self-creation is required for genuine skill development, artistic achievement, or scientific discovery. What matters is not whether agents create themselves ex nihilo, but whether they develop the capacity to participate consciously and skillfully in the ongoing process of becoming what they choose to become. Agency lies not in creating capacities from nothing, but in learning to deploy them systematically in service of chosen ends rather than remaining unconsciously subject to whatever conditioning happens to occur.

The Basic Architecture of Becoming

The capacity for temporal scaffolding does not emerge fully formed; instead, it develops through identifiable stages that can be cultivated through systematic practice and appropriate social support. Understanding this development offers insight into how human agency operates in the world, rather than in philosophical abstractions.

Most human behavior operates through what might be called reactive agency, where actions emerge from immediate responses to environmental stimuli mediated by established habits and emotional reactions. This is not mechanical determinism but sophisticated biological programming that enables rapid adaptive responses to complex social and physical environments. Even reactive agency involves genuine choice among alternatives, but these choices are constrained by unconscious conditioning and immediate contextual pressures. The person responds to stress by automatically engaging established coping patterns without systematic awareness of how these patterns develop or persist.

The development of metacognitive awareness enables individuals to observe their own psychological processes and behavioral patterns, creating possibilities for conscious evaluation and modification. This reflective agency emerges through various pathways: therapeutic work that enhances psychological insight, contemplative practices that cultivate mindful awareness, educational experiences that teach psychological literacy, or life experiences that create sufficient disruption to motivate systematic self-examination. The same person now recognizes their stress responses as patterns that can be observed and evaluated rather than inevitable reactions they must endure.

At the most advanced level, individuals become skilled at systematically constructing decision environments that support their long-term values and goals. This architecturally sophisticated agency requires the integration of psychological understanding, practical wisdom about behavior change, and a systematic commitment to ongoing self-improvement. The individual approaches their own development as a long-term project requiring systematic attention and skillful intervention. They understand that behavioral change occurs through environmental modification, social influence, habit formation, and cognitive restructuring rather than through pure willpower or magical self-transformation.

This developmental understanding suggests that human freedom is not a metaphysical given but a practical achievement that emerges through sustained effort and appropriate social support. We are neither born free in some ultimate sense nor condemned to mechanical determination. We possess the potential to develop genuine agency through conscious participation in the natural processes that shape human behavior and experience.

The ghost in the machine reveals itself as neither supernatural intervention nor mechanistic illusion, but as a natural capacity for sophisticated temporal self-organization that enables conscious participation in our own becoming. This capacity represents not the violation of natural law but its most sophisticated achievement. We are nature becoming conscious of itself, matter organized in such exquisite complexity that it can observe and modify its own organization through processes that remain entirely natural while transcending what seemed possible from simpler forms of material organization.

In grasping this truth, we discover that the freedom we seek lies not beyond nature but within its deepest creative processes. The question that frames our ongoing development is no longer whether we are free in some impossible metaphysical sense, but rather how consciously and skillfully we will participate in the ongoing process of becoming what we have the potential to become.

The Ghost of the Past

"But what examines the examiner? What observes the observer?"

HUMAN CONSCIOUSNESS EMERGES through observing itself, revealing the deeper complexity of consciousness observing consciousness, mind monitoring mind, and the strange loop of awareness becoming aware of its own operations. Here lies what I dubbed metacognitive compatibilism: not consciousness as a separate substance floating above the machinery of the brain, but consciousness as the brain's capacity to observe and modify its own operations through recursive processes that create genuine possibilities for self-transformation.

The dismissal of traditional free will debates does not mean dismissing the profound insights of philosophical traditions that grappled with human agency long before our contemporary conceptual straightjackets hardened into place. The greatest minds of antiquity and early modernity developed sophisticated accounts of human action that remain instructive even when their metaphysical assumptions prove untenable. Yet each tradition contains what we might call perceptual limits, failures of vision that prevented adequate treatment of the extended processes through which human behavioral patterns develop and can be systematically modified, and they remind us that integrating historical insight with careful observation of present-day cognition can deepen our understanding of human choice.

These perceptual limits reveal persistent conceptual barriers that continue to constrain contemporary discussions of human agency. The ancients were prisoners of their own temporal horizons, unable to see beyond the immediate moment of choice to the vast architectures of becoming that stretch across seasons of human development. They glimpsed something crucial without possessing the conceptual tools to understand how present cognitive work constructs the decision environments that will shape future behavior. At the same time, their efforts illuminate the long continuum of reflection and practice that allows humans to refine understanding, plan strategically, and cultivate the capacity to act in ways that transform both self and context.

Humans did not always possess this capacity for reflection. It developed gradually through experience, education, and deliberate practice. Ancient thinkers built it by cultivating habits of attention, reasoning, and moral reflection. They trained themselves to notice patterns in their own behavior and to anticipate the consequences of their actions. Philosophical exercises, dialogue, meditation, and engagement with art and literature all helped extend the mind's capacity to observe itself. Metacognition was never a sudden discovery, but a slow achievement shaped by effort and context, influenced by social structures, cultural norms, and the subtle interplay between individual insight and collective learning.

The Aristotelian Moment

Aristotle's account of voluntary action in *Nicomachean Ethics* remains one of his most precise achievements. An act is voluntary when the agent understands the circumstances, acts without external force, and originates the deed. The definition secures a lasting framework for responsibility, yet the sharpness of its boundaries also reveals the limits of his larger ethical project.

Consider the simple elegance of this framework. When someone donates money to earthquake victims, their action appears voluntary because they understand the situation, choose freely without coercion, and initiate the action themselves. When someone hands over money only because of being threatened at gunpoint, their action lacks voluntariness because external compulsion bypasses their agency. When someone accidentally harms another while reasonably believing they provide help, their action lacks full voluntariness because ignorance prevented a clear understanding of the circumstances.

Yet this crystalline analysis embeds assumptions that prevent adequate treatment of the temporal complexity characterizing all genuine human development. Aristotle's framework focuses on discrete moments of action rather than the extended developmental processes through which the capacity for virtuous action emerges and can be systematically cultivated. He captures the surface of choice while remaining blind to the vast networks of influence and development that make choice possible, what we now understand as the hierarchical cognitive architecture that enables metacognitive observation and behavioral modification.

The requirement that voluntary action originates "in the agent" assumes a unified self serving as the ultimate source of choice. This assumption made sense within Aristotle's metaphysical framework, where the soul functioned as the organizing principle of the body and the source of rational direction. But this unified agent dissolves under contemporary analysis into dynamic interactions between multiple neural systems operating across different timescales, each shaped by evolutionary pressures, developmental experiences, and ongoing environmental influences.

When someone chooses to help earthquake victims, this choice emerges from complex negotiations between prefrontal systems evaluating long-term consequences, limbic systems processing emotional responses to suffering, memory systems retrieving relevant past experiences, and social cognition systems modeling the reactions of others. The unified "agent" of Aristotelian analysis fragments into a coalition of specialized processing systems, each contributing to behavioral outcomes through processes largely opaque to introspection.

More problematically, Aristotle's focus on discrete voluntary acts obscures the extended temporal processes through which behavioral patterns develop and can be modified. His analysis asks whether someone's charitable giving represents genuine virtue by examining their knowledge, freedom from compulsion, and role as the originating source. However, this approach overlooks a necessary question: how did their generous character develop over years of moral education, social modeling, reflective practice, and environmental influences that made charitable giving feel natural rather than effortful?

The person attempting to develop greater courage in social situations faces a psychological constitution that generates anxiety and avoidance in precisely the situations where courage is needed. Their fear responses emerge from deep neurobiological patterns shaped by evolutionary history, developmental experiences, and current social contexts. Simply willing themselves to act courageously proves insufficient because courage requires not just behavioral compliance, but also appropriate emotional responses to danger and social challenges.

This is where Aristotle's temporal blindness becomes most apparent. He could not envision how someone might engage in systematic temporal scaffolding, using present cognitive resources to gradually reconstruct the emotional and environmental conditions that generate fear responses. The anxious person learning to develop courage might practice meditation to cultivate metacognitive awareness of anxiety patterns, seek gradual exposure to increasingly challenging social situations, foster relationships with people who model confident behavior, and create environmental supports that make courageous action more probable than avoidant retreat.

Aristotle's doctrine of the mean illustrates both the insights and limitations of his approach to character development. Courage represents the mean between cowardice and recklessness, temperance lies between self-indulgence and insensibility, and generosity occupies the middle ground between stinginess and profligacy. This analysis captures important truths about virtue, which involves balanced responses appropriate to circumstances rather than mechanical rule-following.

Yet the doctrine provides little guidance for how someone whose emotional and behavioral patterns currently generate extreme responses might systematically work to develop more balanced dispositions. The person prone to cowardice experiences genuine fear that makes moderate responses feel impossible. The person prone to recklessness experiences excitement and confidence that make cautious responses feel unnecessary. Moving toward the mean requires not just intellectual understanding of appropriate responses but systematic modification of the emotional and cognitive patterns that generate inappropriate responses.

His concept of prohairesis represents Aristotle's most sophisticated attempt to capture distinctly human agency. Unlike mere appetite responding to immediate pleasure or passion reacting to perceived threats, prohairesis involves the integration of rational deliberation with emotional motivation. It represents the capacity to choose actions based not merely on immediate impulses but on reasoned consideration of what promotes authentic existence over time.

This concept anticipates certain features of metacognitive compatibilism by recognizing that human choice involves more than immediate response to present stimuli. Prohairesis can consider long-term consequences, weigh competing values, and choose actions that sacrifice immediate gratification for the sake of distant benefits. The temperate person demonstrates prohairesis by choosing moderate pleasures that support lasting well-being rather than intense pleasures that undermine it.

Yet Aristotle's analysis of prohairesis remains anchored to individual choice episodes rather than the extended temporal processes through which the capacity for wise choice develops. The young person learning temperance does not simply acquire new information about which pleasures promote authentic existence. They must reconstruct their attention patterns to notice previously ignored consequences, modify their emotional responses to immediate gratification, develop social relationships that support rather than undermine beneficial choices, and create environmental conditions that make temperate behavior more probable than intemperate alternatives.

This reconstruction occurs across extended time periods and involves precisely the kind of systematic self-modification that Aristotelian categories struggle to accommodate. Contemporary research reveals that effective character development requires what might be called architectural reconstruction of the psychological systems that generate choice. Someone developing courage must learn not merely to override fear responses but to modify the cognitive and environmental conditions that generate excessive fear through deliberate temporal scaffolding.

The Aristotelian framework cannot adequately accommodate such systematic psychological reconstruction because it treats character as a relatively stable disposition rather than an ongoing architectural project. The temporal processes through which psychological architecture changes remain largely invisible within traditional virtue ethical frameworks.

Aristotle glimpsed fundamental truths about human excellence while being constrained by temporal blindness, which prevented him from seeing how excellence develops through the hierarchical cognitive structures that enable conscious participation in behavioral modification. We inherit both his insights and his limitations, carrying forward his vision of human flourishing while recognizing the extended temporal processes through which such flourishing becomes possible.

The Stoic Paradox

The Stoics recognized fundamental problems with Aristotelian approaches to human agency and developed more sophisticated analyses of the relationship between rational agency and natural necessity. Beginning with Chrysippus in the third century BCE and continuing through Epictetus and Marcus Aurelius in the first and second centuries CE, they argued that genuine freedom consists not in exemption from causal determination but in rational understanding of and alignment with natural processes. Their insight penetrated deeper than Aristotle's, yet their cosmic vision ultimately trapped them in a paradox that undermined the very agency they sought to preserve.

Epictetus articulates the essential Stoic insight: we are actors in a play written by another hand, yet we retain freedom in how we perform our assigned roles. This captures the Stoic recognition that while we cannot choose the roles assigned to us in the cosmic drama, we retain genuine agency in our responses to circumstances.

This framework resonates with profound truths about human existence that anticipate key insights of metacognitive compatibilism. We do not choose our genetic inheritance, family circumstances, historical moment, or many of the defining challenges we face. Yet, within these constraints, we possess genuine agency in how we respond to circumstances, what meaning we derive from our experiences, and how we align our attitudes with a rational understanding of natural processes. This represents a form of agency that operates through rather than despite causal determination.

External events, including the behavior of others, natural disasters, political upheavals, and even the ultimate consequences of our own actions, lie beyond our direct control and therefore should not be sources of attachment or distress. What is "up to us," according to the Stoics, is our judgment about external events and our subsequent attitudes and responses. This creates an internal sanctuary of freedom that no external force can violate.

This framework addresses the problem of moral luck that would later be identified as undermining responsibility attributions. Someone might act with perfect virtue yet face disaster due to circumstances beyond their control, while another person might act carelessly yet achieve successful outcomes through good fortune. The Stoic response eliminates this problem by locating virtue entirely within the domain of rational judgment and appropriate response rather than in external outcomes that depend partly on factors beyond the agent's control.

Epictetus develops this framework with particular sophistication in his analysis of impressions and assent. External objects and events create impressions in our minds automatically; we cannot prevent these initial representations from arising. But we possess the capacity to examine these impressions and choose whether to give assent to the judgments they suggest. When faced with an impressive rhetorical performance, we might have an initial impression that the speaker is trustworthy and their arguments sound. But rational reflection can examine this impression, consider alternative interpretations, and withhold assent if the evidence proves insufficient.

This capacity for rational examination of our own cognitive processes represents genuine freedom even within a completely determined natural order and points toward the metacognitive hierarchies that enable conscious observation and modification of mental processes. The discipline of assent requires ongoing attention to the formation of judgments and the capacity to modify them based on rational reflection. The discipline of action involves aligning behavior with rationally justified values rather than immediate emotional impulses. The discipline of desire involves modifying attachments and expectations to align with a realistic understanding of what can and cannot be controlled.

These practices point toward forms of systematic self-modification that work across time through what we now understand as temporal scaffolding. Present cognitive work examining impressions, reflecting on values, and practicing disciplined attention modifies the conditions under which future choices will emerge. Someone who regularly practices the discipline of assent will be less likely to accept initial impressions uncritically in novel situations. Someone who has practiced aligning actions with rational values will be more likely to act on these values even under emotional pressure.

Chrysippus offered one of antiquity's most sophisticated attempts to reconcile human agency with causal determinism through his doctrine of "co-fated" events. Human actions are both fated, because they follow from antecedent causes, and free, because they arise from the agent's own rational nature. He illustrated this with the image of a cylinder rolling down a hill. The descent begins with an external force, yet the manner of rolling depends on the cylinder's own shape. Similarly, external circumstances trigger human action, while the specific character of the action depends on the inner constitution of the agent's rational faculties.

This suggests that an action can be both caused and free if it flows through the agent's own evaluative capacities rather than bypassing them. A person who aids another out of compassion acts freely, even if that compassionate character was itself formed by prior causes, because the action proceeds through rational judgment and appropriate emotional response rather than external compulsion or internal compulsion that bypasses rational evaluation.

Yet the Stoic framework contains a fundamental limitation that prevents its development into a comprehensive theory of behavioral modification. The cosmological assumption that rational alignment with natural necessity represents the ultimate goal of human life creates what might be called the resignation problem, or the potential collapse of active agency into passive acceptance of whatever occurs.

Marcus Aurelius exemplifies this tendency in his *Meditations* when he writes: "Accept the things to which fate binds you, and love the people with whom fate brings you together." This transforms Stoic freedom into refined acceptance of predetermined conditions. Someone living under political oppression is encouraged to align inner attitudes with the rational necessity of their circumstances rather than work for change. Someone suffering a personal loss is urged to accept the cosmic wisdom of their grief rather than explore ways to prevent similar losses in the future.

The resignation problem emerges most clearly in Stoic responses to systematic injustice and preventable suffering. If everything that occurs reflects rational cosmic order, then resistance to existing conditions becomes a form of irrationality. The Stoic sage who perfectly aligns with natural order achieves tranquility by accepting whatever happens as expressions of rational necessity rather than as problems requiring an active solution.

Marcus Aurelius voices this tension in his darker reflections: "What is man? A poor soul carrying around a corpse." Here, the very agency celebrated in Stoic ethics appears as a brief flicker of self-awareness within an otherwise mechanical process. The emphasis on acceptance, even in the face of preventable suffering, reveals the limitations of a philosophy that offers sophisticated tools for endurance but provides inadequate resources for systematic transformation of circumstances that cause unnecessary harm.

The temporal blind spot in Stoicism lies in its treatment of psychological development as movement toward a fixed ideal of rational perfection rather than ongoing adaptation to changing circumstances and evolving goals. The Stoic sage represents an endpoint of development rather than a capacity for continued learning and behavioral flexibility that contemporary environments require.

Yet the Stoics discovered something profound about human capacity for conscious participation in psychological development through what we now recognize as metacognitive observation of mental processes. They saw that we can observe our own cognitive processes and systematically modify our responses to external circumstances. But their cosmic vision, for all its grandeur, trapped them in resignation rather than opening possibilities for creative transformation of the conditions that shape human existence. They glimpsed the reality of hierarchical cognitive control without understanding how such control could be deployed in service of systematic behavioral modification rather than merely philosophical acceptance.

A Descartes Division and Cartesian Rupture

René Descartes approached the problem of human agency by tearing reality in half, creating a wound in the fabric of existence that philosophy has never been able to heal. His systematic doubt led to the cogito argument: even if everything else is doubted, the fact that I am thinking proves that I exist as a thinking being. This established thinking substance as more certain than material substance and provided the foundation for metaphysical dualism that would both liberate and constrain philosophical discussions for centuries.

The *Meditations on First Philosophy* presents the mind as essentially a thinking thing, distinct from the extended physical body that occupies space and moves according to mechanical laws. This dualistic framework offers an elegant solution to the problem of human agency within a mechanistic natural order. If human beings are composed of both a material body subject to physical causation and an immaterial mind exempt from mechanical determination, then mental choice can influence physical behavior without being constrained by the same causal laws that govern purely physical processes.

Cartesian dualism preserves human dignity by exempting the essential self from reduction to mechanical processes. The capacity for rational judgment, moral evaluation, and free choice belongs to the immaterial soul rather than the physical brain, protecting these distinctively human capacities from scientific explanation that might undermine their reality or significance. This framework enables the development of mechanistic science for understanding the physical world while preserving spiritual and moral domains that transcend purely material causation.

The Discourse on Method outlines systematic procedures for intellectual development that represent sophisticated approaches to cognitive self-modification, anticipating key insights of metacognitive compatibilism. Methodical doubt eliminates false beliefs by subjecting all opinions to rigorous skeptical examination. Analysis breaks complex problems into simple components that can be understood clearly. Synthesis constructs solutions by proceeding from simple to complex in logical order. A comprehensive review ensures that nothing has been omitted from consideration.

These methodological principles can be applied reflexively to examine and modify one's own cognitive processes rather than merely external subject matters. Someone seeking to improve their reasoning might systematically doubt their current beliefs to eliminate those based on inadequate evidence, analyze complex problems into manageable components rather than being overwhelmed by their complexity, construct solutions through careful logical progression rather than intuitive leaps, and review their reasoning process to identify and correct systematic errors. This represents a form of temporal scaffolding operating through methodical cognitive practices.

Descartes' analysis of error offers a particularly sophisticated account of how rational agency operates in cognitive processes, pointing toward the hierarchical structure of cognitive control. Error arises when the will affirms or denies judgments that exceed the clear and distinct understanding provided by the intellect. The will is infinite in scope, capable of affirming or denying any proposition presented to it, while the understanding is finite and achieves clarity only regarding limited subject matters.

Error occurs when infinite will operates without sufficient intellectual constraint. Someone might affirm complex metaphysical doctrines based on inadequate reasoning or deny mathematical truths due to emotional resistance to their implications. The solution involves disciplining the will to give assent only to propositions that the intellect perceives clearly and distinctly.

This analysis suggests a model of rational agency where freedom and truth-seeking can be reconciled through what we now understand as metacognitive monitoring and control. When the intellect achieves clear and distinct perception of truth, the will naturally aligns itself with these perceptions without sacrificing freedom. Descartes claims that his perception of God's existence, once achieved through proper reasoning, compels assent in a way that enhances rather than diminishes freedom because alignment with truth represents the proper exercise of rational capacity.

Yet Cartesian dualism faces decisive objections that have only grown stronger with advances in neuroscience. The interaction problem, first articulated by Princess Elisabeth of Bohemia in her correspondence with Descartes, asks how an immaterial mind could causally influence a material body. If mental and physical substances share no common properties, causal interaction between them becomes impossible.

Contemporary neuroscience makes the interaction problem acute by demonstrating systematic correlations between mental events and brain processes. Cognitive capacities can be eliminated or modified by localized brain damage. Psychoactive drugs systematically alter mood, perception, and reasoning by modifying brain chemistry. Brain stimulation can evoke specific memories, emotions, or motor behaviors. Every mental capacity that has been carefully studied appears to depend on identifiable brain mechanisms that can be modified through physical interventions.

The machinery of choice reveals itself under scientific scrutiny not as the sovereign moment of immaterial decision but as a temporal process where consciousness arrives as witness to decisions already crystallizing in neural activity. What we experience as the moment of choice appears to be the conscious registration of a decision-making process that has already largely completed itself through unconscious neural activity.

More fundamentally, Cartesian dualism poses conceptual barriers to investigating how cognitive modification occurs across time. If psychological processes operate through an immaterial substance exempt from natural causation, there is no way to systematically study how present mental effort shapes future cognitive states. This isolates human psychology from natural science and prevents investigation into how behavioral change actually occurs through comprehensible mechanisms.

The problem deepens when considering the Cartesian treatment of the will as infinite and exempt from rational constraints. If the will can affirm or deny any proposition regardless of evidence, then human agency becomes fundamentally arbitrary rather than rational. There is no principled reason to cultivate disciplined thought over intellectual laziness, or to prefer virtuous behavior over vice, because the infinite will transcend the very standards that could guide such preferences. This creates what might be called a normative void within Cartesian psychology.

The infinite freedom of the will undermines the framework needed to understand why some choices advance authentic existence while others hinder it. Someone struggling with destructive patterns of thought or behavior finds no systematic guidance beyond the arbitrary exercise of infinite will. The framework cannot explain why disciplined attention should be preferred over scattered focus, or why emotional regulation should be cultivated over reactive impulse, because such preferences would limit the will's infinite freedom.

Descartes glimpsed the reality of conscious cognitive control while mislocating its source in immaterial substance. His methodological insights about systematic doubt and logical analysis remain valuable, but they require grounding in a naturalistic understanding of cognitive development rather than metaphysical exemption from natural processes. What Descartes took to be evidence of the mind's separation from nature is better understood as evidence of nature's sophistication, the emergence of hierarchical cognitive architectures that enable conscious participation in behavioral modification through entirely natural processes.

The Spinozan Resolution

Baruch Spinoza rejected Cartesian dualism as incoherent and proposed a monistic view that treats apparent mental and physical processes as different aspects of the same natural reality. *The Ethics* presents this with geometric rigor, demonstrating that everything that exists represents modifications of a single substance that can be described either as thought or as extension, but never as requiring mysterious interaction between separate realms.

This view resolves the mind-body problem by treating mental and physical processes as dual aspects of a single, unified event. Deciding to lift an arm and the neural activity that produces the movement represent the same natural occurrence described from different perspectives rather than a mysterious causal interaction between separate substances. The apparent problem of mental causation dissolves because there is no separate mental realm requiring causal connection to physical processes.

Spinoza's geometric method emphasizes the rational necessity that governs all natural processes, including human psychology. Just as each step in a geometric proof follows necessarily from prior definitions and axioms, each thought, desire, and action follows necessarily from antecedent natural causes. A child learning to speak, a person navigating social conflicts, or an adult developing exercise habits all represent natural processes unfolding according to rational necessity rather than arbitrary choice or supernatural intervention.

The Ethics begins with a thoroughgoing critique of anthropocentric illusions that prevent adequate understanding of human psychology. Spinoza writes: "Men believe themselves free, simply because they are conscious of their actions, and unconscious of the causes whereby those actions are determined." Our sense of freedom arises from consciousness of our desires combined with ignorance of the complex causal histories that generate those desires. We feel free because we experience wanting various things while remaining unaware of the genetic, developmental, and environmental factors that created our specific pattern of wants. The experience of choosing represents conscious registration of deterministic processes rather than exemption from natural causation.

This naturalistic analysis of human psychology anticipates contemporary findings in neuroscience and social psychology. Emotions, desires, and actions emerge from interactions between our biological constitution and environmental circumstances, guided by universal natural principles. Joy arises when our power of action is enhanced, sadness when it is diminished. Hope and fear emerge from imaginative projections of future possibilities. Love and hatred flow from joy and sadness associated with external causes.

Spinoza's determinism does not eliminate authentic human development or systematic self-modification. *The Ethics* presents intellectual love of God or Nature as the highest form of human achievement, arising from understanding the eternal and necessary connections that govern natural processes, including one's own psychological life. Such understanding transforms how events affect us by enabling appropriate emotional responses based on adequate rather than inadequate ideas about causation.

Someone who grasps the natural causes of human conflict is less likely to respond to interpersonal difficulties with resentment and more likely to respond with patience and understanding. Someone who recognizes the environmental and psychological factors that maintain their habitual behavior patterns is better positioned to modify those factors systematically rather than simply willing themselves to act differently.

Achieving this understanding requires what Spinoza calls emendation of the intellect: methodical effort to correct inadequate ideas and replace them with adequate ones. Inadequate ideas are partial, confused, or imaginary representations that produce ineffective actions and emotional instability. Adequate ideas clearly represent causal connections and universal principles, supporting stable joy and effective decision-making.

This intellectual development occurs through systematic study of natural processes, reflective analysis of emotional patterns, and gradual refinement of conceptual frameworks for understanding human psychology and social dynamics. Present cognitive work shapes future intellectual capacity, creating cumulative improvements in understanding that enable increasingly sophisticated approaches to behavioral modification.

However, Spinoza's philosophy faces significant limitations when extended into a comprehensive theory of systematic self-modification. The most serious problem lies in his treatment of intellectual understanding as sufficient for beneficial behavioral change. While Spinoza recognizes that intellectual development requires time and favorable circumstances, he provides an inadequate analysis of how individuals with confused ideas and problematic emotional patterns might systematically improve their condition.

Contemporary environments often present supernormal stimuli: artificial rewards, manipulative social pressures, and technological systems designed to exploit psychological mechanisms in ways that produce behaviors individuals recognize as contrary to their deeper interests. Someone might intellectually understand that social media use interferes with sleep, productivity, and face-to-face relationships, yet continue their habitual checking behaviors despite this clear comprehension.

Spinoza underestimated the environmental and social modifications required for translating intellectual understanding into behavioral change. Someone who understands the causes of their procrastination must also modify their work environment to reduce distractions, develop implementation strategies that make task initiation more automatic, create accountability systems that provide external motivation, and gradually build habits of focused work through systematic practice. Intellectual understanding provides a foundation for such systematic modification but cannot substitute for the architectural work of behavioral change.

Spinoza saw further than his predecessors into the naturalistic foundations of human psychology while remaining trapped by intellectual pride. He believed that understanding necessity would be sufficient for wisdom, failing to see that wisdom requires not just understanding but skillful intervention in the very processes that generate understanding itself. He glimpsed hierarchical cognitive control without recognizing how such hierarchies could be systematically modified to support beneficial behavioral change rather than merely philosophical contemplation.

What the Ancients Could Not See

Each tradition examined offers profound insights into human agency yet remains constrained by a focus on immediate psychological states rather than extended developmental processes. Aristotelian analysis examines discrete moments of voluntary action. Stoic disciplines cultivate rational acceptance of present circumstances. Cartesian dualism exempts the mind from natural causation. Spinozan intellectualism assumes that understanding generates behavioral change.

These limitations reflect shared assumptions about the nature of human agency that continue to constrain contemporary discussions. All traditions assume that agency operates primarily through discrete moments of rational choice rather than extended processes of environmental and psychological construction. All focus on individual psychological states rather than the social and cultural systems that shape individual development. All emphasize backward-looking questions about the ultimate sources of action rather than forward-looking questions about how behavioral patterns can be systematically improved.

Excavating these limitations reveals resources for more adequate approaches that honor the insights of philosophical tradition while transcending their conceptual constraints. The Aristotelian emphasis on character development suggests the systematic cultivation of beneficial dispositions through environmental design, rather than merely repeating virtuous acts. Stoic disciplines suggest sophisticated approaches to cognitive modification that could be extended beyond acceptance toward active transformation of circumstances. Cartesian methodical procedures provide systematic approaches to intellectual development that could be applied to behavioral architecture rather than merely abstract reasoning. Spinozan naturalism enables investigation of psychological modification as a natural process amenable to scientific understanding and practical intervention.

What these traditions could not fully comprehend was the capacity for metacognitive compatibilism.

We are inheritors of wisdom and blindness in equal measure. What the ancients saw clearly, we must preserve. What they could not see, we must learn to perceive. The question is not whether Aristotle or Spinoza was right, but how their partial truths can be woven into an understanding adequate to our time and our possibilities.

The nature of human becoming eluded them not through a failure of intelligence, but through the limitations of their age. They could not have imagined the mechanisms we now understand, could not have foreseen the challenges we now face, and could not have envisioned the possibilities we now glimpse. Yet they prepared the ground on which we stand, and their insights remain essential components of any adequate understanding of human agency.

What emerges from this investigation is not supernatural mystery but a natural capacity for temporal scaffolding. Their struggles with agency point toward what we can now recognize as hierarchical cognitive architectures that enable conscious participation in behavioral development through entirely naturalistic processes.

This capacity represents neither Cartesian exemption from natural law nor Spinozan intellectual contemplation, but something more practical and more powerful. It is the ability to become architects of our own conditioning rather than merely its products. The ancients saw fragments of this truth scattered across their different systems. In understanding how their insights point toward metacognitive compatibilism and temporal scaffolding, we discover not exemption from the natural order but our deepest participation in its creative processes.

The Mind Observing Mind

"What if the controller and the controlled were the same system learning to conduct itself?"

SOMETHING CURIOUS HAPPENS WHEN we turn our attention inward. We discover that the very act of looking changes what we see. The mind, examining its own operations, finds itself in the peculiar position of being both observer and observed, detective and suspect, scientist and specimen. This recursive capacity may be the most remarkable achievement in the long history of evolutionary development, yet philosophy has barely begun to grasp what it means for human agency.

We speak casually of "self-awareness" as though it were the most natural thing in the world. In reality, it represents perhaps the strangest phenomenon in nature:

matter organized in such a way that it can observe its own organization. A hurricane does not watch itself spin. A river does not monitor its own flow. But human consciousness can step outside its immediate operations and examine them as objects of investigation. This ability transforms everything we thought we knew about choice, control, and the possibilities for deliberate self-modification.

When you notice your mind wandering during a conversation and gently redirect your attention back to the speaker, what exactly has occurred? Something within your cognitive system has observed another part of that same system and initiated a corrective response. The observer and the observed exist within the same biological boundaries, yet they function as distinct processes capable of influencing one another. This is not the simple mechanical feedback of a thermostat, where temperature sensors trigger heating or cooling systems according to predetermined parameters. Human metacognitive awareness involves one part of the mind evaluating another part according to standards that can themselves be examined and modified.

Consider what happens when someone catches themselves in a moment of harsh self-criticism. They recognize the critical voice, observe its effects on their emotional state, and perhaps choose to respond with greater compassion. But who is doing the observing? Who chooses the response? And what allows this observer to transcend the very patterns it observes? We find ourselves confronting a puzzle that touches on the deepest questions about human nature. How can a system modify itself from within? How can consciousness lift itself by its own bootstraps?

The answer lies in understanding that consciousness is not a thing, but a process; not a unified command center, but a dynamic coalition of specialized capacities that have learned to monitor and influence one another. What we experience as unified decision-making reveals itself under examination as intricate architectures where multiple systems evaluate, regulate, and modify each other in cascading hierarchies of control. The person choosing whether to help a struggling colleague operates not through simple will but through coordinated activity between networks that detect social cues, assess long-term consequences, monitor emotional responses, and implement behavioral strategies.

This hierarchical organization fundamentally transforms our understanding of human agency. We are not unified commanders issuing orders to passive mental machinery. We are dynamic coalitions of specialized systems, each capable of observing and modifying the operations of others within the same cognitive architecture. Here lies the groundwork of metacognitive compatibilism, which posits that consciousness is the brain's evolved capacity for recursive self-observation and regulation.

The apparent mystery of mental causation dissolves when we recognize that higher-order patterns of neural organization can constrain and influence lower-order processes through mechanisms that operate entirely within natural law while enabling unprecedented forms of behavioral sophistication.

These hierarchical structures did not emerge overnight. They represent the culmination of evolutionary developments in behavioral flexibility, the gradual emergence of cognitive architectures capable of stepping outside their own immediate operations to evaluate and modify them across extended time horizons.

The Long Apprenticeship of Self-Observation

The capacity for self-observation represents no supernatural addition to natural processes but the culmination of evolutionary developments in behavioral flexibility. We are the heirs of creatures who learned to watch themselves think, and in this watching discovered the seeds of transformation.

Early nervous systems functioned as simple relay networks, transmitting information from sensory organs to motor systems with minimal intermediate processing. Touch triggered withdrawal reflexes through direct pathways requiring no central integration or behavioral choice. Such systems permitted rapid protective responses but provided limited behavioral flexibility when environmental circumstances changed.

The development of centralized nervous systems created new possibilities for integrating multiple information sources before generating responses. Central processing permitted coordinated responses to complex environmental situations by evaluating multiple sensory inputs simultaneously rather than each input triggering a separate motor output. A predator's approach detected through visual, auditory, and olfactory channels simultaneously permits more refined escape responses than any single channel could support, weaving separate threads of information into coherent patterns of meaning. The past became a prologue to present action, as experience transformed into wisdom.

Memory systems permitted response modification based on past experience rather than relying entirely on genetically programmed reflexes. An animal encountering a particular predator in a specific location might modify its behavior when approaching that location again, demonstrating primitive learning that improves survival through experience rather than immediate environmental feedback. Predictive systems carried this development further, permitting response generation based on anticipated future states rather than merely current inputs. Rather than waiting for environmental changes to occur before responding, predictive networks could initiate behavioral adjustments based on patterns detected in environmental changes over time.

Human metacognitive abilities represent refined extensions of these basic functions for behavioral integration, learning, and prediction. Yet they involve qualitative advances that create unprecedented possibilities for deliberate self-modification. Human consciousness can observe not merely environmental states but its own psychological states as objects of attention and evaluation.

This recursive ability creates unique possibilities for deliberate modification of the very mechanisms that generate behavior. The crucial development lies in the emergence of hierarchical processing architectures where higher-order systems can monitor and regulate the operations of lower-order systems within the same cognitive architecture. We are nature learning to observe itself. In this observation lies the seed of transformation that exceeds anything possible in unconscious natural processes while remaining entirely natural in its mechanisms.

Consider how this capacity manifests in everyday experience. When someone notices themselves becoming irritated during a traffic jam and recognizes this irritation as counterproductive, they engage in a form of recursive observation. The irritation arises from lower-level systems responding to environmental frustration, but higher-level systems can observe this response, evaluate its utility, and potentially modify it through various strategies. They might reframe the delay as an opportunity for quiet reflection, practice breathing exercises to regulate physiological arousal, or essentially accept the situation as beyond their immediate control.

This capacity for recursive observation extends far beyond simple emotional regulation. Consider someone learning a complex skill, such as playing a musical instrument. They must not only coordinate their physical movements and attend to auditory feedback but also observe their own learning process. They notice when their attention wanders, when frustration interferes with practice, and when certain practice strategies prove more effective than others. They develop strategies for managing their own motivation, structuring their practice sessions, and pushing through plateaus in skill development. Learning involves not just acquiring the target skill but developing expertise in managing the psychological processes that support skill acquisition.

The recursive nature of this capacity creates extraordinary possibilities for self-modification that extend across virtually every domain of human experience. Someone can observe their social anxiety, understand the thoughts and behaviors that maintain it, and develop strategies for gradual exposure that reduce anxious responses over time. They can notice patterns in their decision-making, identify cognitive biases that lead to poor choices, and develop frameworks for more effective deliberation. They can observe their habitual responses to stress, conflict, or disappointment and cultivate alternative responses that better serve their long-term flourishing.

Yet this capacity also creates characteristic challenges and paradoxes. The very act of observing psychological processes can modify them in unintended ways. Excessive self-monitoring can create anxiety, self-consciousness, or obsessive patterns that interfere with natural psychological functioning. Someone who becomes too focused on monitoring their social performance might develop social anxiety that proves more problematic than their original social awkwardness. The attempt to observe and control mental states can create secondary problems more difficult to address than original difficulties.

The Architecture of Recursive Control

The brain reveals itself not as a simple command structure but as a federation of specialized systems, each capable of observing and influencing the others. Modern neuroscience provides detailed maps of these networks, revealing sophisticated architectures that support deliberate self-modification through entirely natural mechanisms.

Different regions of the prefrontal cortex specialize in distinct aspects of self-monitoring and behavioral regulation, working together to create hierarchical control networks. As mentioned before, when someone notices their attention wandering during a conversation and redirects it toward the speaker, specific prefrontal networks maintain representations of both wandering attention and conversational goals while computing the discrepancy between actual and desired states. This region permits the cognitive comparison and planning necessary for deliberate behavioral modification.

Other brain regions serve complementary functions in this architecture of self-control. The anterior cingulate cortex functions as a conflict monitor, recruiting prefrontal control networks when automatic behaviors conflict with our goals. When someone committed to healthy eating encounters tempting but nutritionally poor food, anterior cingulate networks detect the conflict between immediate desire and long-term health commitments, generating signals that recruit prefrontal control networks to implement regulatory strategies.

This conflict detection demonstrates remarkable sensitivity to different types of conflicts between competing psychological activities. Some regions specialize in detecting conflicts between competing thoughts or judgments, while others detect conflicts between immediate desires and long-term values. This functional specialization enables the targeted recruitment of appropriate regulatory systems, depending on the specific nature of the control challenges.

The medial prefrontal cortex integrates emotional and social information with cognitive control processes, enabling complex self-regulation in interpersonal contexts and supporting identity-based behavioral modification. This region is activated when people think about their future selves, evaluate whether their actions align with their values, or consider how their behavior affects others. It provides crucial links between abstract self-concepts and concrete behavioral choices, translating values into action.

Rather than residing in a single brain region, metacognitive control emerges from coordinated interactions between distributed networks that contribute specialized capabilities to overall self-regulatory functioning. The default mode network, active during rest and introspection, constructs and maintains temporal identity narratives that provide motivational frameworks for sustained behavioral change. When people engage in what feels like mind-wandering, this network performs essential temporal integration: connecting past experiences with present circumstances and future goals, constructing coherent stories about personal development possibilities, and maintaining a sense of continuous identity across time that makes long-term behavioral consistency psychologically meaningful.

The salience network directs attention to internal psychological states and external environmental features relevant to current goals, serving as a switching mechanism that permits flexible attention regulation between external focus and internal self-monitoring. This network enables the attentional flexibility necessary for effective metacognitive observation while remaining responsive to environmental demands requiring external attention.

Executive control networks implement specific regulatory strategies once monitoring systems identify the need for intervention. These networks demonstrate remarkable specialization, with different sub-networks handling different types of cognitive control, including attentional regulation, emotional regulation, response inhibition, and working memory updating. Each network serves as a specialized tool in the cognitive toolkit, enabling deliberate self-modification.

Effective cognitive self-regulation involves characteristic patterns of coordinated activity across these distributed networks rather than simple activation of individual brain regions. When people successfully regulate emotional responses, maintain attention on difficult tasks, or resist immediate temptations in favor of long-term goals, brain imaging reveals patterns of prefrontal activation combined with modulation of activity in regions associated with the psychological processes being regulated.

The brain emerges not as a simple machine but as a symphony of specialized systems, each capable of monitoring and influencing the others in intricate hierarchies of control that make conscious self-transformation possible.

Yet this neuroscientific understanding creates fundamental questions about the nature of mental causation that threaten to undermine the entire framework of metacognitive agency.

The Paradox of Mental Causation

As we have seen, the very idea of a mind observing and modifying its own operations raises a profound challenge. If mental events depend on brain events, and brain events unfold according to physical laws, how can higher-order mental processes genuinely influence lower-order ones? The problem of mental causation threatens to reduce apparent self-modification to a mere byproduct of underlying neural processes, leaving consciousness as a powerless spectator of its own neural drama.

When someone notices anxious thoughts and successfully redirects their attention to calm breathing, neuroscience reveals that this process involves the prefrontal regions monitoring conflict detection systems and implementing attentional control through the modulation of attention networks. But if all these processes unfold according to prior neural states and physical laws, what genuine causal work does the conscious recognition of anxiety perform? Does awareness make a difference, or does it merely witness differences already determined by prior neural events?

Several approaches preserve genuine mental causation while remaining consistent with naturalistic frameworks, revealing that the apparent threat to agency dissolves under closer examination. Recent work in complexity science suggests that emergent properties can possess genuine causal efficacy through the setting of constraints and boundary conditions, rather than the application of force. Higher-order patterns create contexts that channel lower-order processes in specific directions without violating physical laws, much as riverbanks shape water flow without adding energy to the system.

Metacognitive awareness might constrain neural processing by establishing attentional priorities, goal hierarchies, and regulatory contexts that influence how neural networks process information, creating genuine top-down causation through organizational constraint rather than mysterious intervention in physical processes.

Non-reductive physicalism maintains that mental events are physical events described at higher levels of organization, but that these higher-level descriptions capture causal patterns invisible at lower levels. Just as biological explanations remain valid even though biological events are ultimately physical, psychological explanations capture real causal relationships even though psychological events are ultimately neural. The conductor influences the orchestra through entirely physical mechanisms, yet the musical patterns that emerge transcend any description that focuses only on individual instruments.

Interventionist approaches ground causation in counterfactual relationships rather than mechanisms, defining causes as factors whose manipulation would make a difference to their effects under appropriate conditions. Mental events count as genuine causes if manipulating them would make a difference to their effects, regardless of the mechanisms through which this influence operates. Cognitive interventions that successfully modify behavior demonstrate genuine mental causation regardless of their neural implementation.

Meditation training provides compelling evidence for genuine mental causation. Deliberate cultivation of metacognitive awareness produces measurable changes in brain structure and function including increased cortical thickness in attention-related regions, enhanced connectivity between control and emotional processing networks, and reduced activity in mind-wandering networks. These neural changes correlate with improved attention regulation, emotional stability, and stress resilience, suggesting that mental training produces physical changes that support enhanced psychological function.

The evidence supports genuine mental causation operating through natural mechanisms. Cognitive behavioral therapy produces both symptomatic improvement and measurable brain changes. Meditation training enhances attention regulation abilities while modifying neural structure and function. Cognitive training programs improve working memory performance through both behavioral and neural modifications.

These interventions work by modifying higher-order cognitive patterns that then influence lower-order psychological processes through entirely natural mechanisms. The fact that the mechanisms are natural does not eliminate their causal efficacy or reduce their significance for human agency. The mind emerges from matter while transcending its limitations through hierarchical organization that creates genuine novelty within natural law.

Developing Metacognitive Expertise

Metacognitive awareness exists on a continuum that can be developed through training. Understanding these levels reveals both possibilities and limitations of human cognitive self-regulation while providing practical guidance for developing more refined self-modification abilities.

Basic metacognitive awareness involves simple recognition that cognitive processes are occurring. This includes noticing thoughts, feelings, or desires without engaging in a detailed analysis of their content or dynamics. Most adults possess this level, enabling elementary cognitive control such as recognizing attention lapses, identifying emotional responses, or detecting conflicts between different goals or desires. Even this basic level represents a remarkable achievement, distinguishing human consciousness from simpler information processing systems.

The ability to recognize "I am thinking about tomorrow's meeting" involves higher-order processes that can observe and categorize lower-order cognitive content while maintaining some independence from that content. This basic awareness enables simple cognitive control strategies, including attention redirection, emotional labeling, and basic impulse regulation. Someone who notices their mind wandering during reading can redirect attention to the text. Someone who recognizes feeling anxious can implement simple calming strategies.

Yet basic metacognitive awareness often remains sporadic and reactive rather than methodical and proactive. People may notice attention wandering only after extended periods of distraction, recognize emotions only after they have intensified significantly, or detect goal conflicts only when they create obvious problems.

Intermediate metacognitive awareness involves detailed observation of cognitive content, quality, and dynamics. Someone at this level might notice not just anxiety but specific environmental triggers that activate anxiety, physical sensations accompanying anxious feelings, thought patterns maintaining or intensifying anxiety, and behavioral impulses generated by anxious states.

This level enables refined cognitive control strategies, including cognitive reappraisal, attentional regulation, and complex emotional regulation. Someone noticing anxiety patterns in specific social situations can develop targeted strategies addressing particular triggers and maintaining factors rather than attempting general anxiety elimination through willpower alone.

Intermediate awareness also enables recognition of cognitive biases and errors in thinking. Someone might notice their tendency to catastrophize about uncertain outcomes, to focus selectively on negative information while ignoring positive evidence, or to make attributions about others' behavior that reflect their own insecurities rather than accurate assessment.

The development of intermediate metacognitive awareness often involves learning to distinguish between different types of mental events, including thoughts, emotions, sensations, and motivational states that basic awareness treats as undifferentiated mental content. This differentiation enables more precise intervention strategies tailored to specific types of psychological processes.

Advanced metacognitive awareness involves a refined sensitivity to subtle mental qualities combined with frameworks for understanding psychological phenomena. Someone at this level might observe micro-emotions occurring within seconds, notice relationships between different thought types and their effects on mood and energy, or recognize subtle attentional movements preceding obvious changes in focus.

Expert meditators often describe observing mental phenomena with nuanced attention, much like a wine connoisseur's discerning taste. They might notice peaceful concentration beginning to shift toward restlessness by observing specific sequences, such as a slight increase in mental activity, followed by physical restlessness, and then evaluative thoughts about the quality of their concentration.

Advanced practitioners report awareness of what might be called cognitive architecture, recognizing structural patterns and relationships between different mental processes. They observe how certain types of thoughts cluster together, how emotional states influence accessibility of different memories, and how changes in physical posture affect mental clarity and stability.

This architectural awareness enables approaches to cognitive modification that work with rather than against natural psychological patterns. Rather than fighting unwanted mental states through effortful suppression, advanced practitioners learn to modify conditions that give rise to these states, creating cognitive environments that naturally support beneficial mental patterns.

At its highest development, metacognitive awareness approaches what contemplatives call "witnessing consciousness", which is a fancy way of saying a stable capacity to observe all mental phenomena with equanimity, neither grasping at pleasant states nor pushing away unpleasant ones but maintaining clear awareness of whatever arises in the field of consciousness.

Developing Metacognitive Capacity

Advanced metacognitive awareness develops through several key components that can be cultivated through appropriate training and practice. Understanding these components provides practical guidance for developing refined self-observation abilities, enabling effective temporal scaffolding.

Attentional flexibility enables redirection from external stimuli to internal psychological states and sustained observation over extended periods. This ability can be developed through meditation practices that involve attention training, mindfulness exercises, and contemplative practices that cultivate present-moment awareness and strengthen sustained attention.

Someone developing attentional flexibility might begin by observing their breath for brief periods, gradually extending the duration while learning to notice when attention has wandered and gently return it to the chosen focus. Over time, this practice develops the ability to observe internal psychological states with the same sustained attention initially applied to breathing.

Cognitive decentering involves the ability to observe thoughts and feelings as mental events rather than identifying completely with their content. This creates psychological distance, enabling more objective evaluation while reducing emotional reactivity that can interfere with clear observation. Someone with strong decentering ability can observe thoughts like "I'm inadequate" or "This situation is hopeless" as mental events that arise and pass, rather than as accurate descriptions of reality that require an emotional response.

Decentering develops through practices that cultivate an observer perspective toward mental phenomena. Meditation practices that involve noting or labeling mental events help establish psychological distance from mental content. Cognitive therapy techniques that teach people to examine evidence for and against automatic thoughts develop the ability to evaluate rather than immediately believe mental content.

The development of decentering often involves recognizing the difference between experiencing emotions and being emotions, having thoughts and being thoughts, or encountering sensations and identifying with sensations. This recognition creates space for conscious response rather than automatic reaction to psychological content.

Emotional regulation provides the psychological stability necessary for sustained self-observation even when observing difficult or distressing mental states. Without adequate regulation ability, metacognitive observation can become overwhelming or create secondary problems such as anxiety about anxiety or depression about depression.

Developing emotional regulation often involves learning to relate differently to difficult emotions rather than trying to eliminate them entirely. Someone might learn to observe anxiety as a temporary physiological activation rather than evidence of danger, or to experience sadness as an appropriate response to loss rather than a sign of personal inadequacy.

Acceptance-based approaches to emotional regulation teach people to experience difficult emotions without judgment or avoidance, while maintaining the ability to take effective action. This involves developing tolerance for emotional discomfort rather than requiring immediate relief, recognizing emotions as temporary experiences rather than permanent states, and understanding emotions as information about circumstances rather than commands for action.

Conceptual frameworks for understanding mental phenomena provide organizational structures that support the observation and categorization of psychological processes. Various psychological theories, philosophical frameworks, and contemplative traditions offer different conceptual tools enhancing metacognitive observation ability.

Understanding different theoretical perspectives enables more refined metacognitive observation by providing multiple conceptual lenses for interpreting psychological phenomena. Someone familiar with both Buddhist and Western psychological frameworks can recognize mental events from multiple perspectives, potentially gaining a richer understanding than either framework alone would provide.

The cultivation of metacognitive expertise represents perhaps the most refined expression of human cognitive evolution. We have the ability for our consciousness to observe and modify its own operations with precision, which enables our conscious participation in psychological development.

Hierarchical Intervention Strategies

Metacognitive hierarchies enable different types of cognitive interventions operating at various levels of organization and temporal scales. Understanding these intervention hierarchies reveals how self-modification can address cognitive and behavioral patterns across multiple levels of psychological organization.

Immediate-level interventions operate through direct modification of ongoing psychological processes as they occur. Attentional interventions redirect attention away from stimuli that trigger problematic responses or toward stimuli that support desired responses. When someone notices becoming anxious during a social interaction and deliberately shifts attention to their breathing or to positive aspects of the interaction, they engage in attentional intervention that can produce immediate effects.

These interventions work by modifying inputs to psychological systems rather than changing the systems themselves. By controlling what receives attention, individuals can influence which cognitive and emotional processes become activated without directly modifying those processes. The effectiveness of immediate interventions depends on the strength of competing psychological processes and the availability of cognitive resources for implementing control strategies.

Cognitive reappraisal interventions operate at the level of interpretation and meaning-making by changing how situations are mentally represented and evaluated. Instead of viewing a challenging work project as a threat to reputation, cognitive reappraisal might frame it as an opportunity for skill development. These interventions modify the conceptual frameworks that determine how situations are interpreted and what emotional and behavioral responses are generated.

Reappraisal strategies include perspective-taking, which involves considering alternative viewpoints; temporal distancing, examining situations from a future perspective; and benefit-finding, which identifies the positive aspects of challenging circumstances. Research demonstrates that cognitive reappraisal can effectively reduce negative emotions while maintaining or enhancing positive emotions.

Behavioral-level interventions address patterns of action that maintain or reinforce problematic psychological states. For instance, someone struggling with social anxiety might practice social behaviors that contradict anxious avoidance patterns, creating a new behavioral repertoire that supports different psychological responses to social situations. Similarly, a person coping with depression might deliberately schedule small, manageable activities that provide a sense of accomplishment, gradually disrupting the cycle of withdrawal and passivity that sustains depressive states.

These interventions recognize that psychological and behavioral patterns influence each other through complex feedback loops. Avoidant behaviors maintain anxiety by preventing learning experiences that would reduce anxiety, while confident behaviors can generate psychological states that support continued confidence.

Environmental modification interventions address external conditions that trigger or maintain problematic psychological patterns. This might involve changing physical environments to reduce exposure to triggers, modifying social relationships to increase support for beneficial behaviors, or restructuring daily routines to create conditions that naturally foster a desired mental state.

Identity-level interventions operate at the deepest level by modifying narrative frameworks and self-concepts that organize psychological and behavioral patterns across extended time periods. Someone might transition from seeing themselves as "a person with anxiety" to "a person learning to manage anxiety effectively," creating identity frameworks that support sustained behavioral change efforts.

These intervention levels interact in complex ways within metacognitive hierarchies, creating possibilities for coordinated change efforts that address multiple levels simultaneously. The architecture of intervention reveals consciousness as the engineer of its own transformation, capable of working across multiple levels of psychological organization to create change that transcends the limitations of any single approach.

The Observer Paradox and Recursive Control

The most refined forms of metacognitive control involve recursive self-modification, which is the use of higher-order cognitive processes to modify the operation of these same higher-order processes. This represents the pinnacle of human self-regulatory ability while creating complex philosophical challenges about the nature of the self engaging in such modification.

Someone who recognizes that their self-criticism patterns interfere with their ability to learn from mistakes begins by using metacognitive awareness to observe their self-critical thoughts. They then evaluate these observation processes themselves, noticing that their self-observation sometimes becomes another form of self-criticism. They might then develop strategies for observing their self-observation processes with greater compassion and acceptance, creating what cognitive scientists call "strange loops" where the system recursively applies its operations to itself.

This recursive structure creates possibilities for cognitive self-engineering, which involves modifying cognitive processes through the application of these same processes to themselves. Unlike simple behavioral conditioning or habit formation, recursive self-modification involves deliberate restructuring of cognitive architecture, generating thoughts, emotions, and behaviors.

Meta-attention involves using attention to observe and modify attentional patterns themselves. Someone might notice that their attention habitually focuses on negative aspects of situations and practice redirecting attention toward positive or neutral aspects. Over time, this meta-attentional training modifies default attentional patterns, creating lasting changes in cognitive and emotional responses without requiring constant effortful control.

Meta-emotional regulation involves using emotional awareness and regulation strategies to modify emotional regulation processes themselves. Someone might recognize that their attempts to suppress negative emotions intensify these emotions, and thus develop more effective approaches, such as acceptance-based strategies or cognitive reappraisal techniques.

Yet recursive self-modification creates characteristic challenges that reveal complex relationships between observation and modification within conscious systems. The observer paradox emerges from recognition that observing cognitive processes necessarily modifies these processes, sometimes in unintended ways that complicate regulatory efforts.

Excessive self-monitoring can create anxiety, self-consciousness, or obsessive cognitive patterns that interfere with natural cognitive functioning. Someone who becomes too focused on monitoring their social anxiety might develop "anxiety about anxiety" that proves more problematic than the original anxiety.

Recursive control problems emerge when metacognitive processes become targets of metacognitive regulation in ways that create self-defeating loops. Someone might develop criticism of their self-criticism, anxiety about their tendency toward anxiety, or sadness about their depression. These recursive loops can amplify rather than resolve problematic patterns by creating additional layers of problematic mental content.

Managing recursive dynamics requires an understanding of metacognitive processes and their interactions. It often involves what contemplative traditions call "effortless effort," which means sustaining mindful attention without imposing excessive control or self-conscious manipulation on natural psychological processes.

The key insight is that effective recursive self-modification requires a delicate balance between active intervention and passive acceptance. Too little intervention leaves problematic patterns unchanged, while too much intervention creates additional problems through excessive self-consciousness and control. Skilled practitioners learn to intervene just enough to guide psychological processes in beneficial directions without disrupting their natural flow.

In the recursive depths of metacognitive control, we encounter consciousness at its most refined, with the mind observing the mind observing the mind in an infinite regress that somehow achieves practical transformation through the very paradox that seems to make it impossible.

The Paradox of the Self-Modifying Self

Recursive self-modification raises fundamental philosophical questions about the nature of the self engaging in such modification. If all cognitive processes, including metacognitive processes, operate through deterministic mechanisms, what exactly is the "self" that observes and modifies these processes? How can a determined system genuinely modify itself rather than simply following predetermined patterns of apparent self-modification?

Traditional notions of a unified controlling self become problematic when examined through cognitive science and metacognitive theory. What we experience as "self" appears to be ongoing construction emerging from complex interactions between multiple cognitive processes rather than a thing that controls these processes from outside the system.

Yet metacognitive experience clearly involves something that feels like a self observing and modifying other aspects of itself. When someone recognizes "I am becoming anxious" and implements anxiety regulation strategies, there appears to be an observer, decision-maker, and regulator that coordinates these activities. The challenge is explaining this phenomenology without requiring supernatural agents or mysterious exemptions from causation.

The emergent self hypothesis suggests that the sense of self emerges from recursive interactions between cognitive processes rather than existing as separate controlling entity. The "self" engaging in temporal scaffolding represents pattern of cognitive organization that maintains some consistency across time rather than thing that exists independently of cognitive processes.

This emergent self possesses genuine causal efficacy within the cognitive system because it represents higher-order patterns of organization that constrain and influence lower-order processes. The fact that these higher-order patterns emerge from lower-order processes does not eliminate their causal influence, just as the fact that hurricanes emerge from atmospheric processes does not eliminate their ability to influence weather patterns.

The narrative self constructed through autobiographical memory, future planning, and identity formation provides continuity and coherence that permits sustained behavioral modification across time. This narrative self is clearly constructed rather than discovered, but this does not make it arbitrary or ineffective. The stories we tell about ourselves have genuine consequences for behavior and experience.

An individual who constructs an identity narrative around being "a person who takes care of their health" will be more likely to make behavioral choices consistent with this identity than someone who lacks such a narrative structure. The narrative provides a motivational framework that influences decision-making, even though the narrative itself is constructed rather than an objective fact about personal essence.

The distributed self model suggests that self-experience emerges from interactions between multiple cognitive subsystems rather than residing in any particular brain region or cognitive process. Different aspects of self-experience, including autobiographical memory, future planning, value evaluation, and social identity, are implemented in different neural networks that coordinate to create unified self-experience.

This distributed architecture explains why different types of brain damage can selectively impair different aspects of self-experience while leaving others intact. The distributed model also explains individual differences in self-experience and metacognitive ability. People vary in the strength and coordination of different cognitive subsystems that contribute to self-experience, leading to differences in narrative coherence, temporal reasoning, value consistency, and behavioral control ability.

The self capable of temporal scaffolding is neither an uncaused agent exempt from natural processes nor a mere illusion with no causal efficacy. It is an emergent pattern of cognitive organization that arises from natural processes while possessing a genuine ability to influence these same processes through recursive loops of observation and modification.

This understanding preserves both naturalistic accounts of human psychology and the practical reality of self-modification without requiring mysterious exemptions from causation or reductions of human agency to mechanical determinism. We are neither masters of an internal kingdom nor slaves to neural machinery. We are patterns of organization that have learned to observe and modify themselves, natural phenomena that have become conscious of their own nature and acquired the ability to participate in their own evolution.

Implications for Temporal Scaffolding

The metacognitive hierarchies examined here provide a foundation for understanding how human agency operates through temporal processes rather than discrete moments of choice. The ability for metacognitive awareness permits individuals to observe their own behavioral patterns, identify environmental and psychological factors that influence these patterns, and design interventions that modify these factors in beneficial directions.

An individual who develops refined metacognitive awareness can recognize that their attention tends to fragment in digital environments, understand how this fragmentation affects their learning and productivity, and deliberately modify their technological environment to support sustained focus. The hierarchical structure of metacognitive control permits coordinated interventions operating at multiple levels of psychological organization simultaneously.

Immediate attentional interventions can provide short-term management of distracting thoughts, while environmental modifications create conditions that reduce the frequency of such distractions. Identity-level interventions that frame technological challenges as opportunities for developing stronger attention regulation can provide motivational frameworks that sustain modification efforts across time.

The neuroplasticity of metacognitive systems means that present training in self-observation and cognitive control creates lasting enhancements in capacity for future self-modification. Regular meditation practice not only improves current attention regulation but also strengthens neural networks that support attention regulation in future situations. This creates positive feedback loops where successful self-modification enhances capacity for further self-modification.

Yet the analysis also reveals important limitations of metacognitive approaches to behavioral change. Excessive self-monitoring can create secondary problems that interfere with natural psychological functioning. Recursive control loops can amplify rather than resolve problematic patterns when interventions become targets of further intervention.

These limitations suggest that effective temporal scaffolding requires a balanced approach that combines deliberate self-observation with environmental design and social support, rather than relying exclusively on individual metacognitive effort.

The observer paradox demonstrates that conscious awareness necessarily modifies the processes being observed, creating opportunities for beneficial change while also creating risks of unintended consequences. Understanding these dynamics enables more skillful approaches to self-modification that work in harmony with, rather than against, natural psychological processes.

The emergent nature of the self engaging in metacognitive control means that temporal scaffolding represents genuine self-modification rather than external manipulation of a passive system. The patterns of cognitive organization that constitute the self can genuinely modify themselves through recursive feedback loops, creating possibilities for continued development that transcend initial biological and environmental constraints.

This analysis provides naturalistic foundations for human agency that avoid both libertarian fantasies about exemption from causation and determinist reductions that eliminate genuine self-modification capacity.

Metacognitive compatibilism reveals human agency as neither supernatural intervention nor mechanical illusion, but as a sophisticated natural capacity for recursive self-organization that enables conscious participation in behavioral development.

The mind emerges as a process rather than a thing, a verb rather than a noun. In recognizing this, we open possibilities for conscious participation in psychological development that neither require supernatural intervention nor reduce human agency to mechanical determinism. We are the process by which nature has learned to modify itself through conscious observation and intentional intervention.

This capacity represents the most sophisticated expression of evolutionary development: matter organized in such complexity that it can observe its own organization and systematically modify that organization in pursuit of goals that transcend immediate survival imperatives. In exercising this capacity skillfully through temporal scaffolding, we honor both our natural origins and our transcendent possibilities while remaining grounded in understanding that makes continued development possible rather than mysterious.

The Architecture of Becoming

"But what if habits themselves could be architected? What if excellence became not accidental repetition but deliberate construction?"

THE IMPASSE SEEMS COMPLETE. Libertarian free will requires impossible causal breaks. Hard determinism eliminates responsibility. Traditional compatibilism fails to distinguish genuine agency from sophisticated manipulation. Each approach to moral responsibility founders on problems that appear insurmountable within its own conceptual framework.

Yet humans demonstrably possess capacities that these frameworks struggle to explain. We observe our own mental processes with a clarity no other creature achieves. We design environments that shape our future behavior in predictable ways. We create social structures that support beneficial choices while making harmful ones more difficult. We deliberately modify the conditions that influence our decisions in ways that alter what we will likely choose when decision points arise.

Something these traditional frameworks miss entirely becomes visible once we shift attention from the moment of choice to the architecture of time itself. The question is not whether we could have chosen otherwise at the instant of decision. The question is what capacities we possess for systematically constructing the conditions under which decisions occur.

This changes everything.

The Mechanism Revealed

Human agency operates through time in ways that make the libertarian search for ultimate origination irrelevant while preserving everything worth wanting in the concept of free will.

Present cognitive resources can construct future decision environments in ways that shape what we will choose when those futures arrive. This capacity for deliberate architectural modification through time represents genuine agency operating through entirely deterministic mechanisms. We become free not by standing outside of causation, but by participating skillfully in causal processes, using our present understanding to build future conditions that support the kinds of choices we reflectively endorse.

Consider what happens when someone recognizes a destructive pattern in their intimate relationships. Perhaps they consistently choose partners who recreate the emotional unavailability they experienced in childhood. The pattern operates largely below conscious awareness. They feel attracted to certain people, pursue relationships with them, and only after the relationship fails do they recognize the familiar dynamic. The same absence. The same desperate attempts to earn love. The same ultimate abandonment.

Traditional frameworks are unable to explain this situation adequately. The libertarian suggests they freely choose these partners at each decision point, but this ignores the systematic nature of the pattern and the unconscious factors driving attraction. The hard determinist notes that childhood experiences create neural patterns that generate these attraction responses, but this provides no guidance for change. The compatibilist observes that they act on their own desires without external compulsion, yet they desperately want to desire different partners and cannot understand why they repeatedly choose the same type.

The answer lies not in the moment of choice but in the architecture preceding it. By the time they feel attracted to someone, the decision environment has already been constructed by factors, including childhood attachment patterns, current emotional state, social context, and accumulated relationship history. These factors do not eliminate agency. They constitute the landscape within which agency operates.

But here emerges the crucial insight that dissolves the free will problem. While they cannot choose whom they feel attracted to at the moment attraction arises, they can observe the pattern across relationships. They can notice that the people who trigger the strongest attraction share specific characteristics. They can recognize that these characteristics correlate with emotional unavailability. They can understand that the attraction itself reflects childhood attachment patterns rather than genuine compatibility.

This metacognitive awareness creates temporal distance between the arising of attraction and the decision to pursue a relationship. In that distance, agency becomes possible. Not through libertarian exemption from the causes generating attraction, but through conscious construction of decision architectures that modify how attraction influences behavior.

They might establish a practice of discussing potential partners with trusted friends who can recognize warning signs they themselves cannot see through the fog of attraction. They might implement a waiting period before pursuing new relationships, allowing initial attraction intensity to diminish enough that rational evaluation becomes possible. They might work therapeutically to understand childhood patterns while developing new neural associations between security and love. They might consciously choose to date people they find interesting rather than intensely attractive, allowing different relationship dynamics to emerge.

None of these interventions eliminate the unconscious factors generating problematic attraction patterns. But they modify the decision architecture in ways that prevent attraction from automatically determining relationship choices. The interventions work not by breaking causal chains but by adding new causal factors that shape outcomes differently.

This is temporal scaffolding. The present self uses available cognitive resources to construct conditions that the future self will encounter when making decisions. The construction operates through entirely deterministic causal processes. Present observations cause therapeutic insights. Therapeutic insights cause new neural patterns. New neural patterns cause modified attraction responses. Modified attraction responses cause different relationship choices. Each step follows from prior causes in ways that science can investigate and predict.

Yet the person exercises genuine control over their developmental trajectory precisely through conscious participation in these causal processes. They architect their own transformation by understanding and deliberately modifying the factors that determine their behavior. The agency operates through causation rather than standing apart from it.

The temporal dimension proves essential. Present and future selves exist in different contexts with different resources available. The present self possesses perspective, emotional distance, and freedom from immediate attraction that the future self will lack when attraction arises. The future self will have an immediate choice opportunity but will lack the calm observation and rational evaluation that the present self can access. By using present advantages to compensate for future limitations, the person creates behavioral continuity across time that would be impossible if each moment stood in isolation.

The metaphor of scaffolding captures this temporal process precisely. Builders erect temporary structures that enable the construction of permanent architecture. The scaffolding itself serves no purpose in the final building, but the building could not exist without the scaffolding that enabled its construction. Similarly, present interventions create structures that enable future behavioral patterns to become stable enough to operate without continued conscious scaffolding.

But the metaphor also illuminates something deeper about human agency. We are simultaneously the builders and the building. The present self constructs the architecture that the future self will inhabit. The future self then becomes a new present self, capable of further architectural modification. The process continues recursively without terminus, each present self inheriting and modifying the architecture constructed by past selves while building conditions for future selves.

This recursive temporal structure explains what libertarians sought through ultimate origination but could never find. We do originate our own development, not by standing outside causation but by participating consciously in causal processes that shape our own becoming across time. The origination is real, but it operates through natural mechanisms rather than supernatural exemption from determinism.

Why This Isn't Behaviorism

Someone might object that temporal scaffolding reduces to nothing more than sophisticated behaviorism. After all, both emphasize environmental modification, systematic reinforcement, and observable behavior change.

The difference lies in whether consciousness does causal work. Behaviorism treats mental states as either nonexistent or causally irrelevant. The "black box" need not be opened. B.F. Skinner's operant conditioning works whether the organism understands what's happening or not. A rat doesn't need to observe its own learning patterns, recognize environmental contingencies, or design future conditioning schedules. The behavior changes through mechanisms operating entirely below awareness.

Temporal scaffolding requires the opposite. Metacognitive awareness is the enabling condition for systematic self-modification. The woman breaking her relationship patterns must consciously recognize the pattern across multiple relationships. She must understand how childhood experiences created current attraction responses. She must deliberately design interventions based on this understanding. She must observe when interventions fail and adjust her approach accordingly. Remove conscious understanding, and the entire process collapses.

The scaffolding is intentional architecture, not accidental conditioning. Someone using behavioral techniques on themselves deploys those techniques because they understand the mechanisms and can evaluate outcomes against chosen goals. This recursive self-application, where consciousness modifies the conditions that will determine its own future states, is precisely what behaviorism excludes by treating consciousness as causally impotent.

The difference matters practically. Behavioral modification imposed externally often fails once the external structure is removed. Self-imposed scaffolding, grounded in understanding, tends to persist because the person has internalized both the methods and the reasons for using them. They become architects of their own development rather than merely well-trained subjects of someone else's conditioning.

The Long Ascent

This capacity for temporal self-construction did not appear miraculously. It represents the culmination of evolutionary developments spanning millions of years, each innovation building upon previous achievements in ways that eventually created something unprecedented in the history of life on Earth.

The story begins not with consciousness but with sociality. Our earliest hominid ancestors lived in small groups, where survival depended on cooperation, coalition formation, and navigating complex social dynamics. Natural selection in these environments favored cognitive capacities for tracking social relationships, predicting others' behavior, and coordinating group activities.

Chimpanzees and bonobos, our closest living relatives, demonstrate sophisticated social cognition that provides glimpses into the cognitive capacities our common ancestor likely possessed. These apes recognize dozens of individual group members and remember their past interactions across months or years. They form alliances that shift strategically in response to changing circumstances. They engage in political maneuvering, including deception, reconciliation after conflicts, and coalition formation, to challenge dominant individuals.

Yet something crucial remains absent in chimpanzee cognition that fundamentally distinguishes it from human thought. They predict behavior without understanding minds. A chimpanzee learns that a particular individual shares food and approaches them when hungry. But this behavioral prediction differs categorically from understanding that the individual holds beliefs about food availability, desires to share based on social bonds, and intentions to maintain alliances through generosity.

The chimpanzee operates with what philosophers call first-order intentionality. They have beliefs and desires about the world. They want food, fear predators, and prefer certain companions. But they lack second-order intentionality—beliefs about beliefs. They cannot represent "He believes the food is hidden" or "She wants me to think she's submissive." Social prediction operates through the recognition of behavioral patterns without a metacognitive representation of internal mental states, distinct from observable actions.

Early hominids, confronting increasingly complex social challenges, faced selection pressures that favored enhanced social cognition. Groups grew larger, requiring tracking of more relationships across time. Social structures became more complex, with nested alliances and shifting coalitions that could shift depending on the situation. Competition intensified as population densities increased and resources became contested in ways that simple dominance hierarchies could not resolve. These pressures created evolutionary bottlenecks where enhanced social intelligence provided decisive advantages that accumulated across generations.

The crucial transition involved developing theory of mind, the capacity to attribute mental states to others as distinct from their observable behavior. This did not require consciousness in the full modern sense. It required neural systems capable of representing that others have beliefs, desires, and intentions that may differ from one's own and from objective reality.

The adaptive advantages proved enormous. An individual who could represent "He believes the fruit is in that tree" could manipulate that belief through deception, leading rivals away from actual food sources while securing them for oneself or one's allies. Someone who could represent "She wants to form an alliance with me" could predict behavior in ways that simple pattern recognition of past actions could never achieve. Someone who understood "They intend to challenge the alpha male" could position themselves strategically before conflicts erupted, supporting the likely victor or avoiding dangerous confrontations entirely.

Theory of mind enabled a form of social chess where moves could be anticipated multiple steps ahead through modeling others' likely thoughts and reactions. The person who played this game well secured better alliances, avoided dangerous conflicts, coordinated more effectively with group members for collective action, and ultimately achieved greater reproductive success. Natural selection would have strongly favored any genetic variations enhancing these capacities, creating powerful directional pressure toward increasingly sophisticated social cognition.

But theory of mind about others creates an unstable cognitive situation that carries within itself the seeds of something far more radical. Once neural systems can represent that others have minds with beliefs and desires distinct from observable behavior, those same systems can turn inward. If I can model your beliefs as potentially false, I can model my own beliefs as potentially false. If I can represent your desires as distinct from reality, I can represent my own desires as psychological states rather than simply experiencing them as immediate motivations demanding satisfaction.

This inward turn of social cognitive capacities marks the origin of metacognitive awareness, the observation of one's own mental processes as objects that can themselves be observed and evaluated. The systems that evolved for understanding other minds became available for understanding one's own mind, creating unprecedented possibilities for behavioral self-modification.

Yet this application proved far from automatic or inevitable. Many species show evidence of rudimentary theory of mind without developing sophisticated self-awareness. Dolphins, elephants, and corvids exhibit behaviors that suggest they can to some degree represent others' mental states. But none have developed the elaborate metacognitive architecture that characterizes human consciousness. The crucial factor driving deeper metacognitive development in hominids involved the specific ways in which self-awareness enhanced social cognition, rather than operating independently of it.

Consider the strategic implications of metacognitive awareness in intensely social environments, where reputation, alliance formation, and social manipulation significantly influence reproductive success. An individual who can observe their own emotional responses can learn to control or disguise them, presenting strategic facades to others that serve social goals. Someone displaying anger might actually feel quite calm but recognize that anger display will discourage challengers. Someone concealing fear might feel terrified but understand that fear display invites aggression. The capacity to observe and regulate one's own emotional displays enables social deception that goes far beyond the simple behavioral mimicry other species can achieve.

Someone who can recognize their own beliefs as beliefs rather than facts can evaluate whether those beliefs serve their social goals. They might believe themselves more capable than they actually are, which could be adaptive if such confidence attracts allies and deters rivals. Or they might recognize their genuine limitations and adjust their social strategies accordingly. The metacognitive capacity to examine one's own cognitive states creates possibilities for strategic belief management that unconscious creatures cannot access.

Someone who can identify their own behavioral patterns across situations can modify those patterns to improve social outcomes. Perhaps they notice their tendency toward aggressive responses during status conflicts. This self-observation enables them to recognize anger arising before it escalates to violence that might be costly or deadly. They can implement primitive forms of self-regulation, such as temporarily withdrawing to calm down or redirecting aggressive energy toward safer targets that won't threaten crucial alliances.

These capacities would have been enormously valuable in the complex social environments where hominid evolution occurred. Natural selection would have strongly favored individuals who could observe and modify their own behavioral patterns to navigate social challenges more successfully. But the truly revolutionary aspect of metacognitive awareness involves not just its immediate strategic advantages but its recursive nature that creates possibilities for indefinite elaboration.

Once you can observe your mental states, you can observe yourself observing those states. Once you can recognize patterns in your behavior, you can recognize patterns in your pattern recognition. This recursion creates hierarchical cognitive architecture where, again, higher-order processes monitor and regulate lower-order processes in loops that could in principle extend indefinitely, though in practice they typically operate at two or three levels.

Someone might observe themselves becoming angry (first-order metacognition). Then they might observe that they tend to become angry in situations involving perceived disrespect (second-order metacognition recognizing patterns). Then they might observe that their anger responses often backfire by creating enemies rather than commanding respect, leading them to develop strategies for managing anger more effectively (third-order metacognition evaluating the effectiveness of their patterns and strategies).

This hierarchical structure enables what we now recognize as temporal scaffolding. The person who recognizes their anger patterns can design environmental modifications to reduce triggers, practice alternative responses in safe contexts, and develop internal narratives that reframe perceived slights as unimportant rather than threatening. Each intervention operates through present cognitive work that modifies future behavioral possibilities.

The neurological evidence reveals how evolution created this unprecedented cognitive architecture. The prefrontal cortex, particularly regions including the medial prefrontal cortex and dorsolateral prefrontal cortex, underwent significant expansion during hominid evolution. These regions show dramatically increased size and complexity in humans compared to other great apes, suggesting that their functions became increasingly important for fitness.

What do these regions do? They implement exactly the capacities required for temporal scaffolding. Working memory systems that can hold multiple considerations simultaneously during deliberation. Executive control systems that can override automatic responses based on strategic evaluation. Prospective thinking systems that can simulate possible futures to evaluate choices before committing to them. These are not incidental abilities but fundamental cognitive tools that enable the kind of strategic, long-term oriented behavior that complex social competition rewards.

But evolution created more than just enlarged prefrontal regions. It created intricate networks connecting these control systems with limbic regions generating emotions, hippocampal systems encoding memories, and sensory systems processing environmental information. The result is hierarchical architecture where higher-order prefrontal processes can observe and regulate lower-order limbic and sensory processes while themselves being subject to observation and regulation by still higher-order reflective processes.

This architecture does not require mysterious homunculi or infinite regress. The observation emerges from functional relationships between neural systems operating at different levels of processing hierarchy. Higher levels monitor lower levels through neural connections that transmit information about current processing states. This monitoring enables regulatory interventions that modify lower-level processing based on strategic goals, learned patterns, and predicted consequences.

The capacity for self-observation and self-regulation thus emerges from entirely natural neural mechanisms that evolution shaped because they provided survival advantages in environments where social competition rewarded strategic behavior and long-term planning. We are not ghosts inhabiting machines but sophisticated biological systems whose architecture enables forms of self-monitoring and self-modification that create what we experience as conscious agency.

When Thought Learned to Speak

The evolutionary development of metacognitive capacity created the potential for temporal scaffolding. But language represents the cultural innovation that expanded this potential far beyond what biology alone could achieve, transforming human consciousness in ways that continue to reverberate through every aspect of contemporary life.

Every other species exists trapped in immediate experience shaped by biological memory and associative learning. A dog can remember past experiences and anticipate future events based on learned associations. When you pick up the leash, your dog becomes excited because a past correlation between the leash and walk has created a strong expectation of an imminent pleasant experience. But a dog cannot reflect on the concept of memory itself, discuss with other dogs the nature of anticipation, or systematically examine whether their expectations typically prove accurate.

The dog's temporal consciousness remains bound to concrete experiences without abstract representation, enabling manipulation of temporal concepts themselves. They live in what we might call the extended present, a now that reaches backward through memory and forward through anticipation but never quite escapes immediacy into genuine past and future as distinct temporal locations.

Human language breaks through this limitation by creating symbolic representations that can be combined recursively to generate infinite possible meanings. This recursive symbolic capacity enables forms of temporal thinking that remain impossible for creatures lacking language, transforming human consciousness in ways we are only beginning to understand.

The linguistic innovation occurs at multiple levels simultaneously, each contributing to the expansion of temporal consciousness beyond biological constraints. Most fundamentally, language enables precise temporal reference through tense markers and temporal adverbs, which create shared frameworks for coordinating actions across time. We can distinguish between "I am hungry," "I was hungry," and "I will be hungry" through grammatical structures that represent different temporal locations with remarkable precision.

This might seem trivial until you recognize what it makes possible. Prelinguistic hominids could coordinate immediate group action through gestures and vocalizations. Hunt this animal now. Flee this predator now. Share this food now. But coordinating action across temporal distance requires linguistic representations of when things will happen relative to now. Meet at the hunting grounds tomorrow morning. Gather these plants before the rains come. Prepare shelters for winter before snow arrives.

These temporal specifications enable forms of planning and coordination that remain impossible in the eternal present of animal consciousness. The ability to say "in three days we will hunt the deer near the river" creates shared temporal frameworks that allow multiple individuals to coordinate complex activities across time without remaining in constant contact. Language extends the temporal reach of social cooperation from immediate joint action to elaborately planned collective endeavors spanning days, seasons, or even years.

But language does far more than enable temporal reference. It enables temporal manipulation through counterfactual thinking, which operates by constructing linguistic scenarios that explore alternatives to what actually occurred. When you think "If I had chosen differently, things would be better now," you use language to construct alternative temporal sequences that never happened in reality. This counterfactual capacity proves essential for learning from mistakes and planning better future choices.

The linguistic construction "if X, then Y" enables hypothetical reasoning that projects possible futures conditionally. "If I pursue this relationship, then I will likely experience the same pattern as before." The conditional statement creates a hypothetical future scenario that can be evaluated before being actualized through behavior. You can explore the implications of choices linguistically before committing to them behaviorally, testing possibilities in the imagination before testing them in reality.

This hypothetical reasoning requires not just language but specifically the recursive embedding that language enables. "I think that if I do X, then she will think that I believe Y" involves multiple levels of embedding where thoughts nest inside thoughts in ways that would be impossible without linguistic structures that can themselves contain linguistic structures. The recursion in language mirrors and enables the recursion in temporal thought that characterizes sophisticated planning and strategic social interaction.

Language also enables what cognitive scientists call mental time travel through episodic memory and prospective thinking, which operates through the linguistic and visual reconstruction of experiences. When you remember a specific past experience, you don't simply retrieve information about what happened. You reconstruct the experience itself using many of the same neural systems that were active during the original experience, placing yourself mentally in the past moment and re-experiencing it from that temporal perspective while knowing that it is past rather than present.

Similarly, when you imagine future experiences, you project yourself forward in time and simulate what that future moment might feel like using the same neural systems that generate current experience. The simulation draws on memories of past experiences, an understanding of causal patterns, and linguistic representations of possible futures to create detailed scenarios that feel almost as real as current perception, while remaining clearly marked as imaginary rather than actual.

This temporal simulation operates largely through linguistic frameworks that organize and structure the imagined experiences. You don't just see random images when imagining future possibilities. You construct narratives with beginnings, middles, and ends. You represent causal relationships between events using linguistic structures like "because," "therefore," and "in order to." You evaluate different possibilities by representing them linguistically and reasoning about their likely consequences through internal dialogue that unfolds much like a conversation with another person.

Crucially, language enables recursive temporal thinking, allowing you to reflect on your own thinking across time in ways that create unprecedented opportunities for self-modification. You can observe "I tend to think X when in situation Y" and then think about how to modify that thinking pattern through environmental changes, practice of alternative thoughts, or development of metacognitive awareness about triggers. You can reflect on your own past reflections, noticing patterns in how your thinking changes over time and what factors influence those changes.

The recursive nature of language itself models and enables the recursive nature of temporal consciousness. Just as linguistic structures can embed within linguistic structures infinitely ("I think that you think that she thinks..."), temporal thoughts can embed within temporal thoughts ("I plan to remember to evaluate how this planning process worked"). This parallel structure is not coincidental. Language may have evolved partly to enable the temporal recursion necessary for sophisticated planning and strategic social behavior, which gave our ancestors decisive advantages over their competitors.

The social dimension of language proves equally important for expanding temporal consciousness beyond individual biological limits. Language enables the transmission of temporal knowledge and planning strategies across individuals and generations in ways that create cumulative cultural evolution of temporal thinking abilities. The person who figures out an effective approach to storing food for winter can explain it linguistically to others, enabling cultural accumulation of survival knowledge that proceeds far faster than biological evolution could accomplish.

Each generation inherits linguistic representations of effective temporal strategies discovered by previous generations, enabling cultural evolution of temporal scaffolding practices that builds upon rather than merely repeating past achievements. The hunter who develops a new tracking technique can teach it explicitly to younger hunters through linguistic instruction combined with demonstration. The plant gatherer who discovers which preservation methods prevent spoilage can share this knowledge through stories that embed practical wisdom in memorable narratives.

This cultural transmission of temporal knowledge accelerates human adaptation to changing environments while creating new selection pressures that favor biological capacities for cultural learning and linguistic communication. Individuals who can learn efficiently from linguistic instruction outcompete those relying solely on individual discovery through trial and error. This creates gene-culture coevolution where biological evolution shapes brains increasingly capable of linguistic cultural learning while cultural evolution creates environments favoring biological traits supporting sophisticated language use.

Language also enables social accountability structures that support individual temporal scaffolding through mechanisms that remain impossible for prelinguistic creatures. When you tell others about your plans and commitments, you create linguistic representations existing in shared social space rather than merely private mental space. These shared representations create social pressure for behavioral follow-through that private commitments alone cannot generate.

The power of accountability partnerships, support groups, and public commitments derives largely from creating shared linguistic frameworks for temporal commitments that make failure socially costly in ways that motivate continued effort even when individual motivation flags. You might break a private resolution to exercise regularly without much consequence beyond personal disappointment. But breaking a public commitment to exercise with a friend creates social costs including letting someone down, damaging your reputation for reliability, and potentially losing the relationship.

Yet language also introduces new vulnerabilities for temporal consciousness that require metacognitive awareness to navigate successfully. Linguistic self-narratives can become rigid stories that constrain rather than enable development by fixing identity in ways that resist change. Someone who adopts the linguistic identity "I am an anxious person" may inadvertently reinforce anxiety patterns by making them central to self-understanding and difficult to modify without threatening their sense of who they are.

The linguistic representation of self becomes self-fulfilling prophecy limiting possibilities for change because actions inconsistent with the self-narrative feel inauthentic or threatening. "I'm just not the kind of person who speaks up in meetings" becomes both description and prescription, making speaking up feel like violation of authentic identity rather than expansion of behavioral repertoire.

Effective temporal scaffolding requires sophisticated linguistic awareness about how self-narratives either support or constrain development. The language we use to describe ourselves shapes the possibilities we can imagine for change. Someone who shifts from "I am an anxious person" to "I experience anxiety that I am learning to manage" creates different developmental possibilities through the linguistic reframing alone. The first statement treats anxiety as essential identity. The second treats it as temporary state subject to modification through learning.

The narrative structure of language also affects temporal consciousness in ways that require careful attention to avoid self-deception. Human memory is not video recording but narrative reconstruction that occurs anew each time we remember. Each remembering potentially modifies the memory itself through the reconstruction process, introducing current knowledge, emotions, and interpretations that may not have been present during the original experience.

The stories we tell about our past literally reshape the past by modifying the memories that constitute our personal history. This narrative malleability creates both opportunities and risks for temporal scaffolding. Someone working to modify relationship patterns can deliberately reconstruct their narrative about past relationships in ways that support rather than undermine change. They might shift from a victim narrative where others always hurt them to an agency narrative where they repeatedly chose unavailable partners but are learning to choose differently.

The narrative shift itself becomes intervention that enables different futures by changing how they understand their past and what possibilities they can imagine for themselves. But narrative reconstruction can also serve defensive avoidance where people rewrite their histories to avoid confronting uncomfortable truths about their patterns. The person who narratively reconstructs each failed relationship as entirely the other person's fault prevents the pattern recognition necessary for beneficial change by maintaining the fiction that they bear no responsibility for outcomes they actually helped create.

Language thus represents both the greatest tool for temporal scaffolding and a potential obstacle when linguistic patterns become rigidified in ways that prevent genuine development. The capacity for recursive symbolic thought that language enables makes sophisticated temporal consciousness possible, creating unprecedented opportunities for conscious self-modification through environmental design and behavioral architecture. But the same capacity for abstract representation can generate linguistic prisons where self-narratives constrain possibilities for change and defensive stories prevent the honest self-observation necessary for identifying patterns that need modification.

Conscious agency requires metacognitive awareness about language itself, recognizing how linguistic representations shape temporal consciousness while maintaining flexibility to revise representations when they no longer serve development. We use language to construct temporal scaffolding through planning, commitment-making, and narrative construction. But we must also observe how language constructs us through the self-narratives we adopt, the temporal frameworks we internalize, and the stories we tell about why we are the way we are.

How Scaffolding Actually Works

Understanding the evolutionary and linguistic foundations reveals why humans possess capacities for temporal scaffolding that other creatures lack. But how does this capacity actually operate in concrete situations where someone seeks to modify established behavioral patterns?

The core mechanism involves using current understanding to shape the conditions under which future choices occur in ways that alter what will likely be chosen when those futures arrive. This sounds abstract until you examine actual cases where people successfully modify long-standing patterns through systematic architectural work.

Consider someone attempting to develop a consistent meditation practice after years of failed attempts. They understand intellectually that meditation would benefit their attention regulation, emotional stability, and psychological well-being. They have read extensively about the advantages of meditation. They genuinely believe that regular practice would significantly improve their quality of life.

Yet they struggle to maintain consistency. They meditate for a few days, then skip a session. They resume for a week, then stop for a month. The pattern repeats despite genuine belief in meditation's value and sincere desire for consistent practice. Why does intellectual understanding fail to generate behavioral consistency?

Traditional frameworks struggle with this common situation. The libertarian might suggest they lack sufficient willpower to freely choose meditation over competing activities, but this merely labels the problem without explaining it. The hard determinist might trace their inconsistency back to childhood experiences that created neural patterns prioritizing immediate gratification over delayed benefits, but this provides no guidance for change. The compatibilist might observe that they act on their own authentic desires when choosing not to meditate, but this ignores their equally authentic desire for the consistency they cannot achieve.

The temporal scaffolding framework reveals the situation differently. The person faces a fundamental mismatch between the cognitive resources available at the time of planning to meditate and the resources available when meditation time arrives. In the present, calm and reflective, they can clearly see how meditation serves their long-term goals. The benefits feel real and motivating. The activity seems manageable and worthwhile.

However, in the moment when meditation time arrives, different cognitive resources come into play.

They feel tired from a long day. The couch looks inviting. Their phone offers immediate stimulation. The meditation cushion feels uncomfortable, and meditation itself feels like additional effort after a day of effort. None of the long-term benefits that motivated their commitment in the calm present moment feel real or compelling in the stressed future moment.

This temporal mismatch between planning resources and execution resources explains much of the gap between intention and action that plagues human behavioral change efforts. The person planning is not the same person executing in crucial psychological ways, even though they inhabit the same body and share the same goals in abstract terms.

Temporal scaffolding works by using the present cognitive resources to construct environmental and psychological conditions that support the desired behavior even when future cognitive resources prove insufficient. Rather than relying entirely on future willpower and motivation, the person architects their future decision environment to make the desired behavior more probable, regardless of how they feel when the moment arrives.

They might establish a specific time and place for meditation each day, creating routines that make the behavior more automatic rather than requiring fresh decision-making. Morning immediately after waking might work better than evening when tired. A dedicated meditation space that cues the activity might work better than meditating in spaces associated with other activities.

They might remove barriers that create friction. Laying out meditation cushion the night before. Setting out comfortable clothing. Ensuring the space is warm enough in winter and cool enough in summer. Each barrier removed makes the desired behavior slightly more probable by reducing the effort required to begin.

They might add accountability structures that provide external motivation, supplementing internal motivation. Joining a meditation group that meets regularly. Committing to a friend who also meditates. Using an app that tracks consistency and sends reminders. These external structures provide motivation that persists even when internal motivation falters.

They might implement identity frameworks that make meditation feel like an expression of who they are rather than an effortful activity requiring constant motivation. Someone who adopts the identity "I am someone who meditates" experiences skipping meditation as violating their self-understanding rather than merely missing an instrumental activity. The identity commitment creates psychological pressure for consistency that instrumental motivation alone cannot generate.

Most importantly, they might develop metacognitive awareness of the patterns that interfere with consistency. They notice that they skip meditation most often when stressed, which is precisely when meditation would be most beneficial. This awareness enables them to recognize stress as a trigger for skipping rather than allowing the automatic pattern to operate below conscious awareness. Recognition creates the possibility for intervention.

When they notice stress arising, they can implement countermeasures specifically designed for this trigger. Perhaps stress makes meditation feel like an additional burden rather than a relief. Reframing meditation as stress relief rather than additional task might help. Or modifying their meditation approach to better address stress—perhaps using more active techniques like walking meditation rather than sitting meditation when feeling agitated.

Each intervention operates through present cognitive work that constructs future conditions supporting desired behavior. None of the interventions eliminates the fundamental reality that the future self will feel different from the present self or that motivation will fluctuate. But they create decision architectures that work with rather than against these psychological realities, making desired behavior more probable even when motivation wanes and circumstances become challenging.

This architectural approach contrasts sharply with willpower-based approaches that assume people simply need to try harder or care more. Someone attempting meditation through willpower alone faces continuous psychological struggle between their commitment to meditate and their immediate desire to avoid effort. Each session requires a conscious decision to override immediate impulses in favor of long-term goals. This constant effortful control depletes motivation and eventually leads to the abandonment of the practice when willpower reserves are exhausted.

Architectural approaches eliminate much of this struggle by creating conditions where meditation becomes easier than not meditating. When the environment supports the practice through routines, triggers, accountability, and identity frameworks, meditation happens more automatically rather than requiring constant conscious effort. This doesn't eliminate all difficulty. Honestly, developing any new capacity involves real work. But it channels effort efficiently into behavioral change rather than wasting it on continuous willpower struggles that eventually fail.

The same principles apply across all domains of behavioral modification. Someone attempting to change their eating patterns, develop exercise habits, improve social skills, manage time more effectively, or modify any other established pattern faces the same fundamental challenge. There is the possibility of an architectural mismatch between planning resources and execution resources. Success requires utilizing current resources to design future decision architectures that support desired behaviors, even when future resources prove insufficient for implementing desired choices through willpower alone.

The Resolution of Ultimate Origination

The framework of temporal scaffolding dissolves the problem of ultimate origination that destroyed libertarian free will while preserving everything worth wanting in human agency.

The libertarian sought exemption from causation, or a first cause that would originate decisions from nothing. This proves impossible because it requires mechanisms contradicting our best understanding of natural processes. Every event, including decisions, follows from prior causes according to causal regularities that science investigates. Nothing stands outside this causal order as an uncaused cause.

But temporal scaffolding reveals that ultimate origination was always the wrong requirement for moral responsibility. What matters is not whether we stand outside causation but whether we possess capacities for conscious participation in causal processes that shape our own development across time.

Return to the person modifying destructive relationship patterns through therapeutic work and conscious architectural design. They did not ultimately originate the childhood experiences that created their attachment style. They did not choose their genetic endowment, early developmental environment, or the neural mechanisms generating attraction responses. Every factor contributing to their relationship choices traces back through causal chains that extend to the moment of their birth and beyond, into their ancestral history, which stretches back millions of years.

Yet they possess genuine agency in modifying these patterns precisely through conscious participation in causal processes operating in the present. Their metacognitive awareness enables them to recognize patterns across relationships. Pattern recognition causes therapeutic engagement, where they work to understand childhood origins of their attraction patterns. Therapeutic engagement causes new neural connections to form between prefrontal control systems and limbic attraction systems. New neural connections cause modified attraction responses when they encounter potential partners. Modified attraction responses lead to different relationship choices based on genuine compatibility rather than the unconscious repetition of childhood dynamics.

Each step operates through entirely deterministic causation where every effect has prior causes that science can investigate and increasingly predict. Yet the overall process represents genuine self-modification that justifies moral evaluation because the person participated consciously in causal processes rather than remaining unconscious of the patterns determining their choices. The agency is real, even though it operates through entirely natural, deterministic mechanisms. The person is both caused by their history and causing their own future development through present scaffolding efforts.

This dissolves the regress problem that haunted libertarian approaches to free will. When libertarians were asked what caused the supposedly uncaused choices, they faced infinite regress. If choices are truly uncaused, how do they connect to anything about the person making them? But if the person's character causes them, what caused that character? The regress continues until it reaches factors clearly beyond individual control, including genetic inheritance, developmental experiences, and environmental influences.

Temporal scaffolding accepts this regress while transforming its implications for moral responsibility. Yes, the current character was caused by past circumstances beyond initial control. But the present character causes the future character through scaffolding processes operating now. The person becomes responsible not for their initial conditions, which were indeed determined by factors beyond their control, but for their current engagement or non-engagement with processes of deliberate self-modification, given their current circumstances and capacities.

Someone born into difficult circumstances that created problematic behavioral patterns bears no responsibility for the initial pattern formation, which occurred before they possessed capacities for metacognitive awareness or environmental modification. But they bear increasing responsibility as they develop capacities for recognizing patterns and implementing modifications that address underlying causes rather than merely suppressing symptoms. The responsibility grows gradually as metacognitive awareness develops, therapeutic resources become available, social support emerges, and environmental modifications become possible through accumulated knowledge and resources.

Someone with extensive therapeutic resources, strong social support, sophisticated metacognitive awareness, and favorable environmental conditions bears more responsibility for continued problematic patterns than someone lacking these resources. But both possess some degree of agency because both can engage with self-modification efforts to whatever extent their circumstances permit, and both can work to develop greater capacity even when starting from difficult baselines.

This graduated responsibility framework proves far more sophisticated than the binary libertarian approach, where people either possess complete free will or lack it entirely. Responsibility comes in degrees corresponding to actual capacities for temporal scaffolding that vary across individuals and circumstances while developing across time through conscious practice and environmental support.

The framework also addresses the luck problem that libertarians struggled with unsuccessfully. If everything traces back to factors beyond our control, how can anyone deserve praise or blame for their actions? The answer lies in recognizing that the relevant question is not whether we ultimately originated our capacities but whether we exercise the capacities we currently possess given our actual circumstances.

Two people might start with vastly different natural endowments for metacognitive awareness and self-regulation. One finds self-observation easy and natural, developing sophisticated temporal scaffolding through minimal effort. The other must work hard to develop even basic self-awareness and behavioral modification skills. This initial difference reflects pure constitutive luck. Neither person chose their starting capacities.

But what matters morally is not the initial endowment but what each person does with their current capacities through engagement or non-engagement with temporal scaffolding practices appropriate to their circumstances. Someone born with exceptional self-regulatory capacities who never exercises them through deliberate development deserves less moral credit than someone born with limited capacities who works persistently to develop whatever abilities they can achieve. The evaluation tracks engagement with development relative to circumstances rather than absolute level of achievement.

This also explains why we distinguish between people at different developmental stages. A four-year-old who hits another child in anger lacks the metacognitive capacity to observe their anger arising, recognize it as potentially problematic, and implement alternative responses. The neural systems supporting such awareness remain underdeveloped. Holding them morally responsible in the same way we hold adults responsible would be absurd, not because they lack metaphysical freedom but because they lack the temporal scaffolding capacities that ground moral responsibility.

As the child develops, we appropriately increase moral expectations as their capacities develop. The twelve-year-old possesses greater metacognitive awareness and self-regulatory capacity than the four-year-old and bears correspondingly greater responsibility for managing anger appropriately through the capacities they now possess. The adult with fully developed prefrontal systems bears still greater responsibility because they possess sophisticated capacities for recognizing patterns, understanding triggers, and implementing systematic modifications.

This developmental gradient makes far more sense than libertarian approaches that struggle to explain when free will begins or why it should depend on brain development at all. Temporal scaffolding reveals responsibility as naturally graded according to actual capacities that develop gradually through biological maturation and cultural learning rather than appearing magically at some threshold age determined by legal convention.

The Defeat of Hard Determinism

Hard determinism claimed that causal determination eliminates moral responsibility because our actions flow inevitably from causes we did not create. Temporal scaffolding reveals this argument as deeply confused about the relationship between causation and agency.

The hard determinist notes correctly that all behavior follows from prior causes. Someone who acts violently did not choose their genes, childhood experiences, or the immediate circumstances triggering violence. Tracing causation backward far enough always reaches factors beyond the person's control, extending back before their birth.

The hard determinist concludes they bear no responsibility for violence because they did not create the causal factors generating it. But this conclusion follows only if we accept that responsibility requires ultimate origination of the sort libertarians sought and could never find. Once we recognize temporal scaffolding as the capacity grounding responsibility, the hard determinist argument collapses into incoherence.

Yes, all behavior is determined by prior causes. However, some of those causes include the person's own temporal scaffolding efforts to modify the conditions that determine their behavior. The person exercising agency does not stand outside the causal order but participates in it by using present causal powers to shape future causal conditions in systematic rather than random ways.

Consider someone with genetic and developmental risk factors for substance abuse. Perhaps they inherited genes affecting impulse control and reward sensitivity. Perhaps they experienced trauma creating associations between substance use and emotional relief. Perhaps they grew up in environments where substance use was normalized and readily available. All these factors causally contribute to substance use patterns in ways the person never chose.

The hard determinist concludes they bear no responsibility for substance abuse because they did not create these causal factors. Should we overlook the question of whether they possess and exercise the capacity to recognize patterns and implement modifications that address underlying causes?

Someone with substance abuse risk factors who never develops awareness of how their particular psychology responds to substances, who never modifies their environment to reduce access and triggers, who never builds support structures to assist during vulnerable periods, and who never works to understand and address trauma driving use exercises minimal temporal scaffolding despite potentially possessing the capacity to do so. They bear a different moral evaluation than someone who systematically develops metacognitive awareness, implements environmental modifications, seeks therapeutic support, and works persistently toward behavioral change even when facing frequent setbacks.

The causal determination does not eliminate responsibility because the person's own scaffolding efforts or failures to make such efforts themselves function as causes determining outcomes. The presence or absence of scaffolding represents a causal factor just as genetic endowment and developmental experiences do. Responsibility tracks whether people engage in these scaffolding capacities given their circumstances rather than whether they ultimately originated the capacities themselves through some impossible act of self-creation.

The hard determinist might object that scaffolding efforts themselves were causally determined by prior factors, including personality traits, metacognitive capacities, and circumstances that either enable or prevent scaffolding. This is correct, but it is irrelevant to questions about moral responsibility. Responsibility does not require that scaffolding efforts be uncaused, which would be impossible. It requires only that scaffolding efforts function as genuine causal factors in developmental outcomes.

The question is not whether someone's decision to engage temporal scaffolding was ultimately up to them in some metaphysically libertarian sense requiring exemption from causation. The question is whether they possess scaffolding capacities and whether they exercise them through systematic efforts that causally contribute to behavioral outcomes. Both possession and exercise vary across individuals in ways that justify differential moral evaluation, even though prior factors causally determine both.

This reveals the fundamental error in hard determinist reasoning. They assume that if an action is caused, it cannot be free in any sense relevant to moral responsibility. This reasoning conflates two different concepts of freedom. Libertarian freedom requires exemption from causation through impossible causal breaks. The freedom relevant to moral responsibility requires only that action flow from the person's own psychology operating through temporal scaffolding capacities rather than from external compulsion or internal compulsion that bypasses metacognitive awareness and environmental modification capacities.

Someone who acts violently due to a brain tumor, eliminating their capacity for impulse control, differs morally from someone who acts violently despite possessing intact capacity for impulse control but having never developed it through practice and environmental design. Both acts are causally determined by prior factors beyond ultimate control. But only the second involves the person's intact agency capacities operating through mechanisms that could have developed differently through scaffolding but didn't. The first represents genuine compulsion bypassing agency. The second represents agency that remains underdeveloped despite possessing potential for development.

We discover that causal determination, far from eliminating agency, makes genuine agency possible by providing the reliable causal patterns that temporal scaffolding deploys to shape developmental trajectories. Without causation operating reliably, scaffolding could not work because present efforts would not reliably influence future outcomes through predictable mechanisms. The causation that the hard determinist treats as eliminating freedom proves to be the necessary foundation for the only form of freedom worth wanting.

Beyond Compatibilist Identification

Traditional compatibilism failed by focusing on whether actions flow from the agent's own desires and values. Someone acts freely if they act on desires they identify with rather than desires they wish they did not have. But this criterion proves inadequate because desires and values themselves can be products of manipulation or circumstance beyond the person's control.

Temporal scaffolding succeeds where traditional compatibilism failed by focusing not on whether desires are one's own but on capacities for observing and modifying whatever desires happen to be present through systematic architectural work.

Harry Frankfurt's manipulation cases exposed identification criteria as insufficient. Imagine someone whose higher-order desires were engineered through sophisticated conditioning to identify with first-order desires serving the manipulator's goals. They fully embrace their desires and would not change them if they could. Traditional compatibilism must classify them as free despite the profound unfreedom created by manipulation that prevented the development of capacities for recognizing and resisting the manipulation itself.

Temporal scaffolding avoids this problem by focusing on capacities rather than identification. The manipulated person lacks genuine agency, not because they fail to identify with their desires, but because manipulation prevented the development of capacities for recognizing patterns, understanding causes, and implementing modifications. Their metacognitive awareness has been compromised or bypassed by conditioning operating below conscious threshold in ways that prevent the self-observation necessary for beneficial change.

Normal socialization differs crucially from manipulation, not because socialized individuals possess ultimate origination but because normal development includes opportunities for metacognitive observation of social conditioning combined with capacities for evaluating and modifying it through conscious effort. The socialized person can recognize when responses reflect unexamined social learning rather than reflective endorsement. They can work to change responses misaligned with their considered values through temporal scaffolding practices, including therapeutic work, environmental modification, and social support.

The manipulated person lacks these crucial capacities. Their metacognitive systems were prevented from developing normally through conditioning that bypassed conscious awareness, or their awareness was systematically directed away from recognizing the manipulation through sophisticated deception, or their capacities for behavioral modification were undermined by conditioning operating through mechanisms immune to conscious intervention.

This distinction proves robust across manipulation cases that defeated traditional compatibilism. In each case, we can ask whether the person possesses intact capacities for metacognitive awareness and temporal scaffolding or whether these capacities have been compromised by manipulation that prevented their normal development.

Consider someone who experienced severe childhood trauma versus someone who grew up in a healthy family environment. Both are profoundly shaped by circumstances beyond their initial control. However, the person from a healthy family typically develops intact capacities for metacognitive awareness and self-regulation through developmental experiences that encourage independent thought, emotional expression, and autonomous choice. They can observe their patterns, evaluate whether they serve their goals, and work systematically to modify problematic patterns through conscious effort.

The person who experienced severe trauma often emerges with compromised metacognitive capacities and self-regulatory systems because trauma occurred during critical developmental periods when these capacities were forming. The result is not that they lack agency entirely but that their scaffolding capacities require therapeutic support to function effectively rather than operating naturally through normal developmental processes.

This explains why we appropriately reduce moral responsibility for actions resulting from severe trauma without eliminating responsibility altogether. The trauma compromised but did not destroy scaffolding capacities. With appropriate therapeutic support, these capacities can develop sufficiently to enable beneficial self-modification. Until that development occurs, holding the person to the same standards as someone with intact capacities would be unjust because it ignores genuine differences in scaffolding ability that matter for behavioral change.

Temporal scaffolding thus preserves the insight motivating compatibilism, that genuine agency requires actions flowing from the person's own psychology rather than external compulsion, while avoiding compatibilism's failures by focusing on metacognitive and architectural capacities rather than simple identification with desires. The person acts freely when they exercise intact capacities for observing their psychology and modifying the conditions that shape it, regardless of whether they identify with their current desires or whether those desires originated through processes they controlled.

Implications for Human Agency

The recognition that temporal scaffolding grounds genuine agency while operating through entirely deterministic mechanisms profoundly transforms our understanding of human freedom and responsibility, with implications that matter significantly for individual lives and collective institutions.

We discover that the freedom worth wanting was never exemption from causation but the capacity for conscious participation in causal processes that shape our own becoming across time. This capacity proves compatible with complete causal determination because it operates through causation rather than standing apart from it in mysterious ways that would make scientific understanding impossible.

Someone exercises maximum agency not by somehow exempting themselves from natural law but by developing a sophisticated understanding of how causal processes operate and using that understanding to construct developmental trajectories aligned with their reflective values and considered goals. The person who understands psychology, neuroscience, and behavioral modification possesses greater potential for beneficial self-change than someone who understands their own psychology as mysterious or magical precisely because causal understanding enables systematic intervention rather than hoping for miraculous transformation.

This reveals education as perhaps the most important form of temporal scaffolding support that societies can provide. When people understand how their attention systems, emotional patterns, habit formation, and social influences actually operate through natural mechanisms, they gain tools for systematic self-modification that remain unavailable to those who lack such understanding or who view psychology through frameworks emphasizing pathology rather than natural adaptive processes.

Yet education alone proves insufficient without environmental and social structures supporting agency development. Someone who understands temporal scaffolding but lives in conditions of severe poverty, violence, or instability may lack the basic security necessary for implementing long-term developmental projects. Someone who possesses knowledge but faces technological environments deliberately designed to exploit their psychological vulnerabilities may find scaffolding efforts constantly undermined by commercial manipulation operating through mechanisms more sophisticated than individual resistance can overcome.

A genuine commitment to human agency requires attention to the full range of conditions that support or constrain scaffolding capacities across diverse populations. Economic policies, urban design, technological regulation, educational approaches, and social institutions all either enhance or undermine individual agency depending on whether they support or prevent effective temporal scaffolding through the resources and opportunities they provide.

The framework also reveals connections between individual and collective agency that traditional approaches missed entirely. Just as individuals exercise agency through temporal scaffolding at the personal scale, societies exercise collective agency through institutional scaffolding at the social scale. Democratic institutions, educational systems, technological infrastructures, and cultural practices all function as collective temporal scaffolding, shaping the behavioral possibilities available to future individuals and communities.

Understanding these collective structures as scaffolding rather than fixed constraints reveals opportunities for deliberate architectural modification at the social scale. Societies can consciously redesign institutions, technologies, and cultural practices to support individual agency development better while serving collective welfare. The choices contemporary humans make about collective scaffolding will shape human developmental possibilities for generations to come.

We discover ourselves as simultaneously determined and determining, caused and causing, shaped and shaping through processes that science can investigate while enabling authentic self-creation that gives human life meaning and moral significance beyond mere mechanical causation.

The Metacognitive Hierarchy

"What if the architect of the self discovers themselves to be architecture?"

THE OBSERVER PARADOX haunts any attempt to ground agency in self-awareness. If consciousness enables genuine agency by observing and modifying mental processes, what observes the observer? If metacognitive awareness represents the foundation of human freedom, what grounds that awareness itself?

The threat of infinite regress appears unavoidable. Either we accept an endless tower of observers watching observers, or we admit that observation terminates something that cannot itself be observed, undermining the entire framework.

Philosophy has circled this paradox for centuries, finding no resolution that preserves both naturalism and genuine consciousness. The materialist eliminates consciousness to save naturalism. The dualist preserves consciousness by abandoning naturalism. Neither proves satisfactory because both treat consciousness as a given rather than an achieved phenomenon, as a metaphysical fact requiring explanation rather than as a biological capacity that evolved through natural processes over time.

Yet John Donne's meditation on human interconnection suggests an escape from the paradox. He once wrote, "No man is an island, entire of itself; every man is a piece of the continent, a part of the main." What if the observer is not a single entity that must itself be observed, but a distributed capacity that emerged through evolutionary pressures favoring increasingly sophisticated forms of social cognition? What if hierarchical self-observation developed not to create isolated islands of awareness but to enable coordination among minds that were never truly separate?

The resolution lies not in metaphysics but in architecture. Consciousness, as we experience it, represents no supernatural addition to natural processes, but rather the culmination of evolutionary developments in behavioral flexibility that have created unprecedented forms of self-monitoring. The capacity for hierarchical self-observation emerged gradually through natural selection operating in complex social environments where understanding others' minds and one's own mind provided enormous adaptive advantages.

The paradox of infinite regress dissolves once we recognize that observation began and became hierarchical through incremental elaboration rather than requiring infinite towers of observers from the start. Understanding how this happened requires examining both the philosophical structure of hierarchical cognition and the neural mechanisms implementing it through entirely natural processes.

Hierarchy Without Homunculus

Someone catches themselves rehearsing an argument they will never have. The imagined conversation unfolds with cinematic clarity. Their opponent's objections, their devastating responses, the final vindication they will never actually experience because the confrontation will never actually occur. Then awareness intrudes. They notice themselves constructing these fantasies. The recognition feels different from the fantasy itself, like stepping back from a painting to see the frame.

This everyday experience reveals something philosophy has struggled to explain. The mind observes itself without requiring a separate observer standing outside the mind. When you catch yourself lost in fantasy, who does the catching? When you notice your attention wandering, what part of you does the noticing?

The libertarian answer posits a ghost in the machine, an immaterial soul that somehow escapes causation and peers down at mental processes from a transcendent vantage point. But this merely relocates the mystery. If the soul observes mental processes, what observes the soul? The regress begins again, each observer requiring another observer in an infinite tower that collapses under its own conceptual weight.

The hard determinist eliminates the mystery by eliminating the observer. Consciousness becomes a mere epiphenomenon, a powerless shadow cast by neural processes that would operate identically in darkness. The person catching themselves in fantasy experiences not genuine self-observation, but an illusion of observation created by deterministic brain states. The "catching" changes nothing because no real observer exists to make changes based on what is allegedly observed.

Yet this elimination of the observer contradicts what neuroscience reveals about how conscious attention systematically improves learning, how metacognitive monitoring enables error correction, and how deliberate reflection modifies subsequent behavior in ways that unconscious processing alone cannot achieve. The observer matters causally. The question is how observation can operate without observers in the problematic sense that generates infinite regress.

The answer emerges from recognizing that observation need not require observers as separate entities standing apart from observed processes. Hierarchical systems can implement observation through functional relationships between different levels of processing without requiring homunculi at any level.

A thermostat observes temperature. When the heat falls below the set point, the control mechanism activates heating. When the temperature exceeds the set point, the mechanism activates cooling. The thermostat genuinely observes and responds to temperature changes. Yet no one imagines a tiny observer inside the thermostat watching a temperature gauge. The observation emerges from a functional organization that connects sensors to control mechanisms through relationships, creating genuine monitoring without requiring separate observers.

The human brain implements metacognition through vastly more sophisticated versions of these same basic principles. Neural systems generate first-order mental states, including perceptions, emotions, and behavioral impulses, through processes operating largely below conscious awareness. Other neural systems monitor these first-order states through connections that transmit information about their presence and characteristics. Still other systems use this metacognitive information to regulate behavior, learning, and further cognitive processing through executive control.

The monitoring emerges from functional relationships between neural systems operating at different levels of the processing hierarchy, rather than requiring observers at any specific level. Primary sensory cortices generate representations of external stimuli.

Higher-order association cortices integrate these representations into increasingly abstract forms. Prefrontal regions monitor these integrated representations and use the information to guide behavior through conscious deliberation. The monitoring occurs through neural connections that transmit information about processing states, rather than through observing entities that must themselves be observed.

But the thermostat analogy misleads in one respect that matters profoundly for understanding consciousness. Thermostats implement monitoring without anything resembling subjective experience. No one believes that thermostats feel what it is like to detect temperature changes. The monitoring operates entirely in darkness, lacking the phenomenal character that distinguishes human metacognitive awareness from mere information processing in unconscious systems.

This difference points toward what philosophers call the hard problem of consciousness. We can explain how neural systems monitor other neural systems through the process of information processing. We can map the functional relationships by implementing this monitoring through increasingly detailed neuroscience. We can describe what consciousness does for behavior and cognition. Though explaining why monitoring generates felt experience, why there is something it is like to observe one's own mental processes rather than monitoring occurring in darkness, seems to require something more than functional analysis can provide.

David Chalmers argued that consciousness poses a hard problem distinct from the easy problems of explaining cognitive functions. The easy problems involve explaining how the brain performs various functions, including attention, memory, learning, and behavioral control, through mechanisms that science can investigate. These problems prove tractable through standard neuroscientific methods, despite many details remaining unknown. The hard problem involves explaining why performing these functions generates subjective experience. Why does consciousness feel like something from the inside? Why aren't we just sophisticated zombies processing information in darkness, without any inner felt experience requiring explanation?

The explanatory gap between functional descriptions and phenomenal experience has led many philosophers to conclude that consciousness cannot be fully naturalized. Thomas Nagel argued that objective scientific description necessarily misses the subjective character of experience because what it is like to be a conscious system cannot be captured from the third-person perspective that science requires. The bat's experience of echolocation differs fundamentally from human experience in ways that no amount of functional analysis of bat neurology can reveal, because the felt quality of experience exceeds its functional role.

Yet this conclusion about the impossibility of naturalizing consciousness proves too quick. The explanatory gap may reflect limitations in our current conceptual frameworks instead of inherent barriers that scientific progress cannot overcome. Throughout history, phenomena that seemed irreducibly mysterious eventually yielded to naturalistic explanation once appropriate frameworks emerged. Life once seemed to require vital forces beyond physical explanation. The organized complexity of living systems seemed impossible to explain through mechanical processes alone. We now understand life as a sophisticated organization of physical and chemical processes without a mysterious remainder.

Consciousness may follow a similar trajectory once we develop adequate frameworks for understanding how hierarchical functional organization generates phenomenal properties through mechanisms operating entirely within natural law. The key lies in recognizing that hierarchical organization itself generates emergent properties that supervene on, but differ qualitatively from, the properties of individual components considered in isolation.

Water is liquid. Individual H_2O molecules are not. The liquidity emerges from molecular organization through interactions between molecules that create collective properties impossible for molecules in isolation. Similarly, consciousness may emerge from hierarchical neural organization through interactions between monitoring systems that create phenomenal properties impossible for individual neural processes considered separately.

The emergence involves no mysterious non-physical properties magically arising from physical substrates. It involves recognizing that complex organizations of physical components possess properties requiring description at the level of organization rather than reduction to component properties. Water's liquidity is both physically and naturally perfect, yet impossible to locate or predict from individual molecules examined apart from their organizational context.

Consciousness emerges from hierarchical neural architectures where monitoring systems observe and regulate lower-level processes in recursive loops, creating unified experiential fields through mechanisms science can investigate. The phenomenal character, the what-it-is-likeness that seems so resistant to physical explanation, emerges specifically from systems that represent their own processing to themselves in ways that create recursive loops of self-representation.

When neural systems monitor their own states, and that monitoring itself becomes monitored in hierarchical cascades, the result is the peculiar form of self-intimating awareness we call consciousness. The system becomes aware of being aware through functional organization rather than through mysterious properties requiring dualistic explanation. The awareness proves genuinely phenomenal, genuinely felt, genuinely experienced, while operating through entirely natural mechanisms that hierarchical functional organization makes possible.

This explains why consciousness correlates with certain types of neural processing rather than arising in all information-processing systems. Thermostats process information without consciousness because they lack the recursive architecture where systems monitor their own monitoring. They implement first-order observation of temperature but not second-order observation of their own observational processes. The recursion matters because phenomenal consciousness emerges specifically from self-monitoring systems rather than from monitoring alone.

The Neural Machinery of Self-Observation

The anterior cingulate cortex sits deep within the frontal lobes like a sentinel posted between ancient impulse and modern reflection. When you reach for dessert despite having resolved to eat more healthfully, when attraction flares toward someone you know will hurt you, when anger rises at a slight you know is trivial, something in this region detects the conflict between what you want and what you want to want.

The detection happens before conscious awareness catches up. Milliseconds after competing impulses arise, the anterior cingulate signals that something needs attention, that automatic response and strategic goal have collided, that conscious control must intervene, or impulse will win by default. The signal feels like nothing specific, just a vague sense that something is wrong, that you should pause, that this moment requires more than automatic response.

Neuroimaging reveals the anterior cingulate activating precisely when people face such conflicts. Show someone images designed to trigger incompatible responses and watch this region light up as the conflict registers. Ask people to perform tasks where prepotent responses must be overridden and see activation spike when control becomes necessary. Damage this area and watch people lose the capacity to detect their own errors, continuing with failed strategies while insisting everything is fine.

But the anterior cingulate does more than detect conflict. It monitors errors, generating signals when outcomes fall short of expectations. This error detection operates largely below conscious awareness yet connects to consciousness in ways that enable learning from mistakes through reflection. When you realize mid-sentence that you have just said something foolish, when you notice after the fact that you responded to criticism with defensive anger you now regret, when you recognize hours later that you missed an obvious solution to a problem, the anterior cingulate has been signaling error even when conscious awareness lagged behind the neural detection.

The connections this region maintains position it perfectly for bridging automatic reaction and conscious control. It receives information from limbic systems generating emotions, from sensory systems processing environmental information, and from memory systems retrieving past experiences. It sends signals to prefrontal regions capable of implementing strategic responses based on abstract goals and long-term values. The anatomy creates a bridge between the brain systems we inherited from our mammalian ancestors and the uniquely human capacity for deliberate psychological design.

Yet the anterior cingulate cannot enable temporal scaffolding alone. It operates within broader networks, and one network proves particularly important for understanding how consciousness supports agency across time.

The default mode network activates when external attention relaxes, allowing the mind to turn inward toward memory and imagination rather than outward toward immediate environmental demands. Scan someone's brain while they rest quietly and watch this network activate. The medial prefrontal cortex, posterior cingulate, inferior parietal lobule, and medial temporal structures, including the hippocampus, all show coordinated activity that increases when external tasks decrease.

This coordination baffled early researchers who expected brains to show decreased activity during rest rather than this organized pattern of activation. But the confusion dissolved once they recognized what the network does. It enables mental time travel through mechanisms that simulate experiences using many of the same neural systems that generate experience.

When you remember your high school graduation, neural systems that processed the original experience reactivate to reconstruct the memory. Visual areas recreate the gymnasium where the ceremony occurred. Auditory areas regenerate the sounds of names being called. Emotional systems reproduce the mixture of pride and nervousness you felt walking across the stage. The reconstruction draws on stored traces, combined with current knowledge, to create something that feels like re-experiencing the event, despite occurring years later in different circumstances.

Similarly, when you imagine tomorrow's difficult conversation with your supervisor, the same systems activate to simulate an experience that has not yet happened. You see your supervisor's face, hear potential words exchanged, and feel anticipated anxiety, all through neural simulation using systems evolved for processing actual perception and action. The simulation proves imperfect, missing details and distorting probabilities. But it provides enough information to evaluate options and plan responses before the actual situation arrives.

This capacity for mental time travel transforms human agency in ways that creatures lacking it cannot achieve. An animal can remember that a particular location contained food yesterday and return there today. But they cannot imagine themselves in next week's situation, simulate different possible actions, evaluate likely outcomes, and design present interventions to make desired futures more probable. They remain trapped in the extended present, where past and future exist only as shadows cast by current stimuli rather than as distinct temporal locations that can be inhabited through imagination.

The default mode network enables temporal scaffolding by maintaining representations of the self across time, creating continuity between past, present, and future selves. When you plan next month's vacation, you imagine a future where you enjoy experiences you have designed in the present. When you reflect on last year's mistakes, you examine a past whose patterns you can modify through present learning. The network creates the temporal self that temporal scaffolding requires, which is the sense of being the same person extending across time despite constant change in moment-to-moment experiences.

Yet this network creates a paradox that reveals something profound about the architecture of consciousness. It deactivates during focused external attention. When you concentrate intensely on immediate tasks, the systems supporting self-reflection quiet their activity. This creates apparent tension. How can consciousness support both present engagement and temporal planning when these functions seem neurologically incompatible?

The tension dissolves through time itself. You do not need to engage in external tasks and reflect on temporal patterns simultaneously. You alternate between modes, using periods of external engagement to generate experiences and periods of internal reflection to learn from those experiences while planning future engagement. The temporal separation creates synergy rather than conflict. Each mode supports the other through their alternation rather than competing for simultaneous expression.

Someone learning a musical instrument demonstrates this pattern clearly. During practice, full attention is given to physical movements, sound production, and following the score. The default mode network quiets as task-positive networks activate to control immediate performance. But between practice sessions, during rest or commute, or moments before sleep, the network reactivates. The mind replays recent practice, notices patterns in mistakes, imagines alternative approaches, and plans modifications for the next session. The reflection draws on engagement while planning future engagement through mechanisms operating in different neural modes at different times.

The interplay between networks reveals the brain's capacity for shifting between consciousness modes serving different functions. Task-positive networks enable focused attention on immediate demands. The default mode network enables the broader temporal perspective necessary for learning from experience and planning future behavior. Effective agency requires fluid movement between modes rather than remaining trapped in either.

But networks and functional relationships tell only part of the story. The chemistry matters as much as the architecture.

The Chemical Foundation of Conscious Control

Three molecules determine whether hierarchical neural architectures can support conscious behavioral modification. Dopamine, serotonin, and norepinephrine. Each contributes something irreplaceable to the capacity for temporal scaffolding. Remove any of these chemical systems and watch agency collapse despite intact neural structures and preserved intelligence.

Dopamine does not create pleasure, despite popular descriptions reducing it to a happiness molecule. It signals something more subtle and more powerful. It tracks prediction errors, calculating the moment-by-moment difference between expected and actual outcomes across numerous neural pathways that process information about reward and goal achievement.

When outcomes exceed expectations, when something proves better than predicted, dopamine neurons fire intensely. The burst strengthens whatever neural patterns preceded the positive surprise. The strengthening operates automatically, below conscious awareness, gradually shifting behavioral probabilities toward actions that generated better-than-expected results. When outcomes fall short of expectations, when something proves worse than predicted, dopamine firing decreases below baseline. The dip weakens the patterns that preceded disappointment, again automatically, gradually shifting probabilities away from actions that generated worse-than-expected results.

This mechanism enables learning from experience through entirely unconscious processes. The rat that finds food in the left arm of a maze experiences a dopamine burst, strengthening the neural patterns that led there. The rat that finds the left arm empty experiences a dopamine dip, weakening those same patterns. After sufficient repetitions, behavior shifts toward the rewarded option without the rat possessing any conscious understanding of what it has learned or how.

However, humans can consciously tap into these unconscious processes. Someone attempting to develop better eating habits can deliberately experiment with different approaches while observing which generate felt satisfaction indicating dopamine signals. They try eating protein-rich breakfasts and notice that they feel satiated longer than with carbohydrate-heavy alternatives. They try scheduling specific eating times and notice reduced impulsive snacking. They try meal preparation routines and notice both effort and reward in the activity itself.

Each observation of felt reward signals dopamine, strengthening patterns that support beneficial behavior.

The system operates deterministically through chemical mechanisms. But conscious observation transforms unconscious learning into conscious experimentation. Rather than waiting for behavior to shift gradually through accumulated prediction errors, the person actively generates prediction errors through deliberate behavioral variation while attending to which variations generate the chemical signals indicating success.

Dopamine also determines whether effort feels worthwhile through its role in motivation and goal pursuit. When you anticipate reward, dopamine release creates felt motivation that makes effort seem manageable rather than overwhelming. The anticipation matters more than the reward itself. Dopamine spikes before reward arrives, creating the energized state that enables sustained work toward goals despite immediate costs.

This explains patterns that seem puzzling without understanding the chemistry. Someone might genuinely value long-term health while struggling to exercise consistently. They understand intellectually that regular physical activity would benefit them. They want the outcomes that the exercise would create. However, when the moment for exercise arrives, they lack the felt motivation that would make starting seem worthwhile.

The abstract value cannot generate the chemical signal that translates belief into action.

The problem worsens because contemporary environments exploit dopamine systems through mechanisms evolution never prepared us for. Variable reinforcement proves particularly powerful for hijacking motivation through uncertainty. When rewards arrive unpredictably, dopamine systems maintain high activation, processing the uncertainty itself as reward-relevant information requiring attention. The gambling machine, social media notifications, and video game loot boxes each exploit this mechanism by making reward timing unpredictable while ensuring rewards arrive at frequencies that maintain engagement.

Understanding the exploitation enables resistance through conscious architectural work. Recognizing how platforms manipulate dopamine, someone can design technological use that reduces variable reinforcement while preserving genuine benefits. Schedule specific times for checking social media rather than responding to unpredictable notifications. Modify settings to batch communications rather than delivering them as they arrive. Create friction that transforms impulsive checking into a deliberate choice. Each intervention works by altering the chemical conditions under which decisions occur rather than relying on willpower to override chemical signals moment by moment.

Yet dopamine alone cannot support temporal scaffolding without serotonin providing complementary functions that prove equally indispensable.

Serotonin modulates mood, impulse control, and temporal perspective through mechanisms that determine whether someone can maintain long-term goals despite immediate temptations. Low serotonin creates impulsivity, making immediate rewards feel irresistible while future consequences feel abstract and distant. High serotonin enables delay of gratification, making future outcomes feel real enough to influence present choices despite temporal distance.

Someone with well-functioning serotonin systems can observe immediate impulses without acting on them automatically. They feel the pull of temptation but can pause, consider consequences, and choose strategic responses over automatic reactions. Someone with serotonergic dysfunction experiences impulses as commands rather than information. The impulse to eat dessert, to check the phone, to skip the difficult task, each feels like it must be satisfied immediately, despite conscious knowledge that satisfaction undermines longer-term goals.

Depression and anxiety both involve serotonergic dysfunction as core features, and both specifically impair temporal scaffolding through their chemical effects on impulse control and future orientation. The depressed person understands intellectually what would help. They know that exercise would improve their mood, that social connection would reduce isolation, that productive work would restore meaning. But this intellectual understanding cannot generate the chemical foundation for acting on the knowledge. The impulse to remain in bed, to avoid others, to abandon responsibilities, each feels overwhelming despite conscious recognition that giving in maintains the depression.

The gap between knowledge and action feels agonizing to those experiencing it. They possess sophisticated understanding of their condition combined with complete inability to translate understanding into behavioral change. Others interpret this gap as laziness or weakness of will, failing to recognize that the chemical systems enabling translation from thought to action have become dysfunctional through processes the person did not choose and cannot override through mere effort.

Selective serotonin reuptake inhibitors work by increasing serotonin availability at neural synapses throughout the brain. When effective, these medications restore the chemical foundation for impulse control and future orientation that depression had eliminated. The person regains capacity to observe impulses without being controlled by them, to feel future outcomes as real rather than abstract, to maintain goals despite immediate difficulties. Intellectual understanding can finally connect to behavioral implementation through restored chemical function.

But medication alone proves insufficient. The restored chemical foundation enables temporal scaffolding but does not implement it automatically. The person must still develop metacognitive awareness, design environmental modifications, establish social support, practice behavioral patterns. The chemistry creates possibility. The conscious architectural work actualizes possibility through systematic effort operating within favorable chemical conditions.

The third system, norepinephrine, determines whether attention can be sustained long enough for either metacognitive observation or behavioral implementation to occur. This system modulates arousal, regulating whether we experience calm focus, energized engagement, or anxious hypervigilance at any moment.

Optimal norepinephrine creates the attentional state necessary for both observing patterns and implementing modifications. The person can sustain focus on difficult tasks without becoming either drowsy or agitated. They can maintain calm observation of their own mental processes without the intrusion of anxious rumination. They can persist through obstacles without losing energy or becoming overwhelmed.

Dysregulated norepinephrine destroys these capacities despite preserved intelligence and intact motivation. Too little creates lethargy that prevents sustained effort. Tasks that should be manageable feel exhausting. Attention wanders despite attempts to maintain focus. Persistence proves impossible because the chemical foundation for sustained arousal does not exist. Too much creates anxiety that fragments attention while preventing the calm observation necessary for metacognitive awareness. The person cannot sustain focus because anxious thoughts intrude constantly. They cannot observe patterns because anxiety about patterns dominates awareness. They cannot implement plans because agitation prevents the steady persistence that behavioral change requires.

These three systems interact in ways that create conditions either supporting or preventing temporal scaffolding, regardless of how well someone understands what they should do. Optimal levels of dopamine, serotonin, and norepinephrine create chemical conditions that enable intellectual understanding to translate into behavioral implementation through effort that feels difficult yet manageable. Dysregulated neurochemistry creates conditions where the same understanding leads nowhere because the chemical foundation for translation does not exist despite preserved cognitive capacity.

This reveals something philosophy has struggled to acknowledge. Agency requires not just hierarchical neural architecture but also a proper chemical function supporting that architecture. The person with depression possesses intact prefrontal systems, a functional anterior cingulate, and a working default mode network. Their neural architecture remains capable of supporting temporal scaffolding. But serotonergic dysfunction prevents the architecture from operating effectively despite its structural integrity. They face genuine disability, not metaphysical exemption from causation, not weakness of will, but chemical conditions that prevent translation from thought to action through mechanisms medicine can address but philosophy alone cannot.

The Development of Self-Observation

The neural systems supporting metacognitive awareness do not appear fully formed at birth but develop gradually over decades through processes that create the graduated responsibility patterns examined earlier. Understanding this development reveals why we appropriately hold a twenty-five-year-old to different standards than a twelve-year-old, why even adults vary in their capacities, and why conscious practice literally reshapes the brain through mechanisms operating across the lifespan.

A four-year-old hitting another child in anger possesses minimal capacity for observing their own emotional states or implementing alternative responses. When anger arises, it completely dominates the consciousness. The feeling and the child become identical in that moment. No metacognitive distance exists between experiencing emotion and being that emotion. The child is angry. Anger is not something they can observe and potentially regulate.

This is not a moral failure or a character defect but a developmental reality. The prefrontal systems supporting metacognitive observation remain immature. The connections between prefrontal monitoring systems and limbic emotional systems remain weak. The capacity for observing emotion as distinct from being emotion has not yet developed through the neural maturation that will occur gradually across years of development, stretching into adulthood.

By twelve, the same child possesses greater, yet still limited, metacognitive capacity. They can sometimes recognize anger arising before it escalates to violence. They can occasionally implement simple regulation strategies, such as walking away or counting to ten before responding. But the capacity operates inconsistently, failing frequently under stress, fatigue, or provocation. The prefrontal systems have developed sufficiently to enable some self-observation and control. But full maturation remains years away, making consistent self-regulation impossible despite increasing capacity for occasional success.

By twenty-five, assuming normal development, the person possesses a mature neural architecture supporting sophisticated metacognitive awareness. They can observe emotions arising without being dominated by them automatically. They can recognize patterns across situations, understanding what triggers strong responses and how those responses typically unfold. They can implement various regulation strategies depending on context, sometimes preventing problematic responses entirely and sometimes recovering more quickly when regulation fails.

This developmental progression reflects genuine neurological maturation occurring according to biological timetables that parenting or punishment or willpower cannot accelerate beyond natural limits. Expecting a twelve-year-old to demonstrate adult-level metacognitive capacity would be as absurd as expecting them to run as fast as Olympic sprinters before their bodies finish growing. The capacity depends on neural development that simply has not yet occurred, regardless of motivation or training.

Yet development does not terminate at twenty-five. Neural plasticity continues across the lifespan in ways that enable continued enhancement of metacognitive capacities through practice that physically reshapes brain structure. The fifty-year-old who has spent decades developing systematic self-observation possesses neural systems that are literally different from those of someone who never engaged in such practice, despite having identical genetics and similar environments.

The person who consistently practices observing their own thought patterns strengthens the neural pathways connecting monitoring systems to the processes being monitored. The connections become more numerous through synaptic strengthening, more reliable through myelination, and more efficient through pruning of unused alternatives. The result is a literal enhancement of metacognitive capacity beyond the baseline that genetic endowment and normal development created. Self-observation becomes easier, more automatic, more sophisticated through neural changes produced by practice itself.

This creates positive feedback loops where scaffolding practice enhances scaffolding capacity. The person who works systematically to observe their patterns develops a greater capacity for such observation through the work itself. The enhanced capacity enables more sophisticated practice, which further enhances capacity in recursive cycles without inherent limits. The self-modification is a genuine biological change at the neural level, not merely improved behavioral performance using unchanged capacities.

But plasticity also enables negative spirals where neglect degrades capacity over time. Neural systems require activation to maintain their functional strength through mechanisms similar to those that maintain muscle through exercise. Someone who stops practicing metacognitive observation finds these capacities deteriorating as the neural systems supporting them weaken from disuse. The atrophy is genuine, just as muscle atrophy from prolonged bed rest is genuine, creating real loss of function that must be regained through renewed practice if capacity is to be restored.

This developmental reality undermines claims that agency is either possessed completely or not at all. The twelve-year-old possesses genuine but limited capacity. The twenty-five-year-old with normal development possesses substantial but potentially underdeveloped capacity if they never practiced systematic self-observation. The fifty-year-old who has spent decades cultivating awareness possesses an enhanced capacity exceeding the typical baseline. Each variation in capacity justifies a different moral evaluation, social expectations, and forms of support, because capacity determines what can reasonably be expected and what interventions will prove most effective for continued development.

From Architecture to Agency

The hierarchical account of metacognitive awareness builds upon what was introduced in earlier chapters with the concept of temporal scaffolding. We now see how consciousness can observe itself without requiring infinite towers of observers. We see how mental events can causally influence behavior without violating physical law. We observe how capacities develop over time through natural processes of neural maturation and experiential plasticity.

The ghost in the machine dissolves into hierarchical neural architectures implementing recursive self-monitoring through functional relationships between systems operating at different processing levels. The monitoring is real, the causation is real, and the development is real. All operating through mechanisms that neuroscience investigates and that philosophy can no longer dismiss as metaphysically impossible or scientifically inexplicable.

Someone attempting to change established behavioral patterns works with these actual capacities operating through these actual mechanisms. When they observe themselves procrastinating, the anterior cingulate system detects conflict between behavior and goals. When they imagine completing the task, the default mode network simulates future outcomes using past experiences. When they design environmental changes to reduce distractions, prefrontal systems implement control strategies based on metacognitive awareness. When they practice new responses, experience-dependent plasticity gradually reshapes the neural systems that support those responses.

Each step operates through natural causation. Each step contributes to genuine agency. The person is simultaneously determined by neural processes and determining their own development through conscious participation in those processes. The apparent paradox resolves once we recognize that hierarchical organization creates forms of causation where higher levels regulate lower levels through mechanisms that are both deterministic and genuinely agentive.

This understanding transforms temporal scaffolding from philosophical abstraction into concrete biological process implemented through neural architectures we can study, chemical systems we can support, and developmental trajectories we can enhance. The transformation preserves everything worth wanting in human agency while eliminating mysterious properties that made naturalistic explanation seem impossible.

We are not ghosts inhabiting machines. We are sophisticated biological systems whose hierarchical organization enables consciousness to observe and modify itself through recursive loops, creating the subjective experience of agency from entirely objective neural processes. The experience is genuine. The agency is real. Both emerge from nature's most remarkable achievement in the evolution of matter toward conscious self-transformation.

An Expressivist Foundation

"What if strength is not endurance but architecture? What if becoming stronger means not surviving what determines us, but learning to determine what we become?"

A FRAMEWORK REQUIRING moral responsibility must ground that responsibility in something real. Libertarians ground it in impossible ultimate origination. Hard determinists eliminate it by tracing everything to prior causes. Compatibilists locate it in reasons-responsiveness or identification with desires, but manipulation arguments expose these criteria as inadequate.

The self-modification criterion grounds responsibility in actual psychological capacities for temporal scaffolding. However, this raises an unavoidable question. Why should anyone care about developing these capacities beyond what feels natural? If responsibility tracks psychological abilities and not objective moral facts, what prevents the framework from collapsing into relativism, where any responsibility practices are as legitimate as any other?

This requires stepping outside the philosophical voice that has carried us to this point. The question demands engagement with metaethical foundations that resist vivid examples and concrete cases. We must examine what moral judgments are, how they function, and why they matter. This involves theoretical analysis that cannot be dressed in the rhetoric of temporal scaffolding or illustrated through behavioral change.

The answer lies in the intersection of expressivist metaethics, evolutionary psychology, and cultural history. Not because this provides a comfortable resolution, but because it represents the only coherent foundation for connecting moral responsibility to the actual mechanisms through which behavioral modification happens.

What Moral Judgments Do

When you say, "That action was wrong," you are not reporting the discovery of a moral fact floating in platonic space. You are expressing disapproval while inviting others to share that attitude.

This is not relativism. The attitudes you express are not arbitrary preferences, such as favoring chocolate over vanilla. They are sophisticated responses shaped by evolution and culture to track features that matter for human welfare and cooperation.

Consider the judgment "Torture for entertainment is wrong." The expressivist analysis reveals that this statement expresses and elicits strong emotional responses of horror and condemnation. These responses reflect profound insights into human psychology, the conditions under which humans can flourish together, and the emotional capacities that evolution has shaped for maintaining cooperation.

Someone who feels no horror at torture for entertainment has either failed to develop normal human emotional capacities or undergone conditioning that suppresses these responses. We can point to these failures and abnormalities without claiming to have discovered objective moral facts about torture. The normativity emerges not from correspondence with independent moral reality but from what these attitudes accomplish when widely shared: they make cooperation possible, protect the vulnerable, and create conditions under which humans can live together without constant fear.

Expressivists, such as Allan Gibbard and Simon Blackburn, argue that moral language serves to coordinate attitudes and emotions that facilitate social cooperation. When we call someone morally responsible, we do several things at once. We express our reactive attitudes toward their behavior. We invite others to share these attitudes. We communicate expectations about behavioral change. We create social pressure motivating self-modification.

None of this requires moral facts about what the person ultimately deserves. The normative force comes from the role these practices play in making human social life possible. We are creatures who need cooperation to survive. We possess emotional capacities that enable cooperation through guilt, resentment, gratitude, and pride. Cultural evolution refined these capacities into sophisticated responsibility practices. The normative force emerges from this entire package: our nature, our needs, our emotions, and our cultural achievements working together.

Simon Blackburn's quasi-realism shows how moral discourse can have all the surface features of fact-stating discourse while remaining fundamentally expressive. We can say "It's true that breaking promises is wrong" without committing ourselves to free-floating moral facts. The truth predicate signals our endorsement of the attitude, not correspondence with independent reality.

This matters for the self-modification criterion. When we say someone is morally responsible, we express attitudes toward their capacities for recognizing and addressing problematic behavior patterns. We do not discover facts about their ultimate origination or metaphysical freedom. We express evaluations that connect to the actual psychological mechanisms through which behavioral change happens.

The criterion succeeds not by tracking objective responsibility-making properties but by focusing our expressive practices on features that matter for the social functions these practices serve.

Why Evolved Emotions Are Not Arbitrary

The charge of relativism fails once we recognize that evolved emotional responses are not culturally variable preferences, but universal features of human psychology grounded in our evolutionary heritage as cooperative primates.

Guilt, resentment, gratitude, and pride exist across all human cultures because these emotions helped our ancestors solve recurring adaptive problems. Groups whose members lacked guilt for harming cooperators would have dissolved through accumulated defections. Groups whose members never resented exploitation would have been dominated by free-riders. Groups whose members felt no gratitude for the help received would have failed to reciprocate in ways that sustain cooperation. Groups whose members took no pride in prosocial behavior would have lacked internal motivation for costly contributions to collective welfare.

These are not optional cultural preferences that some societies could abandon while maintaining complex cooperation. They are psychological universals that make human social life possible.

The universality becomes visible when examining moral emotions across diverse cultures. Anthropological research spanning dozens of societies, from hunter-gatherer bands to industrial nations, reveals that all human groups recognize obligations to kin, prohibit certain forms of harm to group members, enforce norms through social sanctions, and utilize emotional responses, including guilt and resentment, to maintain cooperation.

The specific behaviors these emotions target vary across cultures. What counts as forbidden harm, appropriate reciprocity, or praiseworthy contribution depends on local social structures and material conditions. But the underlying emotional architecture remains constant. Every human society has members who feel guilt when violating cooperative commitments, resentment when exploited by free-riders, gratitude when receiving benefits, and pride when contributing to collective welfare.

This universality extends to patterns in moral development across cultures. Children everywhere acquire moral concepts in similar sequences. Young children everywhere first grasp prohibitions against harm and obligations to kin. They later develop an understanding of fairness, reciprocity, and group loyalty. They eventually acquire capacities for abstract moral reasoning about justice, rights, and duties.

Cultural variation affects content while preserving the developmental structure. A child growing up in a collectivist society and one growing up in an individualist society traverses the same developmental stages in the same order while learning different specific norms.

The evolutionary explanation for this universality proves straightforward. Natural selection, operating on our primate ancestors over millions of years, shaped neural systems that generate these emotional responses, as they enabled more complex cooperation than competing groups could sustain. The emotions are as much a part of universal human nature as our capacity for language acquisition or our need for social attachment.

Someone who claims moral attitudes are arbitrary, like food preferences, faces an obvious challenge. Try creating a society where people feel no guilt for betraying cooperators, no resentment toward exploiters, no gratitude for help received, and no pride in contributing to collective welfare. Such a society would immediately collapse through accumulated defections and free-riding. No stable human cooperation would be possible.

This is not arbitrary. This is a biological reality that constrains the forms of social organization humans can sustain.

The expressivist recognizes moral judgments as expressions of attitudes, but these attitudes are ones that humans cannot abandon while remaining capable of complex cooperation. The normative force comes not from correspondence with independent moral facts but from the role these attitudes play in enabling the social life our species requires for survival.

Why Guilt Exists

You break a promise to your closest friend. Before conscious thought begins, something recoils inside you. Not fear of consequences, which may never come. Not a calculation about reputation damage. Pure discomfort at having violated a commitment you value.

This response operates automatically through mechanisms that natural selection shaped across millennia. The question is not whether guilt feels bad but why natural selection would create creatures who torment themselves for harming others.

The answer becomes obvious once you recognize guilt as an internal enforcement mechanism, maintaining cooperation without the need for constant external monitoring. Groups whose members felt guilt when causing harm tended to have more complex cooperative arrangements than groups lacking such regulatory mechanisms. Without guilt, human societies would resemble those of other great apes: small hierarchical groups with limited cooperation beyond immediate kinship.

But guilt proves more sophisticated than simple conditioning. Your guilt responses vary predictably based on factors that matter for cooperation and behavioral change.

Breaking a promise due to a genuine emergency generates different guilt than breaking one through careless planning or deliberate choice to do something more enjoyable. Harming someone through negligence feels different than harming them through malicious intent. Violating commitments to close friends generates stronger guilt than similar violations toward distant acquaintances.

These differential responses track features of behavior and circumstances that predict whether similar violations will recur and whether relationship repair remains possible. Evolution shaped guilt to respond precisely to factors that matter most for maintaining social cooperation. The emotion exhibits rational structure without requiring conscious reasoning about evolutionary functions.

Someone experiencing guilt about breaking a promise is automatically motivated to apologize and make amends. They become more careful about future commitments. They learn which situations create high risk for promise-breaking and avoid them. The emotion serves multiple functions simultaneously: repairing damaged relationships, signaling continued commitment to cooperation, and fostering learning that prevents future violations.

Resentment serves complementary purposes by motivating social responses to norm violations. When someone harms you or breaks a commitment, negative emotions elicit responses ranging from confrontation to social distancing. These responses create costs for harmful behavior that discourage repetition while clearly communicating that such behavior is unacceptable.

Yet resentment also exhibits sophisticated calibration to morally relevant factors. You respond differently to accidental versus intentional harm, temporary lapses versus habitual patterns, people struggling with genuine limitations versus those acting with full capacity for better choices.

Pride and moral approval complete the emotional foundation by creating positive reinforcement for prosocial behavior. Acting courageously, generously, and fairly generates positive feelings, making such behavior intrinsically rewarding. Observing others act prosocially generates moral approval, motivating gratitude, respect, and emulation.

These emotional systems create stable motivational structures that support consistent moral behavior, even when external rewards are absent or delayed. Moral behavior becomes personally satisfying, not merely socially expected.

This emotional substrate provides the foundation for all moral responsibility practices. But evolution alone cannot explain the sophisticated frameworks humans have developed. The emotions themselves are universal across cultures. How we express and refine them through institutions varies dramatically across societies and historical periods.

The Recursive Difference

A chimpanzee can learn through experience that attacking higher-ranking group members leads to retaliation. This represents genuine learning that shapes future behavior. But the chimpanzee cannot observe its own emotional response to provocation and evaluate whether that response serves its long-term interests. It cannot distinguish between anger triggered by genuine threats and anger triggered by irrelevant social slights. It lacks the metacognitive architecture necessary for systematic refinement of emotional responses through reflective observation.

Humans possess this architecture. Someone cuts you off in traffic, and rage flares automatically. Then you notice the hospital emergency sign on their windshield. The rage does not vanish through conscious decisions. It transforms through recognition that the situation differs from what your automatic systems assumed.

This recursive capacity creates possibilities that simple emotional reactions cannot achieve. You can notice patterns in when guilt serves beneficial functions and when it sabotages them. You can recognize that shame about childhood trauma maintains destructive cycles without preventing harm. You can distinguish between emotions that track genuine moral features and emotions that track irrelevant factors, such as group membership or status.

Consider someone raised in a community with strong prejudices against a particular ethnic group. They inherit emotional responses of distrust and dislike through social learning operating below conscious awareness. These responses feel natural and justified, like reactions to genuine moral transgressions.

But exposure to members of the stereotyped group through work or school creates opportunities for disconfirming evidence. The person notices their automatic responses do not predict trustworthiness or moral character. Individuals from the stereotyped group exhibit the same variation in ethics and reliability as people from their own group.

Through repeated observation, they recognize their automatic responses track group membership, not morally relevant individual characteristics. This recognition does not immediately eliminate automatic responses shaped by deep social conditioning. But it creates psychological distance. They can observe the emotional reaction arising, recognize it as tracking irrelevant features, choose not to act on it or reflectively endorse it.

Over time, with continued observation and contrary evidence, the automatic responses themselves may weaken or transform.

This operates at multiple levels simultaneously. First-order emotional responses arise automatically based on evolutionary sensitivities and social learning. Second-order metacognitive processes observe these responses and evaluate whether they align with what matters to the person's values and goals. Third-order processes can observe and evaluate second-order observations themselves, creating recursive loops enabling increasingly sophisticated moral judgment.

Someone recovering from addiction experiences automatic cravings when exposed to triggers associated with past drug use. The first-order response is purely automatic, resulting from neural associations formed through the repeated pairing of environmental cues with drug-related rewards. However, second-order metacognitive processes can observe cravings arising, recognize them as conditioned responses rather than genuine needs, and implement coping strategies developed through recovery work.

At a third level, they can observe their own metacognitive monitoring and evaluate its effectiveness. They notice that certain monitoring strategies work better than others, that some situations require different approaches, and that their capacity for managing cravings improves with practice but deteriorates under stress. This meta-metacognitive awareness enables systematic refinement of self-regulatory strategies over time.

Cultural evolution amplifies individual capacities through collective experimentation and the transmission of knowledge. Societies function as laboratories testing different approaches to moral education, responsibility attribution, and behavioral modification. Some approaches prove more effective than others at promoting cooperation while maintaining dignity and enabling growth. Successful innovations get preserved and transmitted across generations. Failures get abandoned or modified.

Cultural Evolution of Responsibility Practices

The historical development of responsibility practices reveals how cultural experimentation refines evolved emotional responses through accumulated wisdom about human psychology and social organization.

Ancient legal codes, such as Hammurabi's Code, emphasized strict proportional punishment for harm. An eye for an eye, a tooth for a tooth. This approach expressed resentment toward wrongdoers while attempting to limit cycles of escalating retaliation that threatened social stability. The system worked adequately for small, relatively homogeneous communities where most people knew each other and repeated interactions made reputation crucial.

But strict proportionality created problems as societies grew more complex. It provided no framework for evaluating mitigating circumstances or psychological factors affecting culpability. It treated all harms within a category as equivalent regardless of intentions, capacities, or contexts. It offered no mechanisms for behavioral rehabilitation beyond deterrence through threatened punishment.

Greek and Roman legal systems introduced more sophisticated distinctions. They differentiated between intentional and accidental harm, voluntary and involuntary actions, and crimes requiring mens rea from strict liability offenses. These innovations reflected growing recognition that moral responsibility depends on psychological factors beyond mere causal contribution to harmful outcomes.

But ancient systems still lacked adequate frameworks for understanding how character develops and can be modified through systematic intervention. They treated character as relatively fixed, either virtuous or vicious, rather than recognizing developmental trajectories shaped by environmental conditions and conscious effort.

Medieval Christian morality introduced concepts of sin, confession, penance, and redemption, acknowledging the possibility of moral transformation. Someone who committed sins could achieve forgiveness through genuine repentance and behavioral change guided by religious practice. This represented genuine insight: responsibility practices should create growth opportunities, not merely impose suffering proportionate to past misdeeds.

Yet medieval approaches located transformation primarily in supernatural grace rather than natural psychological processes. They lacked a scientific understanding of how behavioral change occurs through mechanisms such as metacognitive awareness, environmental modification, and systematic practice.

Honor-based responsibility systems, which dominated many traditional societies, emphasized collective accountability and reputation management. Families bore shared responsibility for individual members' actions. Someone who violated important norms brought shame upon their entire family, creating powerful incentives for internal regulation and mutual surveillance.

Honor systems worked well in small, stable communities with limited institutional capacity for formal law enforcement. Family networks could effectively monitor and regulate member behavior while providing support for those facing challenges. The threat of collective shame motivated families to intervene early when members showed signs of problematic patterns.

But honor systems created serious problems that later innovations addressed. Collective responsibility could punish innocent family members for actions they did not commit and could not prevent. Focus on reputation and face-saving created cycles of violence as families sought to restore honor through retaliation against those who shamed them. Rigid status hierarchies excluded many individuals from full moral standing based on birth, gender, or social position.

Dignity-based systems emerging during the Enlightenment emphasized individual rather than collective responsibility, recognizing the inherent worth of all individuals regardless of their social status or family reputation. They provided institutional mechanisms for adjudicating disputes without private violence. They created legal protections against arbitrary punishment and guaranteed basic rights to all citizens.

These innovations emerged not through philosophical reasoning alone but through centuries of experimentation with different social structures and observation of their consequences. Societies that abandoned collective punishment while preserving individual accountability achieved better outcomes across multiple dimensions. They reduced cycles of violence, protected innocent family members, enabled social mobility, and created more stable conditions for cooperation across diverse populations.

Yet dignity systems brought new limitations. By locating responsibility entirely in individuals, they sometimes ignored environmental and social factors profoundly shaping behavioral possibilities. They often imposed uniform standards without adequate recognition of developmental differences and capacity variations. They emphasized punishment over rehabilitation, retribution over restoration.

Contemporary therapeutic approaches represent another stage of cultural evolution toward more psychologically sophisticated responsibility practices. Drug courts require treatment participation instead of imposing purely punitive sentences. They explicitly assess participants' capacities for self-modification and provide graduated support matching current abilities while promoting development.

Restorative justice programs bring together those who caused harm, those who experienced harm, and affected community members to develop collaborative responses addressing both accountability and repair. These processes focus on understanding what led to harmful behavior and creating conditions preventing recurrence while healing damaged relationships.

Mental health courts address underlying psychiatric conditions while maintaining accountability for harmful actions. They recognize that severe mental illness can compromise capacities for temporal scaffolding while preserving possibilities for capacity development through appropriate treatment and support.

Trauma-informed approaches to criminal justice acknowledge how adverse childhood experiences affect brain development and behavioral regulation. They neither excuse harmful behavior based on trauma history nor ignore how trauma compromises capacities requiring systematic support for effective restoration.

Each innovation reflects accumulated cultural learning about human psychology and behavioral change. They work with the actual mechanisms through which people develop better self-regulation. They acknowledge both individual agency and environmental conditions that support or undermine that agency. They focus on promoting beneficial change, not simply imposing suffering in proportion to moral desert.

The pattern reveals cultural evolution operating through variation and selection. Different societies experiment with different responsibility practices. Those that prove more effective at promoting cooperation while maintaining dignity and enabling growth are preserved and spread. Those creating more problems than they solve get modified or abandoned.

This evolutionary process continues. Contemporary societies face novel challenges, including technological environments exploiting psychological vulnerabilities, economic structures undermining community stability, and media systems fragmenting shared reality. Responsibility practices must continue adapting while preserving the core functions these practices evolved to serve.

Grounding the Self-Modification Criterion

The self-modification criterion states that moral responsibility is linked to capacities for temporal scaffolding, which include observing behavioral patterns, identifying factors that generate problematic behaviors, designing interventions that modify these factors systematically, and developing metacognitive awareness that enables ongoing behavioral refinement.

This criterion succeeds where others fail by directly connecting moral evaluation to the psychological mechanisms that underlie behavioral change.

Someone who lacks the capacity for self-modification through temporal scaffolding cannot benefit from expressions of moral disapproval in the ways these expressions evolved to provide. Resentment toward them serves no useful social function because they cannot recognize what they did wrong, understand why we respond negatively, or modify their behavior in response to this feedback. The moral emotions we would express toward them misfire because the target lacks the psychological architecture these emotions presuppose.

This is not moral relativism. It is moral realism about psychological mechanisms combined with expressivism about moral facts. There are objective facts about whether someone possesses capacities for temporal scaffolding. There are objective facts about whether expressions of moral attitudes will promote behavioral change.

The moral judgment expresses attitudes calibrated to these psychological facts in ways that serve cooperation and human flourishing.

Traditional frameworks sought criteria for moral responsibility in the wrong places. Libertarians looked for ultimate origination. Hard determinists found only causal determination. Compatibilists examined reasons-responsiveness or identification with desires.

Each criterion failed because each focused on features that do not track what matters for the social functions that responsibility practices serve.

When we hold someone responsible, we express attitudes that serve social functions only if the person possesses the capacity to recognize and respond to these expressions. Praising someone for beneficial behavior serves its function only if they can recognize the behavior as worthy of approval and maintain similar patterns in the future. Blaming someone for harmful behavior serves its function only if they can recognize the behavior as problematic and work to prevent similar actions.

The Frankfurt Cases

Harry Frankfurt's famous thought experiment challenged the principle that moral responsibility requires alternative possibilities. Imagine Jones decides on his own to vote for Smith. Unknown to him, a neuroscientist named Black has been monitoring Jones's brain and would have intervened to ensure Jones voted for Smith if Jones had shown any inclination to vote otherwise.

Since Jones decided independently, Black never intervened. Jones lacked genuine alternatives because Black would have prevented different choices. Yet Jones seems responsible for voting for Smith because the decision arose from his own reasons without external interference.

Frankfurt argued that this shows moral responsibility does not require alternative possibilities. What matters is acting from your own authentic reasons, not whether you could have done otherwise.

Frankfurt cases appear to support traditional compatibilism by showing that acting from your own reasons suffices for responsibility even when alternatives are absent. However, they create deeper problems when combined with concerns about manipulation.

Consider a modified case. Jones decides on his own to vote for Smith. Unknown to him, Black installed these political preferences years ago through sophisticated neural conditioning operating below the conscious threshold. Jones's current desires to vote for Smith result entirely from Black's earlier manipulation. Black need not intervene now because his earlier conditioning ensures Jones will vote as intended.

In this version, Jones acts from his own reasons in the sense that the desires and values generating his vote genuinely belong to him now. He identifies with these preferences and would not change them if he could. No external compulsion forces his vote. Yet Jones seems profoundly unfree because his entire motivational structure results from manipulation that bypassed his capacity for reflective evaluation and self-directed development.

Traditional compatibilist criteria cannot distinguish this case from normal socialization. Both involve external influences shaping desires and values. Both result in the person acting from preferences they currently identify with. Both lack alternatives at the moment of choice. Yet our moral intuitions insist that manipulation undermines responsibility in ways normal development does not.

The self-modification criterion cuts through this problem cleanly.

Jones, in the original Frankfurt case, possesses the full capacity to recognize his voting decision as his own, evaluate whether it reflects his authentic political judgment, and modify his decision-making process if it proves problematic. Black's presence does not compromise these capacities because Black never actually intervenes. Jones's decision-making architecture operates normally. His metacognitive awareness functions properly. His capacity for temporal scaffolding remains intact.

Jones, in the manipulation version, lacks these capacities. The conditioning that shaped his political preferences prevented the development of metacognitive awareness about how those preferences formed. He cannot observe his political desires and ask whether they express considered judgments or merely reflect installed programming. He lacks the capacity to recognize the external control itself because manipulation prevented the development of the psychological resources necessary for such recognition.

The criterion distinguishes cases based on current capacity for self-modification, not on whether alternatives existed at the moment of choice or whether the person identifies with their desires.

This resolves the tension the Frankfurt cases create. Alternative possibilities matter not as metaphysical requirements but as indicators of self-modification capacity. When someone lacks alternatives due to external coercion or internal compulsion preventing metacognitive awareness, this signals compromised capacity for temporal scaffolding. When someone lacks alternatives due to strong moral character rendering immoral action psychologically impossible, this signals a highly developed capacity emerging through systematic self-cultivation.

The recovering addict who has worked for years to eliminate drug use and finds themselves psychologically incapable of using again demonstrates advanced self-modification capacity. The impossibility of drug use reflects successful temporal scaffolding that reconstructed psychological architecture through systematic effort. We do not view this lack of alternatives as undermining responsibility. If anything, it demonstrates responsibility at its most developed.

Compare this to the addict in active addiction who finds themselves psychologically unable to refuse drugs despite a desperate desire to quit. This lack of alternatives reflects compromised capacity for self-modification. Addiction has damaged their ability to design effective temporal scaffolding or maintain metacognitive awareness during moments of craving. The impossibility of refusal indicates reduced responsibility, not because alternatives are metaphysically necessary, but because impossibility signals psychological constraints that prevent beneficial behavioral modification.

Frankfurt cases thus become diagnostic tools revealing what matters for moral responsibility: not alternatives at the moment of choice, not identification with desires, but capacity for observing psychological processes and systematically modifying problematic patterns.

Manipulation and Normal Socialization

Harry Frankfurt argued that moral responsibility requires acting from desires you identify with, not desires you wish you did not have. The unwilling addict who hates their drug cravings but acts on them anyway lacks the internal unity necessary for responsible agency. The willing addict who embraces their desires and would not change them if they could acts more freely despite being equally unable to abstain.

But Frankfurt's criterion proves vulnerable to manipulation. Imagine someone whose second-order desires were engineered through sophisticated conditioning to identify with first-order desires serving the manipulator's goals. They fully endorse their motivational structure and would not change it if they could. Yet they seem profoundly unfree because their entire hierarchy of desires is a result of external control, not authentic development.

The self-modification criterion cuts through this problem. The manipulated person lacks the genuine capacity to recognize and resist manipulation. Their metacognitive awareness has been compromised or bypassed by conditioning operating below the conscious threshold. They cannot engage in temporal scaffolding to modify psychological and environmental factors generating their behavior because they cannot recognize these factors as external impositions instead of authentic preferences.

Normal development differs from sophisticated manipulation. Not because the normally socialized person possesses ultimate origination that the manipulated person lacks. Both had their characters shaped by external forces beyond initial control.

The difference lies in whether the person has developed the capacity to observe their own psychological processes, evaluate whether these processes serve their long-term goals and values, and systematically modify problematic patterns.

A child raised by loving parents who encourage independence and critical thinking develops the capacity to question received values and form their own judgments. An adolescent exposed to diverse perspectives and encouraged to reason through ethical dilemmas develops the ability to evaluate whether their emotional responses track genuine moral features. An adult who encounters challenges requiring personal growth develops skills for recognizing behavioral patterns that no longer serve them and works systematically to change these patterns.

This developmental process creates genuine capacity for self-modification, even though the person never possessed ultimate control over the factors that created this capacity. The normally developed person can observe their own values and ask whether these genuinely express considered judgments or merely reflect uncritical absorption of social expectations. They can recognize when emotional responses diverge from reflective evaluations. They can design environmental conditions supporting authentic goals instead of merely replicating childhood conditioning.

Manipulation bypasses or actively prevents this developmental process. The manipulated person's values and preferences were installed without opportunities for reflective evaluation. Their metacognitive capacities were either never developed or systematically undermined by conditioning operating below conscious awareness.

Most importantly, they cannot recognize external control itself because manipulation prevented the development of the psychological resources necessary for such recognition.

This explains why normal socialization does not undermine responsibility in the same way that manipulation does. The criterion is not ultimate origination, which neither person possesses. The criterion is current capacity for temporal scaffolding through metacognitive awareness.

Healthy development typically creates such capacity by providing opportunities and encouragement for independent thought and self-directed behavioral modification. Manipulation prevents or eliminates it by installing values and preferences without creating genuine capacity for reflective evaluation and systematic change.

John Fischer and Mark Ravizza developed guidance control theory to address manipulation problems facing earlier compatibilism. They argued that responsible agency requires not just acting for reasons but acting from mechanisms that are responsive to reasons in appropriate ways. The mechanism must be the agent's own in the sense that it developed through history, involving opportunities for reflection and evaluation.

The self-modification criterion preserves Fischer and Ravizza's key insight while going further. What matters is not merely that the person's decision-making mechanisms are reasons-responsive. What matters is that they possess the capacity for observing how these mechanisms operate, evaluating their effectiveness, and modifying them when they produce outcomes inconsistent with the person's considered values and goals.

Reasons-responsiveness provides necessary but insufficient conditions for responsibility. Self-modification capacity provides both necessary and sufficient conditions because it encompasses reasons-responsiveness while incorporating metacognitive and architectural components.

Someone whose reasons-responsive mechanisms were engineered through manipulation might respond appropriately to moral reasons without any real capacity to recognize or resist engineering itself. They see reasons and respond to them, but cannot step back to evaluate whether their system of caring reflects authentic development or external control.

The self-modification criterion captures this difference.

Weakness of Will and Moral Luck

Weakness of will puzzled Aristotle and continues to puzzle philosophers. How can someone act against their better judgment, knowing their action is wrong but doing it anyway? If moral knowledge should guide action, how do we explain behavior violating the agent's own moral beliefs?

The expressivist framework, with its self-modification criterion, reveals weakness of will as neither mysterious nor impossible. It is simply the absence of effective temporal scaffolding in domains where such scaffolding would be necessary for behavioral consistency.

The person lacks adequate metacognitive awareness of the factors that trigger problematic behavior. They have not implemented environmental modifications, making beneficial behavior more probable. They have not developed social support systems reinforcing desired choices. They have not created identity narratives framing beneficial behavior as expressing their authentic selves.

Consider someone who repeatedly eats unhealthy food despite a genuine commitment to better nutrition. They understand perfectly well that their eating conflicts with their stated values. They can articulate excellent reasons for eating more healthily. They possess strong general willpower and self-discipline in other areas of life. Yet they continue patterns they recognize as problematic and wish to change.

This person does not lack moral knowledge. They know what they should do. They do not lack rational control in some absolute sense. They exercise effective self-regulation in many areas.

What they lack is effective temporal scaffolding specifically for eating behavior. They have not developed a sophisticated understanding of triggers, environmental cues, and psychological patterns that would enable systematic behavioral modification in this domain.

Two versions of this person illustrate the difference. The first version recognizes their eating as problematic but makes no systematic efforts at change. They occasionally resolve to eat better. These resolutions last a few days or weeks before old patterns reassert themselves. They rely entirely on willpower in moments of temptation, which proves insufficient against powerful environmental and psychological factors promoting unhealthy choices.

They lack metacognitive awareness of why their resolutions fail. They implement no environmental changes. They develop no new habits. They seek no external support.

The second version engages in sophisticated temporal scaffolding. They track eating patterns to identify specific triggers, including emotional states, social situations, and environmental cues. They remove tempting foods from their home while stocking healthy alternatives. They establish meal planning routines to make nutritious eating automatic. They cultivate social relationships supporting nutritional goals.

They practice noticing early signs of stress or emotional discomfort that typically precede unhealthy eating. They develop alternative responses to these triggers that address underlying needs without using food as a primary coping mechanism.

Both versions exhibit weakness of will in traditional terms. Both eat in ways that contradict their stated values and considered judgments. But one demonstrates capacity for temporal scaffolding while the other does not.

Moral emotions respond differently to these cases not through arbitrary discrimination but because they track features that matter for behavioral change.

Responsibility attaches not to perfect behavioral control but to sustained engagement with the project of self-modification through temporal scaffolding.

Moral luck presents similar challenges. Thomas Nagel identified four types: constitutive luck involves the kind of person you are based on genetic and developmental factors; circumstantial luck involves situations you encounter through no choice of your own; antecedent luck includes historical events that shaped your character; resultant luck refers to how your actions turn out regardless of intentions.

When two equally reckless drivers speed through a school zone but only one strikes a child who darts into the street, we typically feel a stronger moral condemnation toward the driver who caused harm. Identical intentions, identical recklessness, identical lack of adequate precautions.

Yet our moral responses differ based on outcomes neither could control. This seems to violate principles of moral fairness. Why should someone bear greater responsibility for consequences they could not foresee or prevent?

The expressivist approach dissolves this problem. Our moral emotions respond to multiple factors simultaneously, creating tensions that reflect competing evolutionary pressures, not conceptual confusion.

The sense of fairness, which makes us resist differential treatment based on luck, evolved to support cooperative reciprocity. Our concern for social protection, which heightens our response to actual harm, evolved to prevent future victims. The capacity for empathy, which allows us to tailor responses according to an understanding of others' psychological states, evolved to calibrate social reactions for maximum effectiveness.

These emotional responses need not adhere to a single, coherent principle about when responsibility obtains. They track different features that matter for different social functions that responsibility practices serve.

Resultant luck affects our emotional responses because actual harm creates victims who require protection and triggers community responses that prevent similar future harm. This serves genuine social functions even when a differential response seems unfair from the perspective of comparing intentions and character.

The tension we feel about moral luck cases reflects genuine conflicts between different values and social functions. We care about fairness and proportionality. We also care about victims and consequences. We care about intentions and character. We also care about preventing future harm through whatever mechanisms prove effective.

Moral luck cases force us to navigate competing concerns without the comfort of principles to eliminate tension.

Consider constitutive luck more carefully. Someone born with genetic predispositions toward impulsivity, low empathy, or poor emotional regulation faces behavioral challenges others avoid through mere genetic fortune. Holding such people fully responsible seems unfair when psychological limitations result from circumstances beyond their control.

Yet refusing to hold them responsible at all seems to eliminate any basis for social protection or behavioral modification.

The self-modification criterion suggests a more nuanced approach. Individuals with genetic disadvantages in self-regulation can still develop metacognitive awareness and temporal scaffolding abilities, although doing so may require more effort and support than those with better genetic endowments.

The responsibility question becomes not whether they possess psychological advantages through genetic luck but whether they have developed or can develop capacities for recognizing behavioral problems and systematically working to address them given their starting position.

This shifts focus from backward-looking questions about whether someone deserves blame for factors beyond their control to forward-looking questions about capacities and interventions. Someone with strong genetic predispositions toward impulsive aggression might require more intensive support for developing self-regulation than someone with better baseline emotional control.

But if they can develop such capacities with appropriate support, they can bear moral responsibility for failures to use or develop them.

The expressivist framework treats constitutive luck not as eliminating responsibility but as affecting what level of capacity development we can reasonably expect and what forms of support society should provide. Someone who grows up with genetic and environmental advantages for self-regulation might be held to higher standards than someone who faced significant disadvantages. But both can be held responsible to some degree because both possess or can develop capacities for temporal scaffolding, even if those capacities differ in strength and require different levels of support.

Collective Responsibility and Distributed Agency

Moral responsibility for collective harms presents challenges that individual-focused frameworks struggle to address adequately. When corporations engage in systematic misconduct, when governments commit atrocities, or when communities perpetuate injustice, responsibility often seems too diffused for traditional attribution.

The expressivist framework extends naturally to collective contexts by focusing on capacities for recognizing and addressing systemic problems through available means. Individual members of collective entities bear responsibility proportionate to their capacity for influencing collective behavior through their institutional roles and their efforts to develop such capacity when it proves inadequate.

Consider an engineer working at a technology company that deliberately designs addictive features into products to maximize user engagement and data collection. The engineer writes code implementing these features. They understand technical specifications and can execute them competently. However, they may lack a sophisticated understanding of how their technical work contributes to collective harms, including attention fragmentation, deterioration of mental health, and erosion of human agency.

Several versions of this engineer demonstrate different degrees of moral responsibility.

The first version lacks awareness of systemic problems entirely. They view their work as a neutral technical implementation of product specifications. They never question whether the features they build serve user interests or company profits. They make no effort to understand psychological research on attention, addiction, and well-being. They never discuss ethical concerns with colleagues or managers. They demonstrate minimal capacity for recognizing and addressing collective harms.

The second version possesses some awareness but feels powerless to influence company practices. They understand that the features they implement exploit psychological vulnerabilities. They recognize tension between user welfare and business objectives. But they believe their individual position provides no leverage for institutional change. They never raise concerns because they assume such efforts would prove futile.

They demonstrate limited capacity despite possessing relevant awareness.

The third version combines awareness with active efforts at institutional influence. They educate themselves about psychological research relevant to their work. They raise ethical concerns in team meetings and design reviews. They advocate for alternative approaches that better serve user interests. They build coalitions with like-minded colleagues who share ethical concerns. They document their objections when management decisions prioritize profit over welfare. They develop strategic approaches to ethical influence, working within the constraints of institutions.

These three versions face identical institutional structures and similar limitations on individual power. However, they demonstrate different capacities for self-modification that extend into collective contexts.

The third version possesses metacognitive awareness of how their role contributes to systemic problems. They implement temporal scaffolding through systematic efforts to develop influence capacity and work toward institutional improvement. They deserve a different moral evaluation than the first version, not because they possess ultimate control over corporate behavior, but because they demonstrate the capacity for recognizing and addressing ethical problems through available means.

The responsibility question for collective harms thus becomes not whether an individual's causal contribution mechanistically produced the outcome, but whether they developed or attempted to develop awareness of systemic problems and took available steps to address them, given their institutional position.

This preserves individual moral responsibility while acknowledging genuine constraints that organizational structures create.

Someone working within a harmful institution who possesses no awareness of systemic problems, makes no efforts to understand their role in collective harms, takes no steps to develop greater capacity for ethical influence, shows no commitment to institutional improvement, demonstrates different moral capacities than someone who systematically develops understanding, builds strategic capacity for change, persistently works toward improvement even within strong institutional constraints.

This framework avoids both inadequate individualism, which ignores how institutions shape behavior, and excessive collectivism, which eliminates individual accountability. It recognizes responsibility as a matter of degree, reflecting actual variation in knowledge, position, and commitment to institutional reform.

Someone in senior leadership with extensive authority bears greater responsibility than junior employees with limited influence. However, even those with minimal formal power can demonstrate moral capacity by making efforts to develop awareness and work toward change within their sphere of influence.

The expressivist approach also explains why we appropriately hold people responsible for participating in harmful institutions even when individual contributions seem negligible and the capacity for changing institutional behavior appears limited. The moral emotions expressed through responsibility attributions serve functions beyond imposing deserved punishment.

They communicate moral disapproval, creating pressure for behavioral and institutional change. They motivate individuals to develop greater awareness of systemic problems. They encourage the formation of coalitions that can achieve reforms impossible for isolated individuals.

These functions operate even when individual causal contributions remain small and the individual capacity for institutional change appears limited. The cumulative effect of many individuals developing awareness and working for reform can transform institutions in ways no individual could accomplish alone.

Consider the transformation of corporate environmental practices over recent decades. Individual employees at polluting companies initially possessed minimal capacity for changing corporate behavior. But as more individuals developed awareness of environmental harms, raised concerns internally, advocated for alternative practices, and built coalitions with similarly concerned colleagues, the collective effect created institutional change that no single person could have achieved.

The expressivist framework acknowledges that holding individuals accountable for their involvement in harmful institutions serves important social functions, even when those individuals possess limited direct power. The moral emotions expressed create conditions that make collective transformation possible.

This connects back to the fundamental insight of expressivism. Moral responsibility practices serve social functions enabling cooperation and promoting beneficial change. These functions succeed best when they focus on actual psychological capacities for recognizing problems and working systematically to address them, whether in individual or collective contexts.

The Foundation Secured

The expressivist foundation reveals moral responsibility as neither an objective moral fact nor an arbitrary social convention. It emerges as a sophisticated cultural refinement of evolved prosocial attitudes, built upon accumulated wisdom about human psychology and behavioral change.

Our moral emotions evolved to serve functions for social cooperation. Guilt maintains cooperative commitments through internal enforcement. Resentment creates costs for harmful behavior through social responses. Pride and approval reinforce beneficial actions through positive feedback. These emotions provided the psychological foundation, making complex human cooperation possible.

But evolution alone cannot explain the sophisticated responsibility frameworks humans have developed. Cultural evolution refined these emotions through millennia of experimentation with different institutional approaches. Honor systems emphasized collective responsibility and reputation management. Dignity systems emphasized individual rights and formal legal processes. Therapeutic systems emphasized psychological understanding and capacity development.

Each approach represents collective learning about what promotes behavioral change while maintaining social cooperation and individual dignity.

The result grounds responsibility in biological reality while preserving its normative force and cultural sophistication. We hold people responsible not because we discover objective facts about what they ultimately deserve. We hold them responsible because expressing certain attitudes toward certain types of behavior serves functions, making complex social cooperation possible.

The criterion connecting moral evaluation to psychological reality is the capacity for self-modification through temporal scaffolding and metacognitive awareness. This criterion tracks what matters for the social functions that responsibility practices evolved to serve. It connects moral evaluation to actual mechanisms through which behavioral change happens. It provides practical guidance for individual development and institutional design while avoiding metaphysical mysteries about ultimate origination and philosophical puzzles about reasons-responsiveness.

Understanding responsibility this way transforms questions about moral agency from metaphysical puzzles into practical challenges. How can individuals develop greater capacity for beneficial self-modification? How can institutions create conditions supporting these capacities? How can cultures preserve wisdom embodied in effective responsibility practices while adapting to novel challenges that previous generations never faced?

These questions lend themselves to empirical investigation and practical experimentation. We can study which interventions enhance metacognitive awareness and temporal scaffolding abilities. We can evaluate which institutional structures support individual capacity development. We can experiment with different cultural approaches to responsibility while assessing their effectiveness for promoting both individual flourishing and collective welfare.

The expressivist foundation provides not only philosophical justification for responsibility practices but practical guidance for their continued development. It reveals moral responsibility as an ongoing human achievement. We become responsible not by discovering objective moral truths but by participating in cultural traditions that refine evolved emotional responses through accumulated wisdom about human nature and social cooperation.

The self-modification criterion does not float free from this foundation. It succeeds precisely because it connects to the actual functions that responsibility practices evolved to serve. When we hold someone responsible based on their capacity for temporal scaffolding, we express attitudes calibrated to psychological realities in ways that promote beneficial behavioral change while maintaining social cooperation.

This is not arbitrary. This is a biological necessity, meeting cultural wisdom, meeting philosophical clarity about what moral evaluation actually accomplishes when it works.

The framework faces an obvious challenge. If moral responsibility grounds itself in evolved emotions and cultural practices, what happens when these emotions malfunction or when cultural practices perpetuate injustice? The answer lies in the recursive capacity that makes humans unique.

We can observe our own emotional responses and evaluate whether they track features that matter for cooperation and human flourishing. We can recognize when shame about childhood trauma maintains destructive cycles. We can distinguish between guilt that promotes behavioral improvement and guilt that sabotages psychological health. We can identify when cultural practices express wisdom and when they perpetuate arbitrary cruelty.

This recursive observation enables moral progress without requiring objective moral facts. We refine responsibility practices not by discovering what people ultimately deserve but by better understanding human psychology and what promotes beneficial change while maintaining dignity and enabling growth.

The expressivist foundation thus preserves possibilities for moral criticism and improvement while remaining naturalistic about moral reality. No free-floating moral facts are waiting to be discovered. However, there are better and worse ways of expressing evolved attitudes in light of the accumulated understanding of human nature and social cooperation.

Practices that connect responsibility attributions to actual capacities for self-modification serve their functions better than practices that ignore these capacities. Systems that provide support for capacity development while maintaining accountability achieve better outcomes than systems that only punish without promoting growth. Cultures that enable systematic refinement of responsibility practices through empirical investigation and practical experimentation will better serve human flourishing than cultures that treat their current practices as fixed and unquestionable.

The foundation is secure not because it rests on metaphysical bedrock but because it connects to biological realities, psychological mechanisms, and social functions that make human cooperation possible. This proves more solid than any foundation requiring impossible ultimate origination or mysterious moral facts disconnected from natural explanations.

Graduated Responsibility in Practice

"What if owning yourself means recognizing that you are owned by forces far greater than yourself, while learning to participate consciously in the very process that shapes your becoming?"

OUR INSTITUTIONS LIE TO US daily about moral responsibility.

Courts pretend that guilt exists in binary states, that someone either possesses full agency or no agency at all. Schools punish students as if academic failure reflects moral deficiency rather than developmental complexity. Therapists treat symptoms as if psychological distress occurs in a social vacuum. Communities respond to crime as if individual depravity explains systematic social problems.

These institutional lies persist because they serve the psychological comfort of those who administer them. Binary responsibility judgments eliminate the difficult work of understanding actual human psychology. They permit moral condemnation without the complexity of assessment, punishment without the challenge of development, or exclusion without the burden of support.

But what happens when our institutions stop lying?

When do legal systems acknowledge that agency exists in degrees corresponding to actual psychological capacities for behavioral change? When do educational institutions recognize that learning requires systematic development of cognitive and emotional capacities rather than mere exposure to information? When do therapeutic practices focus on enhancing client capabilities for continued growth rather than expert management of psychological problems?

The possibility terrifies those who benefit from current arrangements. Graduated responsibility demands more sophisticated psychological understanding, more individualized assessment, and more resource investment in human development. It threatens industries built on processing human problems rather than solving them.

Yet this sophisticated approach to moral evaluation represents not utopian idealism but recognition of realities that current systems systematically ignore. Human behavioral capacities exist in degrees.

Environmental conditions profoundly influence individual choices. Punishment without capacity development typically fails to prevent future harmful behavior. These insights challenge institutional structures not because they are radical innovations but because they acknowledge what careful observation of human behavior has always revealed.

The question becomes not whether our institutions should acknowledge these realities but whether they can survive the intellectual and moral costs of continuing to ignore them.

The Collapse of Binary Responsibility

Sarah's fourteen-year-old daughter hasn't been to school in three weeks. The truancy officer sent the warning letter. The school scheduled the mandatory meeting. Sarah sits across from the vice principal, the counselor, and the attendance coordinator, all of them looking at her with that specific blend of concern and judgment that parents of struggling teenagers learn to recognize.

They want to know if Sarah is a neglectful parent or a responsible one. Either she forces her daughter to attend school, proving she takes education seriously, or she allows the truancy to continue, proving she doesn't. The meeting proceeds as if these are the only options. As if Sarah's situation could be reduced to a simple choice reflecting her character and values.

But Sarah's actual circumstances resist this binary. Her daughter has severe social anxiety that manifests as physical illness every school morning. Genuine stomach pain. Real nausea. The pediatrician found no medical cause but referred them to a therapist. The first available appointment is six weeks away. The daughter refuses to go back to school, locks herself in her room, and threatens to run away if forced. Sarah has tried everything she can think of. Reasoning, pleading, punishment, rewards, and even involving her ex-husband, who promptly blamed Sarah for being too soft.

Sarah works as a home health aide with irregular hours. She cannot physically force a teenager who outweighs her into a car and through school doors every morning. She has tried calling the police for help. They told her this was a parenting issue, not a law enforcement issue. She has tried the school counselor's suggestions about setting firmer boundaries, establishing consistent consequences, and being more positive about school. Nothing has worked.

The school officials do not ask about Sarah's capacity to implement their recommendations given her actual circumstances. They do not assess what psychological and practical resources she possesses for addressing her daughter's anxiety. They do not examine what environmental and systemic factors constrain her options. They ask instead if she will ensure her daughter attends school or not.

This captures the fundamental problem with binary responsibility. The institutions assume that parenting reflects simple choices revealing moral character. The complexity of Sarah's actual situation, the limitations of her actual capacities, and the reality of her actual constraints cannot be processed by a system built on binary categories.

Consider the absurdity of forcing Sarah into one of two boxes. Either she's a neglectful parent who doesn't care about education, or she's a responsible parent who will make her daughter attend. But Sarah demonstrates substantial capacity in many domains. She maintains steady employment despite difficult working conditions. She has sought help repeatedly from multiple sources. She understands that her daughter's anxiety is real rather than a manipulation tactic. She recognizes her own limitations and asks for assistance.

Yet she also lacks capacities in other areas. She has no sophisticated understanding of anxiety disorders or evidence-based treatments. She possesses limited skills for managing her own stress response to her daughter's distress. She has never learned techniques for setting boundaries that feel firm rather than either permissive or coercive. She cannot recognize when her attempts to help reinforce avoidance patterns.

Her capacity for temporal scaffolding appears underdeveloped, specifically around parenting challenges, though she demonstrates it well in her work life. At work, she anticipates patient needs, modifies her approach based on what she observes, and develops systems that make difficult tasks easier. But with her daughter, she reacts to each crisis as if it were unprecedented. She has not yet learned to recognize patterns, identify triggers, or design interventions that address the underlying causes rather than just the surface behaviors.

What the binary misses is precisely what matters for effective intervention. Sarah needs capacity development, not classification. She needs psychoeducation about anxiety disorders and school refusal. She needs specific techniques for responding to her daughter's distress without reinforcing avoidance. She needs help developing a structured plan for gradually increasing school exposure. She needs a connection to a parent support group where she could learn from others who have navigated similar situations. She needs assistance coordinating with the therapist when that appointment finally arrives.

But the system cannot offer these interventions because it cannot see what exists. It can only sort Sarah into predetermined categories based on whether her daughter attends school. The classification determines the response. An adequate parent receives encouragement to continue current efforts. An inadequate parent receives an investigation by child protective services. Neither response addresses Sarah's actual capacities nor provides the specific support that would enable her to help her daughter effectively.

The result is predictable. Sarah will be reported for educational neglect. A caseworker will investigate. The investigation will focus on whether Sarah is trying hard enough, rather than on her capacities and what support would be helpful. The daughter's anxiety will continue untreated for six more weeks. The family stress will intensify. The situation will deteriorate. Not because Sarah lacks moral character or parental concern, but because the system cannot acknowledge the graduated nature of parental capacity and the corresponding need for capacity development rather than simple judgment.

The Architecture of Actual Assessment

What becomes visible when we abandon binary categories in favor of graduated assessment? We see human complexity that binary systems cannot process.

Someone experiencing severe depression retains full understanding that stealing from their employer is wrong while experiencing severely diminished capacity for generating behavioral alternatives or feeling motivated by future consequences. They know intellectually that theft will lead to termination and prosecution, but depression has destroyed their ability to feel these consequences as real motivating factors. The knowledge exists but cannot shape behavior in the way binary systems assume it should.

Traditional frameworks struggle with this complexity because they force a choice the facts refuse to provide. Either the person understood their actions were wrong and chose them anyway, making them fully responsible, or their mental illness eliminated their agency, making them not responsible at all. But neither option captures the reality. The person possessed some capacities while lacking others. They could recognize moral rules intellectually but were unable to generate alternatives or maintain forward-looking motivation. They need intervention addressing their specific pattern of intact and impaired capacities rather than being classified as either guilty or not guilty.

Graduated assessment would systematically examine multiple dimensions of capacity. Can this person recognize their own mental state and understand how emotions influence their decision-making? Can they identify patterns in their behavior across different situations? Do they monitor the effectiveness of their attempts at self-regulation? These metacognitive capacities exist in varying degrees across individuals and can be observed and developed.

Someone might recognize anger clearly while remaining blind to anxiety. They might understand emotional patterns in relationships, but miss how environmental factors trigger emotional responses. They might monitor some aspects of their behavior effectively while remaining unconscious of others. Assessment requires careful observation of these specific strengths and limitations, rather than relying on categorical diagnoses, to determine overall competence or incompetence.

Can this person pause between impulse and action? Do they consider alternatives before responding to strong emotions? Can they implement planned behaviors that conflict with immediate desires? These impulse regulation capacities fluctuate in response to stress, fatigue, environmental conditions, and psychological state. Someone might demonstrate excellent impulse control in familiar environments while struggling significantly in novel or threatening situations. They might regulate minor irritations effectively, but become overwhelmed by major provocations.

Understanding impulse regulation requires assessing both baseline capacity and situational variables that enhance or compromise this capacity. The goal becomes supporting optimal functioning rather than demanding uniform performance across all contexts regardless of individual differences and environmental conditions.

Can this person connect present actions with future consequences? Do they maintain motivation for long-term goals despite immediate costs? Can they learn from past experiences to inform current choices? Temporal reasoning represents sophisticated cognitive achievement that develops gradually and remains vulnerable to various psychological and environmental factors. Someone might understand intellectual connections between actions and consequences while struggling to feel motivated by distant outcomes. They might learn effectively from some types of experiences while repeating patterns in other domains.

Can this person recognize how environmental factors influence their behavior? Do they systematically modify conditions to support beneficial choices? Can they identify and avoid situations that predictably lead to problematic behavior? Environmental modification requires both psychological insight and practical resources that vary significantly across individuals and circumstances. Someone might understand environmental influences clearly while lacking resources for environmental change. They might possess modification skills in some domains while remaining helpless in others.

This multidimensional approach reveals moral responsibility as complex psychological reality rather than simple moral category. It enables sophisticated responses that address actual human needs rather than institutional administrative convenience. But it also creates practical challenges that explain why institutions resist this sophistication.

Graduated assessment demands more time, more psychological knowledge, and more individualized attention than binary classification. A judge can quickly determine guilt or innocence using established legal procedures. Assessing someone's actual capacities for metacognitive awareness, impulse regulation, temporal reasoning, and environmental modification requires extended observation, psychological expertise, and willingness to work with ambiguity rather than forcing clean verdicts.

Schools can efficiently classify students as passing or failing, compliant or disruptive, motivated or lazy. Understanding each student's specific capacity profile across attention regulation, emotional control, social cooperation, and academic motivation requires teacher training in developmental psychology, smaller class sizes enabling individualized attention, and assessment approaches that reveal capacity patterns rather than simply measuring performance against uniform standards.

Therapists can diagnose disorders and apply standardized treatment protocols relatively quickly. Assessing each client's specific capacities for self-observation, emotional regulation, impulse control, environmental modification, and social relationship building requires extended collaborative exploration, psychological sophistication beyond diagnostic categorization, and willingness to design individualized interventions rather than applying predetermined treatment manuals.

The resistance to graduated approaches thus reflects not merely ignorance or malice but genuine practical challenges. Institutions face resource constraints, time pressures, and demands for efficiency and accountability. Binary systems deliver clear answers quickly using established procedures. Graduated systems require ongoing assessment, continuous adjustment, and a tolerance for complexity and ambiguity.

Yet the alternative is what we have now. Our current systems may process people efficiently, but scarcely help them, if at all. Legal systems that achieve high conviction rates while failing to prevent recidivism. Schools that maintain behavioral standards while failing to develop the capacities students need for genuine learning. Therapeutic systems that document symptom reduction while failing to enable lasting psychological change.

The question becomes whether we can afford to continue ignoring psychological reality for the sake of administrative convenience. Whether the apparent efficiency of binary systems justifies their systematic failure to promote actual human development and beneficial behavioral change.

When Courts Stop Pretending

The drug court judge has seen hundreds of cases like Marcus's. Possession of methamphetamine. Third offense. The prosecutor is seeking an eighteen-month prison sentence. The defense attorney argues for treatment instead of incarceration. Both sides present their evidence about Marcus's criminal history, his employment record, his family situation, and his previous attempts at rehabilitation.

But the real question facing the judge is one the legal system struggles to articulate. Not whether Marcus is guilty, which is established by his plea. Not whether he deserves punishment, which the sentencing guidelines specify. The question is what Marcus can actually do with his life, given his current psychological capacities, and what intervention might enhance those capacities enough to prevent him from cycling back through the system in six months or a year.

Marcus started using methamphetamine at sixteen after his mother's boyfriend introduced him to it. He's now thirty-two. He's been arrested seven times, served three short jail sentences, and completed two treatment programs. Each time he gets out, he stays clean for a few weeks or months before relapsing. The pattern has repeated so many times that everyone involved, including Marcus, expects it to continue.

Traditional legal analysis treats this pattern as evidence of Marcus's character and choices. He keeps using drugs despite knowing the consequences. He keeps violating probation despite clear warnings. He keeps returning to the same people and places that trigger his use. The conclusion seems obvious. Marcus lacks the motivation or willpower to stay clean. He needs stronger consequences to incentivize better choices.

But this analysis ignores what becomes visible through capacity assessment. Marcus possesses virtually no metacognitive awareness of his addiction patterns. He cannot identify the specific situations, emotional states, or social dynamics that precede his relapses. When asked what triggers his use, he says, "I don't know, I just start thinking about it and then I'm using." He has no systematic approach to avoiding triggers because he cannot recognize them until after he has already relapsed.

His capacity for temporal scaffolding is similarly undeveloped. He makes vague resolutions to stay clean but implements no concrete strategies for managing cravings, no environmental modifications to reduce access to drugs, no alternative activities to fill the time previously spent using or obtaining drugs. When he completes treatment programs, he absorbs information passively but never translates it into systematic behavioral architecture. He leaves treatment with the same limited self-modification capacities he arrived with.

He also demonstrates profound deficits in emotional regulation that drives much of his drug use. Methamphetamine temporarily relieves a chronic sense of inadequacy and social anxiety that has plagued him since childhood. Without the drug, he feels constantly on edge, unable to relax, convinced that others see him as worthless. He has never learned alternative strategies for managing these feelings because the drug worked so effectively for so long.

Environmental factors compound these capacity limitations. Marcus has no stable housing, no job skills beyond manual labor that he can no longer perform due to injuries from a car accident, and no social network that doesn't involve drug use. His family has cut him off after years of stealing from them to support his habit. He has untreated depression and PTSD from childhood abuse. He lives in a neighborhood where methamphetamine is readily available, and many of his acquaintances deal or use.

The traditional legal response would impose eighteen months of incarceration, which does nothing to address any of these factors. He would serve his time, be released with forty dollars and a bus ticket, and return to the same neighborhood with the same limited capacities and the same environmental risk factors. Within weeks or months, he would relapse. Within a year, he would likely be arrested again. The system would have achieved its goal of punishment, but failed entirely in its goal of preventing future crime.

Drug courts emerged from the recognition that this traditional approach fails systematically for defendants with substance use disorders. These specialized courts don't simply punish or treat. They create structured processes in which participants must demonstrate an increasing capacity for self-regulation over a period of twelve to eighteen months. The approach explicitly connects legal accountability to capacity development in ways that traditional courts cannot.

The process begins with intensive external scaffolding compensating for participants' limited internal self-regulatory capacity. Daily or near-daily check-ins with the court. Frequent random drug testing. Mandated treatment attendance. Strict curfews and activity restrictions. Home visits and workplace monitoring. This external structure provides the behavioral regulation that participants cannot yet generate internally.

As participants begin developing basic capacities, the external structure gradually reduces. Daily check-ins become weekly. Random drug testing becomes less frequent. Curfews loosen. Activity restrictions lift. But the reduction happens only as participants demonstrate actual capacity development, not according to predetermined timelines. Someone who shows strong progress might advance quickly through phases. Someone who struggles might remain in intensive supervision for extended periods. The system adapts to individual capacity development rather than imposing uniform requirements.

The court explicitly teaches temporal scaffolding as a learnable skill rather than assuming participants possess this capacity. Participants learn to identify high-risk situations and develop specific plans for managing them. They practice recognizing early warning signs of craving before they become overwhelming. They implement environmental modifications, such as changing phone numbers, avoiding certain neighborhoods, and scheduling their days to minimize unstructured time. They develop detailed relapse prevention plans specifying exactly what they will do when various triggers arise.

Most importantly, the court treats lapses as information rather than simply as failures requiring punishment. When Marcus relapses after three months of sobriety, the court doesn't simply send him to jail and restart his progress. Instead, it conducts systematic analysis. What was Marcus doing in the hours before the relapse? What emotional state preceded it? What environmental factors contributed? What did he try that didn't work? What might work better next time?

This analysis reveals that Marcus's relapse occurred after losing his housing and sleeping in his car for three nights. The stress and hopelessness overwhelmed his still-developing coping capacities. The court responds not with jail time but with help securing stable housing and intensifying support during the period while his capacities remain fragile. Marcus receives consequences that temporarily increase structure, but the focus remains on understanding what his capacities can currently handle and what development needs to happen next.

Research consistently demonstrates that drug courts produce better outcomes than traditional criminal processing. Participants show significantly lower recidivism rates. Communities experience less crime. Public costs decrease despite higher initial investment in treatment and monitoring. These outcomes reflect not mysterious therapeutic magic but systematic application of graduated responsibility principles. The intervention is effective because it assesses actual capacities, provides support tailored to those capacities, explicitly develops self-modification skills, and adjusts responses based on demonstrated progress rather than imposing uniform requirements.

Yet drug courts remain marginal within criminal justice systems rather than central features. They serve only a fraction of eligible defendants. They require judicial willingness to embrace complexity over categorical processing. They demand resources that cash-strapped jurisdictions struggle to provide. They challenge the punitive assumptions that dominate public discourse about crime and punishment.

The resistance reveals how deeply the binary framework is embedded in legal institutions and public consciousness. Punishment feels natural and just. Capacity development feels soft and enabling. The fact that capacity development prevents crime more effectively than punishment doesn't overcome visceral preferences for approaches that feel appropriately harsh toward people who have caused harm.

Restorative justice programs offer an alternative model for graduated responsibility in legal contexts. These programs bring together those who caused harm, those who experienced harm, and affected community members to develop collaborative responses that address both accountability and repair.

Traditional legal processes exclude victims from meaningful participation. The state prosecutes crimes as violations of law rather than harms to specific individuals. Victims become witnesses providing evidence rather than participants determining outcomes. Offenders interact with legal professionals rather than with the people they actually harmed. The entire process focuses on determining guilt and imposing proportionate punishment, rather than preventing future harm and repairing damaged relationships.

Restorative processes invert these priorities. Victims actively participate in determining what constitutes meaningful accountability and repair. Offenders must confront the actual human consequences of their actions rather than simply facing abstract legal penalties. Community members share their perspectives on the social factors that contributed to the harm and discuss community resources that could support repair and prevention.

The process inherently assesses capacity through observation rather than categorical judgment. How does the person who caused harm respond when hearing about consequences? Do they demonstrate genuine understanding and remorse? Can they articulate what led to their behavior? Do they propose meaningful steps for repair and prevention? These questions cannot be answered through legal procedures determining guilt. They require extended dialogue revealing psychological capacities that matter for future behavior.

Someone with minimal capacity might struggle to understand why victims feel harmed, demonstrate no insight into their own motivations, or propose superficial gestures disconnected from actual repair needs. The restorative process reveals these limitations while creating opportunities for capacity development through facilitated dialogue and structured accountability. The person begins to learn to take a perspective, to connect actions with consequences, and to design behavioral modifications that address underlying causes rather than simply avoiding punishment.

Someone with substantial capacity might demonstrate a sophisticated understanding of harm caused, clear insight into behavioral patterns, genuine remorse connected to victim impact, and thoughtful proposals for both repair and self-modification. The restorative process validates and reinforces these capacities while holding the person accountable in ways that strengthen rather than undermine their commitment to change. They experience consequences that feel meaningful and just while developing greater capacity for preventing similar harm in the future.

Research demonstrates that restorative justice yields higher victim satisfaction, lower recidivism rates, and more favorable community outcomes compared to traditional criminal processing. Victims report feeling heard and respected rather than excluded from proceedings affecting them deeply. Offenders develop a greater understanding of how their behavior affects others. Communities engage constructively with crime rather than simply demanding punishment that may or may not prevent future harm.

Yet restorative programs remain marginal, serving tiny fractions of criminal cases. They require trained facilitators, willing participants, and adequate time for meaningful dialogue. They challenge retributive assumptions about punishment as the primary or sole appropriate response to crime. They demand that communities examine their own contributions to conditions that generate criminal behavior, rather than simply blaming individual moral failures.

Legal pluralism offers another direction for graduated responsibility implementation. Different communities within diverse societies might reasonably implement responsibility principles through different institutional frameworks reflecting their cultural values and circumstances while maintaining consistency with psychological insights about capacity development and behavioral change.

Indigenous communities may stress collective approaches that link accountability with communal healing. Urban settings may favor therapeutic interventions supported by social services. Religious communities may highlight spiritual dimensions of change while aligning with psychological accounts of capacity development.

This pluralism treats moral responsibility practices as cultural refinements of evolved emotional responses, not as objective moral truths demanding uniform application. What matters is effectiveness in fostering behavioral change, sustaining cooperation, and upholding dignity across diverse contexts.

The Failure of Uniform Assumption

Jennifer has taken off work for the third time this month to attend a meeting about Tyler. Her seventh-grade son is failing most of his classes. Not because he can't do the work. His test scores suggest he's quite intelligent. But he hasn't turned in homework in weeks. He disrupts class by talking, making jokes, and distracting others. He has detention slips for leaving class without permission, for disrespectful comments to teachers, and for throwing paper airplanes during a math lesson.

The meeting follows a familiar script, one Jennifer has sat through on two previous occasions. The school staff wants to know what's happening at home. Is there conflict? Inconsistent discipline? Too much screen time? Not enough structure? Jennifer explains, as she has before, that Tyler was diagnosed with ADHD at age seven. He takes medication daily. They have structure at home. She sets clear expectations and follows through with consequences.

The special education coordinator asks whether Jennifer has considered increasing his medication or trying a different one. She has. The current medication is the fourth they have tried. Higher doses make Tyler anxious and unable to sleep. Different medications either don't help or cause intolerable side effects.

The teacher expresses frustration. She has thirty students. She cannot spend all her time managing Tyler's behavior. He is disruptive, distracting, and shows no remorse when confronted. Other parents are complaining that Tyler is preventing their children from learning.

Another specialist mentions that Tyler is bright enough that he should be able to control himself if he really wanted to. After all, he can focus when playing video games or building with Legos. This suggests that the problem is one of motivation rather than capacity.

Jennifer feels the familiar tightness in her chest. She wants to scream at these people who have no idea what it's like. Who are they to see Tyler for a few hours on weekdays and think they understand him? Who are they to believe that proper parenting, the right medication, or sufficient motivation could make ADHD disappear?

But she stays calm and asks what they recommend. More consequences, they say. Natural consequences for not turning in homework. Logical consequences for disruptive behavior. Clear communication between home and school so Jennifer can reinforce the school's expectations.

The script never changes. The school views Tyler's behavior as a choice that reflects insufficient motivation or inadequate parenting. When their recommendations inevitably fail, they suggest that Jennifer isn't implementing them correctly or that Tyler needs more serious intervention, possibly a different school setting for students with behavior problems.

What they never acknowledge is that Tyler possesses fundamentally different capacities than the neurotypical students they're accustomed to teaching. His ADHD isn't a choice or a discipline problem or a motivation issue. It represents developmental differences in brain structure and function affecting executive functions, including impulse control, attention regulation, emotional regulation, and working memory.

Tyler cannot "just focus" on boring tasks the way other students can. He cannot pause between impulse and action when something interesting catches his attention. He cannot hold instructions in working memory long enough to write them down. He cannot regulate his emotional responses to frustration or boredom. These aren't choices. They are neurological realities that no amount of consequences, motivation, or parental involvement can eliminate.

The system cannot process Tyler's actual capacity profile. He demonstrates strong abilities in some areas. He can hyperfocus on topics that interest him for hours. He generates creative solutions to problems. He possesses sophisticated verbal skills and abstract reasoning capacity. These strengths indicate genuine intellectual capability that could translate to academic success under appropriate conditions.

But he demonstrates severe limitations in other areas important for traditional school success. He cannot maintain attention on tasks that don't provide immediate stimulation. He cannot inhibit impulses to speak, move, or shift focus when something more interesting presents itself. He cannot manage the multi-step processes required to track assignments, complete homework, and turn it in on time. He cannot regulate his frustration when tasks prove difficult or when he feels criticized.

These limitations don't reflect a lack of effort or poor character. They reflect genuine capacity deficits that require environmental modification and explicit skill development, rather than increased consequences and demands for greater willpower.

What would change if the school acknowledged this reality? The classroom environment might reduce stimulation and distraction. Tyler might sit near the front, away from windows and peers who engage him socially. Visual schedules might break complex tasks into manageable steps. Frequent check-ins might provide external structure compensating for his limited internal capacity to track time and maintain task focus. Movement breaks might allow him to burn energy that otherwise erupts as disruptive behavior.

Instruction might explicitly teach the executive function skills that neurotypical students develop naturally. Tyler might learn specific strategies for managing impulses, techniques for sustaining attention on non-preferred tasks, and systems for tracking assignments and deadlines. He might practice recognizing his own frustration before it escalates to defiance. He might develop environmental modifications he can implement himself as his metacognitive awareness increases.

Social-emotional learning programs represent educational approaches that explicitly acknowledge capacity variation and teach self-regulatory skills systematically. Research consistently demonstrates that students receiving explicit instruction in emotional recognition, regulation strategies, perspective-taking, conflict resolution, and decision-making show improved academic performance, reduced behavioral problems, and better long-term outcomes compared to students receiving only traditional academic instruction.

Yet these programs remain supplementary additions rather than central features of educational practice. The resistance reveals educational institutions' commitment to content transmission rather than capacity development. Teaching emotional regulation requires acknowledging that many students initially lack these capacities. Teaching social skills requires recognizing that cooperative behavior must be learned rather than demanded. Teaching decision-making requires admitting that good choices depend on developed psychological resources rather than simply knowing right from wrong.

Comprehensive social-emotional curricula assess students' baseline capacities across multiple dimensions and teach skills appropriate for different developmental levels. Kindergarteners learn to recognize and name their emotions, identify physical sensations associated with different feelings, and use simple calming strategies when upset. Third-graders learn to identify patterns in their emotional responses, understand how situations trigger different feelings, and implement multiple regulation strategies depending on context. Eighth-graders learn to analyze complex emotional situations, recognize how their interpretations influence their feelings, and design environmental modifications supporting their emotional goals.

This developmental progression treats capacity-building as a fundamental educational purpose rather than a supplemental concern subordinate to academic content. Students develop a sophisticated understanding of their own psychology while acquiring traditional academic knowledge, creating synergies rather than trade-offs between social-emotional and academic learning.

Environmental design either supports or undermines student capacity development depending on how educational spaces are structured. Classroom layouts reducing distracting stimuli support students with attention regulation difficulties. Flexible seating arrangements accommodate different learning styles and energy levels. Natural lighting and access to outdoor spaces support physiological regulation underlying psychological functioning.

Instructional methods connecting abstract concepts to concrete experiences support students with developing reasoning abilities. Project-based learning provides opportunities for sustained engagement and self-directed work. Collaborative learning develops social capacities while advancing academic understanding.

Assessment approaches focusing on growth rather than comparison support students with varied learning timelines. Portfolio assessment demonstrates development over time. Self-assessment builds metacognitive awareness. Varied assessment formats accommodate different strengths and challenges.

These modifications require acknowledging that student performance reflects interaction between individual capacities and environmental conditions rather than individual ability alone. They threaten educational institutions' commitment to standardized approaches that ignore individual developmental needs while permitting efficient processing of large numbers of students through uniform requirements.

Beyond Expert Solutions

Dr. Chen has been treating patients for compulsive sexual behavior for fifteen years. He has seen hundreds of men whose sexual behavior has destroyed marriages, careers, and self-respect. He has developed what he considers a sophisticated clinical approach grounded in trauma theory and attachment psychology. He helps clients understand how childhood wounds created core beliefs about worthlessness that drive their compulsive behavior. He guides them through processing painful memories. He teaches them to recognize how their behavior temporarily relieves shame while ultimately reinforcing it.

His success rate hovers around thirty percent. About a third of his clients achieve sustained change. Another third makes temporary improvements before relapsing. The final third never really engages with treatment in the first place. These numbers have remained stubbornly consistent throughout his entire career.

The therapeutic model assumes that compulsive sexual behavior reflects underlying psychological dysfunction. Address the root causes through insight and processing, and the behavior should improve. When patients don't improve, the model suggests they're not really trying, not really honest, and not really committed to change.

But Dr. Chen has begun to suspect that this framing misses something crucial. His patients vary enormously in ways the standard model doesn't capture. Take two of his current patients, both in their forties, both discovered by their wives to be using prostitutes multiple times per week. Both report similar histories with absent fathers, critical mothers, early exposure to pornography, and shame about sexuality. Both describe the behavior as compulsive, something they desperately want to stop but feel powerless to control.

Robert has been in treatment for six months. He attends his weekly appointments faithfully, participates in a twelve-step group, and discusses his childhood wounds with apparent openness. He has developed considerable insight into how his father's abandonment created core beliefs about his unworthiness and how using prostitutes temporarily relieves this shame while ultimately reinforcing it. He can articulate these dynamics clearly.

Yet Robert continues to use prostitutes weekly. He recognizes the pattern only after the fact. In the moment, he finds himself driving to familiar areas without conscious decision, like watching himself from outside his body. He has tried deleting contacts from his phone but memorizes the numbers. He has tried avoiding the neighborhoods but finds alternative routes. He has tried calling his sponsor but never does it in time. The insight doesn't translate to behavioral change.

Michael started treatment a month after Robert. He displays much less psychological sophistication. He becomes impatient with discussions of childhood wounds and insists he just needs to stop the behavior. He resists the twelve-step model, saying meetings make him feel worse. He has minimal insight into underlying psychological dynamics.

But Michael demonstrates something Robert lacks. Systematic capacity for environmental modification and behavioral architecture. He installed monitoring software on all his devices and gave his wife the password. He identified the specific times when urges were strongest, late evenings after stressful workdays, and scheduled activities during these windows. He mapped the routes he would drive and eliminated reasons to travel to those areas. He developed a concrete plan for what to do when urges arise, such as calling his brother, going to the gym, and taking a walk with a specific audiobook that requires his attention.

Most importantly, Michael treats his behavioral patterns as an engineering problem rather than a psychological mystery. When something doesn't work, he analyzes why and adjusts his approach. When the urges intensify before his designated call time, he moves the call earlier. When he finds himself rationalizing that the monitoring software has loopholes, he adds additional accountability layers. When stress from work increases his vulnerability, he implements stress management earlier rather than waiting for the urge to arise.

After three months, Michael reports no episodes of using prostitutes. Robert, now at nine months in treatment with far more psychological insight, continues to struggle.

The pattern troubles Dr. Chen because it challenges his entire therapeutic framework. The model predicts that Robert should do better. He has more insight, more emotional processing, and more engagement with understanding the roots of his behavior. But Michael is succeeding despite lacking these factors that therapy emphasizes.

The difference appears to be the ability to construct their development across time. Robert possesses psychological insight but lacks the systematic capacity to translate insight into environmental architecture and behavioral modification. Michael possesses minimal psychological insight but a strong capacity for designing interventions that work with his actual psychology rather than requiring heroic willpower to override it.

This suggests something uncomfortable for the therapeutic profession. Maybe treatment success depends less on psychological insight than on capacity for systematic self-modification. Maybe therapy should explicitly teach temporal scaffolding as a skill rather than assuming patients possess this capacity and need only insight to apply it.

Dr. Chen begins experimenting with explicit capacity assessment during intake. He asks not just about psychological history but about how patients have attempted to change other problematic behaviors in the past. What strategies did they try? How did they monitor their progress? What environmental modifications did they implement? How did they respond when initial strategies failed?

The patients who describe sophisticated self-modification efforts in other domains tend to succeed in treatment. Those who describe passive approaches, waiting for motivation to strike or for the problem to be resolved through insight alone, tend to struggle. This pattern holds across different types of compulsive behavior, different psychological histories, and different social circumstances.

Cognitive-behavioral therapy (CBT), dialectical behavior therapy (DBT), and acceptance and commitment therapy (ACT) share a common insight often obscured by their theoretical differences. Effective treatment teaches concrete skills for managing psychological experiences rather than simply providing insight or processing emotions. These approaches explicitly develop capacities for observing thoughts without immediately believing them, tolerating difficult emotions without avoidance, implementing behavioral experiments testing interpretations, and designing environmental modifications supporting beneficial choices.

CBT teaches clients to observe automatic thoughts, examine evidence for and against these thoughts, generate alternative interpretations, and test behavioral experiments. These skills transfer across different psychological challenges rather than requiring expert intervention for each problem. Someone who learns to observe and evaluate catastrophic thinking about social situations can apply the same skills to anxious thoughts about health, work performance, or relationship conflicts.

DBT explicitly focuses on developing psychological capacities, including distress tolerance, emotional regulation, interpersonal effectiveness, and mindful awareness. The curriculum treats these as learnable skills requiring systematic practice rather than as natural capacities some people possess and others lack. Clients practice specific techniques in therapy sessions, implement them in daily life, and receive coaching when facing difficult situations. The treatment aims to make ongoing therapy unnecessary by developing capacities for independent functioning.

ACT develops psychological flexibility through mindfulness, acceptance, cognitive defusion, present-moment awareness, values clarification, and committed action. The goal is to create general capacities for responding skillfully to psychological challenges rather than eliminating specific symptoms. Someone becomes psychologically flexible by learning to notice thoughts and feelings without being controlled by them, to accept difficult experiences rather than struggling against them, and to take action aligned with their values even when doing so creates discomfort.

These approaches succeed not because they provide superior psychological theories but because they explicitly teach temporal scaffolding and metacognitive awareness as learnable skills. They treat therapy as capacity development rather than expert problem-solving. They aim to make ongoing therapy unnecessary rather than creating lasting dependence on professional support.

Yet many therapeutic approaches still emphasize insight over capacity development, processing over skill-building, and understanding over environmental architecture. The resistance reflects professional identities constructed around being the expert who provides insight rather than the collaborator who builds capacity. It reflects economic models requiring ongoing client relationships rather than time-limited capacity development. It reflects training emphasizing theoretical knowledge over practical skill instruction.

Therapeutic relationships based on graduated responsibility emphasize collaborative enhancement of psychological resources enabling continued growth and adaptation. Therapists focus on teaching skills clients can use independently rather than providing ongoing expert management of psychological problems. The relationship aims to become unnecessary as clients develop capacities for ongoing self-modification and environmental management.

This requires fundamental changes in therapeutic training and practice. Therapists need preparation in capacity development and collaborative relationship-building rather than diagnostic assessment and treatment technique implementation focused on expert-driven interventions that maintain professional authority.

The therapy relationship itself would model graduated responsibility. Early sessions might involve substantial therapist guidance and structure as clients develop basic capacities. Middle sessions would involve increasing client initiative and independence as capacities strengthen. Late sessions would focus on consolidating learning and planning for independent application after therapy ends.

Someone recovering from trauma would receive an assessment of their current capacity for managing trauma responses, and then a systematic building of these capacities over time. Early work might focus on basic grounding and safety skills, creating islands of stability amid overwhelming distress. As the client develops these foundational skills, therapy would progress to building more sophisticated capacities, such as recognizing trauma triggers before they escalate, understanding how trauma affects current relationships, developing narrative coherence about traumatic experiences, and implementing environmental modifications that reduce triggering situations.

Final therapy phases would focus on applying these capacities across varied life domains and planning for continued development after therapy ends. The client would demonstrate substantial capacity, occasionally needing therapist consultation but primarily managing independently. The goal is not a permanent cure but a developed capacity for ongoing self-modification as new challenges arise.

Beyond Individual Blame

The neighborhood meeting was called to address rising property crime. Break-ins, car thefts, and package theft from porches. The police presented statistics showing increases over the past year. The city council member talked about budget constraints limiting police presence. Residents shared stories of being victimized and expressed frustration about feeling unsafe.

The conversation inevitably turned to blame. Who was responsible for this spike in crime? The consensus formed quickly around familiar targets. Parents who don't supervise their teenagers. Schools that don't instill values. A justice system that's too lenient. Young people with no respect for others' property or the law.

The analysis treated crime as reflecting individual moral failure. Bad kids from bad families making bad choices. The solution seemed obvious. Stronger consequences, more police presence, and parents taking responsibility for controlling their children's behavior.

What the meeting never addressed was the economic collapse that had devastated the neighborhood over the past five years. The factory had closed, eliminating eight hundred jobs. Businesses failed as disposable income vanished. Property values declined as people left in search of employment elsewhere. School budgets were cut as tax revenue dropped. Youth programs and after-school activities were eliminated. The local food bank now served twice as many families as it had three years earlier.

These systemic factors created conditions in which property crime became a rational response to limited opportunities for legal success. Teenagers who once held after-school jobs at businesses that no longer existed now faced a choice between accepting poverty or engaging in illegal activity. Families struggling to afford basic necessities were faced with hard decisions about whether stealing was justifiable in order to feed their children.

The neighborhood meeting's focus on individual moral failure allowed residents to avoid examining their collective responsibility for creating conditions that predictably generate crime. It enabled them to feel morally superior to the criminals rather than recognizing their shared situation within economic forces beyond any individual's control.

Crime rates correlate strongly with poverty, unemployment, lack of educational opportunity, and absence of youth programming. Communities with comprehensive development approaches show dramatically lower crime rates than those relying primarily on policing and incarceration. These correlations are not mysterious. They reflect the reality that people respond to incentives and opportunities. When legal opportunities for success are plentiful, most people take advantage of them. When legal opportunities are scarce and illegal opportunities are abundant, crime rates tend to rise predictably.

Someone who commits a property crime in response to a lack of legitimate economic opportunities reveals a community's failure to provide viable paths to success, rather than individual moral depravity. Someone who deals drugs because that's the only way to make rent reveals an economic system that has abandoned them rather than a character defect requiring punishment.

This doesn't eliminate individual agency or responsibility. People make choices within the constraints they face. But those choices exist within contexts that profoundly shape what options seem available and what behaviors appear rational. Binary analysis, locating crime entirely within individual moral failure, ignores the environmental and systemic factors that make crime a predictable response to specific conditions.

Graduated responsibility analysis would assess both individual capacities and community conditions. A teenager arrested for stealing car parts might possess a substantial capacity for self-modification, but operate within community conditions that offer minimal legitimate opportunities, combined with powerful incentives for illegal activity.

Traditional approaches punish the individual while ignoring community conditions. The teenager receives consequences, perhaps detention or probation or juvenile facility placement. Nothing addresses the lack of legal employment, the inadequate educational opportunities, or the concentrated poverty that made stealing rational despite its risks. When the teenager returns to the same environment with the same lack of options, the predictable outcome is continued illegal activity.

Graduated approaches would hold the teenager accountable while simultaneously addressing community failures. The teenager might receive consequences focused on capacity development rather than simple punishment, including job training, mentorship, and assistance in securing legitimate employment. Simultaneously, community interventions would address the systemic conditions creating crime by providing economic development initiatives, youth employment programs, educational investments, and after-school activities that provide structure and opportunities.

This integrated approach recognizes that individual and community-level factors interact in ways that make purely individual interventions insufficient. Someone with a strong capacity for self-modification still struggles to succeed in environments that offer no legitimate opportunities. Someone with limited capacity might succeed with adequate environmental support but fails in contexts that provide neither opportunity nor support.

Programs combining individual capacity development with community environmental modification consistently outperform approaches focusing exclusively on individual treatment or community regulation. Communities that invest in development, education, and opportunities tend to experience a decline in crime. Communities that rely primarily on punishment see crime persist or increase. The correlation between economic opportunity and crime rates is so strong that it can be used to predict future crime based on current economic conditions with remarkable accuracy.

The resistance to community-level approaches reflects deep psychological investments in individual responsibility narratives. Acknowledging that crime results from community conditions rather than individual moral failure requires examining collective responsibility for creating those conditions. It threatens comfortable beliefs about meritocracy and just deserts. It suggests that successful community members benefited from advantages rather than simply earning their success through superior character.

Voters prefer narratives where crime reflects individual evil that can be addressed through punishment. This allows them to support punitive policies while avoiding difficult questions about economic inequality, inadequate educational funding, and systematic barriers to opportunity. It preserves the comforting fiction that anyone who works hard can succeed and that those who turn to crime simply didn't try hard enough.

But the empirical evidence proves overwhelming. Graduated responsibility requires acknowledging these realities. Individual capacity matters. People vary in their abilities to resist temptation, delay gratification, and maintain prosocial behavior in the face of stress. But capacity develops and operates within environmental contexts that either support or undermine it. Effective approaches must address both individual capacity development and community environmental modification.

The Architecture of Genuine Accountability

The ghost in the machine reveals itself as a natural capacity for moral development emerging from complex interactions between individual psychology and social environments.

Graduated responsibility provides a framework for expressing appropriate moral attitudes toward behavioral choices while focusing social responses on developing the psychological capacities that make beneficial choices more probable and harmful choices less likely.

Sarah and her daughter need capacity development, not judgment about parental adequacy. Marcus needs systematic scaffolding training within a supportive structure, not incarceration that ignores the psychological factors maintaining his addiction. Robert needs architectural instruction combined with insight, not insight alone that never translates to behavior. Tyler needs environmental modification and explicit skill instruction, not consequences, assuming capacities he doesn't possess. The teenagers stealing car parts need opportunity expansion alongside accountability, not punishment that changes nothing about their circumstances.

Each case reveals the same underlying pattern. Binary responsibility judgments fail because they force complex psychological realities into predetermined categories. They permit institutions to avoid the difficult work of understanding actual human capacities and designing interventions that develop those capacities. They serve administrative convenience and psychological comfort while systematically failing the people they claim to help.

This understanding preserves accountability while eliminating impossible metaphysical requirements that paralyzed traditional approaches to moral responsibility. It provides practical guidance for criminal justice, educational, therapeutic, and community institutions while remaining grounded in actual human psychological capacities rather than abstract philosophical categories.

The framework suggests that our most important collective project involves creating institutional arrangements that enhance rather than undermine individual capacity for beneficial behavioral development while serving collective welfare through more effective approaches to preventing harm and promoting human flourishing.

We discover that true accountability lies not in punishment of past actions but in creating conditions that support future development, honoring both the causal realities that shape human behavior and the genuine possibilities for conscious participation in behavioral change.

The institutions that implement graduated responsibility approaches will face significant challenges. Assessment complexity, resource requirements, and political resistance. Developing reliable methods for evaluating individual capacities across diverse psychological conditions and cultural contexts represents a genuine challenge requiring systematic research and professional development. Cultural variation in responsibility concepts creates opportunities for learning about effective approaches while maintaining sensitivity to diverse value systems.

Resource requirements prove substantial. Graduated responsibility approaches require more intensive individualized intervention than traditional approaches. But these resource investments typically prove more cost-effective long-term than repeated processing of problems that current approaches fail to address. Therapeutic jurisprudence programs show lower recidivism rates and reduced criminal justice costs. Educational capacity development programs show improved academic outcomes and reduced long-term costs. Therapeutic capacity development programs show improved client outcomes and reduced need for ongoing services.

Political resistance reveals deep psychological investments in punitive responses and individual responsibility narratives that protect existing social arrangements from examination. Many voters prefer approaches that appear to punish harmful behavior rather than approaches that are proven to be more effective at preventing future harm.

Yet the moral and practical costs of maintaining current systems continue mounting. Mass incarceration destroys communities while failing to prevent crime. Educational failure perpetuates inequality while wasting human potential. Mental health crises overwhelm emergency services, while people lack basic capacity development resources. Communities fracture while maintaining the comfortable fiction that individual moral failure explains systematic social breakdown.

Those who participate in developing graduated responsibility approaches contribute to cultural evolution that expresses evolved moral emotions in their most sophisticated forms while serving both individual development and collective welfare through institutions designed around human psychological reality rather than administrative convenience or ideological commitment.

The choice facing contemporary societies involves either continuing to operate institutions based on psychological fictions that serve institutional needs while failing to meet human needs or developing institutions that acknowledge psychological reality, requiring a more sophisticated understanding and greater resource investment in human development.

This choice will determine whether human societies evolve toward greater alignment between institutional practices and psychological knowledge, or continue perpetuating approaches that systematically ignore what careful observation of human behavior has consistently revealed about the complex realities of moral agency, behavioral development, and social cooperation.

Collective Cognitive Evolution

"But what if the bridge is not individual but collective? What if humanity's greatness lies not in solitary transcendence but in conscious participation in its own species-level becoming?"

WHAT IF HUMANITY ITSELF has become conscious?

Not in the mystical sense that gives new age thinkers their thrills, but in the precise sense that our species has developed the capacity to observe and modify its own developmental trajectory through conscious participation in evolutionary processes that previously operated below the threshold of awareness.

Individual temporal scaffolding, examined in previous chapters, aggregates into collective patterns that transcend individual lifespans while remaining grounded in entirely natural mechanisms. We have become the first species capable of conscious participation in our own evolutionary development.

This capacity creates both extraordinary opportunities and profound dangers. The same collective intelligence that enables solutions to complex global challenges also enables new forms of manipulation, control, and collective self-destruction that operate through the very mechanisms promising enhanced agency.

Yet before we celebrate or condemn this development, we must understand what it actually means for a species to become conscious of its own becoming. The question is not whether we should embrace collective cognitive evolution but whether we can afford to remain unconscious of processes already reshaping human psychology across populations and generations.

The Mechanism of Cultural-Cognitive Coevolution

Something unprecedented happened when humans developed language sophisticated enough to transmit not just information but systematic methods for modifying information processing itself. We created cultures that could deliberately shape the cognitive architectures of future generations rather than simply passing along adaptive behaviors through imitation.

Consider what this means concretely. A chimpanzee mother teaches her offspring to use stones to crack nuts. This represents genuine cultural transmission. The technique spreads through populations, creating local traditions that vary across groups. Some communities use one method, others use different approaches. The young learn by watching, and the practice persists across generations.

But the chimpanzee cannot teach metacognitive observation of the nut-cracking process. She cannot explain to her offspring: "Notice when your attention wanders from the task. Observe which stone angles work best and why. Recognize the pattern across multiple attempts." She cannot transmit systematic methods for improving the improvement process itself. The cultural transmission remains first-order, limited to specific behaviors rather than general capacities for behavioral modification.

Human cultural transmission transcends these limitations through language that enables recursive instruction. We don't just teach behaviors. We teach methods for observing behaviors, evaluating their effectiveness, and modifying them systematically. We transmit not just what to do but how to think about what to do and how to improve thinking about doing.

This creates feedback loops between cultural innovation and cognitive enhancement that operate across deep time. Agricultural revolution, writing systems, scientific methods, democratic institutions, and each cultural innovation created new selective pressures while enabling new forms of cognitive development that made further innovations possible.

But gene-culture coevolution operated largely unconsciously until very recently. Agricultural societies developed without anyone understanding how agriculture was reshaping human psychology through both cultural learning and genetic selection. Writing transformed consciousness without scribes comprehending what literacy was doing to human cognition. Scientific culture emerged through collective experimentation rather than conscious design of scientific cognitive practices.

Contemporary humans possess something qualitatively different. We understand the mechanisms through which culture shapes psychology. We can investigate how educational practices influence cognitive development, how media environments affect attention patterns, and how social institutions either support or undermine individual agency. We possess systematic knowledge about the processes shaping human minds.

This knowledge creates possibilities for conscious participation in species-level development that no previous generation could access. We can design educational systems based on evidence about how learning occurs rather than old folk theories about knowledge transmission. We can evaluate media environments based on their effects on attention and emotional regulation, rather than simply accepting whatever emerges from commercial incentives. We can modify social institutions to better support human developmental needs rather than assuming current arrangements represent natural or inevitable forms.

Yet this capacity for conscious direction also creates the possibility of catastrophic error. We could systematically reshape human psychology in ways that eliminate the very capacities that make conscious evolution possible. We could create educational systems that undermine rather than support genuine learning. We could design technological environments that fragment rather than enhance attention. We could establish social institutions that constrain rather than enable human development.

The question facing contemporary humanity is not whether to participate in collective cognitive evolution. We are already participating, whether we acknowledge it or not. The question is whether we will participate consciously, with a systematic understanding of what we are doing and why, or unconsciously, allowing commercial interests and technological momentum to shape human psychology according to imperatives that may not serve human welfare.

How Culture Shaped the Mind

The capacity for conscious cultural participation did not appear suddenly. It emerged through feedback loops operating over tens of thousands of years, each cultural innovation creating psychological changes that enabled further innovations in recursive processes, which accelerated without anyone understanding what was happening.

The agricultural revolution ten thousand years ago created more than settled communities. It created selection pressures that literally reshaped human neurology. The ability to delay gratification became survival-relevant in ways it never was for hunter-gatherers, who could eat immediately upon finding food. Plant seeds now, harvest months later. Store grain now, eat through winter. The neural systems supporting temporal reasoning faced new adaptive challenges.

Someone who could maintain motivation across planting seasons despite no immediate reward possessed decisive advantages over someone who abandoned long-term projects when they became tedious. Natural selection favored genetic variants that supported sustained attention on repetitive tasks, tolerance for hierarchical and concentrated authority, and the capacity for abstract reasoning about invisible future outcomes.

These psychological changes occurred through the simultaneous operation of both cultural learning and genetic evolution. Children growing up in agricultural societies developed behavioral patterns that were impossible in nomadic contexts. But they also inherited genetic variants that made agricultural life psychologically easier across hundreds of generations.

The result was gene-culture coevolution, where cultural innovation created new selection pressures that modified genetic foundations, which then enabled more sophisticated cultural innovations. Human psychology became increasingly suited to agricultural life not through genetic determinism but through dynamic interaction between cultural practices and biological evolution.

Yet no one involved understood what was happening. Farmers did not recognize that their way of life was reshaping human neurology across millennia. They simply practiced agriculture because it worked, unaware that each generation was becoming slightly more psychologically adapted to agricultural existence through mechanisms operating far below conscious awareness.

Writing systems five thousand years ago created another transformation whose depth we still fail to comprehend. The invention of external memory storage that persisted across generations without degradation from imperfect human memory did not just preserve information. It transformed human consciousness itself.

Oral cultures developed sophisticated mnemonic techniques. The Homeric epics preserve rhythmic patterns and formulaic expressions that enabled bards to recreate thousands of lines from memory. The cognitive habits required for oral knowledge transmission emphasized episodic memory, narrative coherence, and rhythmic patterns that aided memorization.

Literate cognition operates differently. Writing enables linear reasoning that builds an argument across pages rather than relying on memorable episodes. It permits abstract analysis disconnected from concrete narratives. It creates possibilities for systematic critique of ideas separated from the people who hold them. Someone reading Aristotle can examine arguments without Aristotle present to defend them, creating critical distance that is impossible when knowledge is embedded in living traditions.

The cognitive transformation from orality to literacy involved both gains and losses. Literate cultures typically experience memory deterioration as writing makes memorization less necessary. The narrative skills oral cultures cultivated atrophy when stories can be recorded rather than recreated. The communal knowledge that oral traditions maintain through collective participation weakens when reading becomes a solitary rather than a social activity.

Contemporary humans cannot imagine thinking without literacy. We assume the cognitive habits literacy created represent natural human cognition rather than recognizing them as culturally constructed patterns that differ systematically from preliterate consciousness. This blindness to our own cognitive construction reveals how thoroughly culture shapes the mind while remaining invisible to those who are shaped by it.

Digital technologies may be creating another cognitive transformation comparable to the invention of literacy. The person who learns primarily through screens develops different attention patterns than those who learn through books. Rapid information processing, multitasking, and network-based knowledge access are digital cognitive habits that differ systematically from both oral and print-based patterns.

Yet we remain too close to this transformation to fully understand its impact on consciousness. Future historians may recognize our era as the moment when human cognition underwent its most profound transformation since the emergence of language. Or they may view digital technology as a brief perturbation that humanity has adapted to without any fundamental alteration.

We cannot know from within the transformation which outcome proves accurate. But we face choices about technological development that will determine which outcome occurs, whether we make those choices consciously or allow them to happen through unconscious drift driven by commercial imperatives.

When Humanity Learned to Test Its Beliefs

The scientific revolution created something more profound than new knowledge about nature. It created systematic methods for testing beliefs against evidence and accumulating reliable knowledge through procedures capable of correcting their own errors across generations.

Pre-scientific natural philosophy relied on rational analysis of essential natures, appeal to authoritative texts, and intuitive insight into cosmic principles. These approaches generated sophisticated systems but provided limited capacity for systematic empirical investigation or cumulative knowledge development, building reliably across generations.

Someone reading Aristotle in the seventeenth century encountered essentially the same natural philosophy as someone in the fourth century BCE, with little systematic progress in empirical knowledge over the course of two thousand years. The philosophical systems became more elaborate through commentary but did not generate cumulative empirical knowledge.

The scientific revolution involved collective innovations in observation techniques, experimental methods, and mathematical analysis, enabling systematic investigation through reproducible procedures validated by independent investigators. Galileo dropping weights, Newton analyzing planetary motion, Lavoisier decomposing substances, each contributed not merely new facts but new methods generating further knowledge building upon previous discoveries.

Scientific cognitive practices transformed intellectual culture beyond their original domains. The emphasis on empirical evidence, systematic observation, and reproducible procedures has influenced historical investigation, political analysis, and personal decision-making, leading to systematic changes in collective reasoning patterns.

Someone living in a scientific culture thinks differently from someone in a pre-scientific culture, even without engaging directly in scientific research. In such cultures, people expect beliefs to be justified by evidence, recognize that authorities can be wrong, and understand that knowledge accumulates through systematic investigation rather than revelation. These cognitive habits permeate daily life and transform thought patterns even in domains with little direct connection to scientific practice.

Yet scientific methodology also created cognitive limitations. Its emphasis on quantification, reductive analysis, and objective detachment may interfere with forms of understanding that require holistic perception, empathetic engagement, and intuitive insight into complex wholes resisting decomposition into measurable parts.

The person trained in scientific thinking excels at analyzing systems by breaking them into components studied in isolation. But this analytical strength becomes a cognitive limitation when understanding requires grasping patterns that emerge from component interactions in ways that analysis into parts cannot capture.

The scientist studying psychology through controlled experiments, isolating individual variables, may miss patterns visible only through prolonged immersion in actual communities, where multiple factors interact in complex ways that experimental control eliminates.

Scientific cognition represents cultural evolution through variation and selective retention rather than simple progress toward perfect knowledge. Science enhances certain cognitive capacities while potentially constraining others in trade-offs whose overall value remains open to evaluation rather than obviously and universally positive.

The question becomes not whether science represents progress but what forms of scientific practice support human flourishing versus what forms undermine it through their limitations and blind spots.

Democracy as Distributed Cognition

Democratic institutions emerged from recognition that collective decision-making benefits from distributed intelligence rather than concentrated authority. Information flows upward from citizens possessing local knowledge and specialized expertise rather than decisions flowing downward from leaders lacking access to information distributed throughout populations.

But democracy functions effectively only when citizens possess capacities for informed deliberation, perspective-taking, and collaborative problem-solving. These democratic cognitive habits do not develop automatically but require cultural support through institutions that cultivate them.

Democratic systems need citizens who can evaluate competing claims about complex policy issues without being paralyzed by uncertainty or manipulated by demagogues exploiting ignorance. They need people who consider long-term consequences rather than being driven entirely by immediate self-interest or emotional reactions to current crises. They depend on individuals participating constructively in collective deliberation with people holding different perspectives, rather than treating political disagreement as a form of warfare that requires the destruction of opponents.

These democratic cognitive capacities prove difficult to develop and easy to undermine. The person who learns to evaluate evidence critically, takes multiple perspectives seriously, and deliberates about long-term consequences develops different political cognition than the person who learns to defer to authority, treats opposing views as threats, and prioritizes immediate group loyalty over reasoned analysis.

Contemporary democratic systems face systematic challenges that may exceed the cognitive capacities of democratic institutions. Complex global issues, including climate change, technological development, and international cooperation, require forms of long-term thinking, technical understanding, and coordination across diverse populations that challenge traditional democratic processes designed for simpler problems in more homogeneous communities.

Information environments created by contemporary media systems may undermine rather than support democratic cognitive capacities. Filter bubbles limit exposure to diverse perspectives. Attention fragmentation prevents sustained reflection on complex issues. Emotional manipulation circumvents rational deliberation by appealing to fear and tribal loyalty.

A citizen scrolling through social media encounters information curated by algorithms that prioritize engagement over accuracy or democratic value. The algorithms learn what triggers emotional responses and feed content, keeping them scrolling, regardless of whether that content promotes informed deliberation or democratic citizenship.

The result can be radicalization through exposure to increasingly extreme content that algorithms promote because it generates high engagement. Users can also experience polarization when they encounter information that only confirms their existing beliefs. Manipulation through targeted messaging is designed to exploit individual psychological vulnerabilities that algorithms have mapped through user behavior.

Consider what happened during recent elections across multiple democracies. Targeted disinformation campaigns leveraged algorithmic amplification to disseminate false claims about voting procedures, candidate positions, and policy implications. The disinformation spread not because it was true but because it triggered strong emotional responses that algorithms rewarded with greater distribution.

Citizens encountered this information in contexts that made it appear credible. Social media friends shared it, lending social proof. The algorithmic ranking made it appear popular and, therefore, trustworthy. The emotional resonance made it feel true regardless of factual accuracy. By the time fact-checkers could respond, the false information had already shaped the understanding of millions of voters.

Democratic cognition requires recognizing this as an ongoing achievement demanding conscious maintenance rather than a stable accomplishment taken for granted once democratic institutions are established. Democratic institutions remain fragile because the cognitive habits they require are fragile, easily corrupted through media environments and educational systems that fail to cultivate the capacities democratic participation presupposes.

The question facing contemporary democracies is whether citizens can develop the cognitive habits necessary for effective democratic participation in information environments that are deliberately designed to undermine those habits for commercial profit. The answer remains uncertain because we are living through the experiment rather than observing it from a safe historical distance.

We face a choice between consciously developing a democratic cognitive culture that resists manipulation and drifting unconsciously toward post-democratic systems where the appearance of popular sovereignty hides the subtle influence of algorithms over collective decision-making, shaping how we think, decide, and interact as a society.

Technological Cognitive Evolution

Contemporary technological development creates possibilities for collective cognitive evolution, transcending previous cultural innovations by enabling direct augmentation of human cognitive capacities through tools that amplify intelligence while potentially transforming it unpredictably.

Digital technologies enable unprecedented information storage, processing, and transmission, extending human cognitive capacities while creating new collective intelligence, and integrating human and technological systems in ways that blur the boundaries between mind and tool.

Contemporary smartphones provide access to virtually all accumulated human knowledge, enabling real-time communication with anyone, anywhere, through pocket-sized devices. These tools augment cognitive capacities, transforming how people think, learn, and solve problems while creating new dependencies on technological systems whose failure would prove catastrophic.

Yet, digital cognitive enhancement creates both systematic risks and opportunities. The same technologies extending human capacities also create possibilities for manipulation, surveillance, and control exceeding anything possible in pre-technological societies where power operated through physical force rather than psychological influence mediated by digital systems.

Search engines and social media platforms utilize algorithmic curation to determine what information people encounter, collecting detailed data about preferences, behaviors, and social relationships that can be analyzed to predict and influence future behavior. These systems shape human thought and action in ways that remain largely invisible to users while serving commercial and political interests that potentially conflict with individual welfare and democratic values.

Someone searching for vaccine information encounters results ranked by algorithms, potentially prioritizing engagement over accuracy, and exposing them to misinformation that algorithms promote because it generates clicks, regardless of its truth value. Someone scrolling social media sees content selected by algorithms learning what triggers strong emotional responses, potentially radicalizing them through exposure to increasingly extreme content algorithms promote because extremism generates engagement.

The manipulation exploits cognitive biases and emotional vulnerabilities that evolution shaped for entirely different environments. Psychological mechanisms that enabled our ancestors to navigate small-scale social groups in stable environments are now exploited by algorithms optimized to capture attention and modify behavior, serving commercial interests at the expense of individual and collective welfare.

Artificial intelligence systems present particularly profound challenges and opportunities, as they promise cognitive capabilities that potentially exceed human intelligence, while possibly replacing human cognitive functions entirely rather than merely augmenting them.

AI systems augmenting human cognitive capacities could enable forms of scientific discovery, creative expression, and collaborative problem-solving impossible for purely human intelligence without technological enhancement. Someone using AI to analyze complex datasets might discover patterns invisible to human perception alone. Someone collaborating with AI to generate creative works might achieve artistic expressions impossible through human creativity alone.

However, AI systems that replace rather than augment human cognitive functions could reduce human cognitive capabilities while increasing dependence on technological systems controlled by others who do not share the interests of those being displaced. Automated systems that eliminate human jobs reduce opportunities for humans to develop and exercise their cognitive capacities through meaningful work. Decision-making algorithms removing human judgment from consequential choices reduce opportunities for developing practical wisdom through experience. Recommendation systems manipulating human choices reduce opportunities for developing autonomous judgment through deliberate decision-making.

The difference between augmentation and replacement proves critical for human cognitive evolution. Augmentation enhances capacities while preserving agency and decision-making authority. Replacement eliminates human functions while creating dependence on systems whose operation and purposes humans may not understand or control.

Current AI development often pursues replacement rather than augmentation because replacing human cognitive functions proves more profitable than enhancing human capabilities. The company automating jobs eliminates labor costs. The platform automates decision-making, eliminating the need for human judgment while gaining the power to shape outcomes. The system manipulating human choices generates revenue through behavioral modification while reducing human autonomy.

The direction of technological development depends on social choices regarding research funding, regulatory frameworks, and cultural values, rather than being driven by autonomous technological imperatives that humans cannot influence. We stand at a threshold where technological development could either enhance human cognitive agency or eliminate it entirely, depending on the choices we make about what forms of AI development to pursue and what forms to prohibit or constrain.

Someone designing AI systems faces a choice between maximizing short-term commercial value by replacing human functions and pursuing long-term human welfare through augmenting human capacities. Someone developing algorithms faces a choice between maximizing user engagement through psychological exploitation or supporting user-defined goals through genuine enhancement of human capabilities. Someone creating social media platforms faces a choice between optimizing advertising revenue through manipulation or facilitating authentic human connection through tools that serve users rather than exploiting them.

These individual choices aggregate into collective patterns determining whether technology enhances or undermines human agency at the species level through processes operating below conscious social choice, unless we develop institutions capable of governing technological development democratically rather than leaving it to market forces and commercial interests.

The possibility of conscious collective governance of technological development represents genuine novelty in evolutionary history. Previous cultural innovations emerged through unconscious variation and selection. Contemporary humans can deliberately choose what forms of technological development to pursue based on a systematic understanding of their likely effects on human psychology and social organization.

But this possibility remains largely unrealized. Technological development currently proceeds through commercial imperatives and engineering momentum rather than democratic deliberation about what forms of technology serve authentic human flourishing versus what forms undermine it for profit.

Who Decides Human Becoming?

The recognition that collective cognitive evolution can be consciously directed creates unprecedented political challenges about who controls the direction of human development and according to what values human becoming should be shaped.

Unlike biological evolution, which operates through unconscious variation and selection, cultural evolution can be influenced by conscious social choices regarding educational systems, technological development, media environments, and economic structures that shape human psychology across generations.

This capacity for conscious direction creates both extraordinary opportunities for addressing global challenges and profound dangers from systematic manipulation, which can eliminate individual agency while appearing to serve collective welfare.

Historical examples of directed cultural change include totalitarian attempts to reshape human consciousness through propaganda, education, and social control, eliminating individual autonomy while claiming to serve collective interests in building communist or fascist societies. Yet democratic societies also engage in conscious cultural direction through educational curricula, media regulation, and social policies shaping individual development while attempting to preserve individual autonomy and cultural diversity.

The difference lies in whether cultural direction operates through democratic participation and individual consent or through authoritarian manipulation and coercion backed by force. Democratic participation in collective cognitive evolution requires citizens to understand how technological and cultural systems influence human development, while possessing the capabilities to evaluate different development possibilities according to their implications for individual and collective flourishing.

Contemporary democratic institutions struggle to address questions about collective cognitive development because these questions require long-term thinking about effects that span generations, a technical understanding of complex mechanisms that educated laypeople may lack, and consideration of fundamental values about human nature and purpose that democratic systems traditionally leave to individual choice rather than collective determination.

Yet the alternative to democratic participation involves allowing technological and cultural development to be controlled by economic elites pursuing profit, technical experts pursuing their own visions, or political authorities pursuing power, none of whom can be trusted to serve collective human welfare when their interests inevitably diverge.

Creating effective democratic governance of collective cognitive evolution requires institutional innovations that enable meaningful citizen participation in complex technical decisions while preserving the democratic values of equality and self-determination, which remain non-negotiable even when they make collective decision-making more difficult.

Climate change illustrates these challenges clearly. Addressing climate change requires collective action that constrains individual choices about consumption and lifestyle, while creating technological and social changes that influence human development for centuries through their effects on where people can live, what resources remain available, and what environmental conditions shape human experience.

Yet, these collective constraints and changes require democratic legitimacy to be morally acceptable while serving both individual and collective welfare across diverse global populations, whose interests and values differ in ways that make consensus difficult, if not impossible.

We face responsibilities that no previous generation has confronted, requiring wisdom about species-level development that transcends traditional moral frameworks focused on individual rights and duties, while remaining grounded in democratic participation by living humans affected by decisions about collective becoming.

Contemporary decisions about technological development, environmental protection, and cultural transmission will influence the developmental possibilities available to future generations for centuries, in ways that could enhance or eliminate human agency, depending on how these choices are made through processes that remain largely unconscious, despite their profound importance for human futures.

The institutions governing these choices remain inadequate to the challenges they face. National governments struggle to regulate multinational technology companies whose platforms shape human cognition across borders. International organizations lack enforcement mechanisms making their decisions effective. Democratic processes prove too slow for technological changes occurring at accelerating pace.

Yet the absence of adequate governance structures does not eliminate the need for conscious collective decision-making about human developmental trajectories. It makes such governance more urgent while more difficult to achieve.

The Nietzschean Challenge

Friedrich Nietzsche's concept of human self-overcoming provides a philosophical framework for understanding collective cognitive evolution as an expression of fundamental life processes rather than merely technological achievement or social engineering. But the framework also reveals deep tensions in any attempt to democratize self-overcoming.

Nietzsche's will to power describes the fundamental drive of life to overcome its own limitations, to transcend its current state, and to create new possibilities for existence. Collective cognitive evolution at its best represents this will to power operating at the species level, where humanity systematically transcends previous limitations through the conscious modification of conditions that shape human development.

This aligns with temporal scaffolding at the individual level. Both involve utilizing present capacities to create conditions that enable future transcendence of current limitations. Both operate through entirely natural mechanisms while creating genuine possibilities for creative self-transformation. Both reject the false dichotomy between determinism and libertarian freedom by revealing agency as conscious participation in causal processes rather than exemption from them.

Yet Nietzsche would reject everything about the democratic framework proposed here. His philosophy explicitly embraces hierarchy, celebrates aristocratic values, and despises the masses, whom he calls "the herd." The idea that everyone can develop sophisticated self-modification capacities through appropriate social support would strike him as precisely the leveling mediocrity that drags everyone down to common denominators.

Consider Nietzsche's contempt for what he calls slave morality, the value system that celebrates equality, mutual support, and collective welfare. He views these values as life-denying, expressions of weakness that seek to constrain the strong rather than enabling them to transcend limitations. Democratic institutions designed to support universal capacity development would, for Nietzsche, represent the systematic repression of human excellence in the name of equality.

The tension cannot be resolved philosophically. It reflects fundamentally different empirical assumptions about human psychological variation. The democratic framework assumes that sophisticated self-modification capacities exist as potential in most humans, which can be developed with appropriate support. Nietzsche assumes a natural aristocracy where only exceptional individuals possess a genuine capacity for self-overcoming, while most humans require direction from above.

Which assumption proves correct remains an empirical question. Do sophisticated metacognitive capacities and temporal scaffolding abilities represent universal human potential requiring proper cultivation, or do they represent rare achievements possible only for cognitive elites? Can democratic institutions systematically develop these capacities across diverse populations, or does democratization inevitably produce mediocrity by constraining excellence?

Contemporary evidence suggests the democratic assumption has merit. Educational research demonstrates that explicit instruction in metacognitive strategies, emotional regulation techniques, and systematic planning methods improves performance across diverse student populations. Therapeutic research indicates that capacity-building approaches facilitate beneficial behavioral change across diverse psychological presentations. Community development research reveals that systematic support enables populations previously written off as incapable of developing sophisticated self-modification abilities.

Yet Nietzsche would remain unimpressed by this evidence. He would argue that teaching everyone metacognitive techniques produces skilled technicians of self-observation rather than genuine self-overcoming. That therapeutic capacity-building creates well-adjusted mediocrity rather than creative excellence. That community development programs raise everyone to adequate functioning while preventing anyone from achieving greatness.

The Nietzschean critique reveals an authentic danger in collective cognitive evolution. The exact mechanisms enabling systematic capacity development across populations could lead to conformity rather than creativity, standardization rather than innovation, and mechanical optimization rather than genuine self-improvement.

When educational systems teach metacognitive techniques through standardized curricula, they risk creating uniform approaches to self-observation that eliminate diversity in how people think about thinking. When therapeutic programs implement evidence-based capacity-building protocols, they risk reducing human psychological variation to diagnostic categories and treatment manuals. When institutions design environments to support beneficial choices, they risk eliminating the obstacles that genuine self-overcoming requires.

This danger becomes particularly acute with technological cognitive enhancement. AI systems designed to augment human cognition could easily replace human cognitive diversity with algorithmic uniformity. Everyone thinks better, perhaps, but everyone thinks the same way, using the same technological prosthetics, optimized according to the same efficiency metrics.

The Nietzschean critique demands that collective cognitive evolution preserve and enhance the very diversity and experimentation it risks eliminating through systematization. This requires maintaining space for individual creative rebellion against collective norms, preserving cultural variation rather than imposing universal standards, and celebrating rather than pathologizing psychological differences that enable innovation.

Authentic collective self-overcoming would create conditions that support individual creativity while enabling collective achievements that transcend individual limitations. The goal is coordination rather than subordination, enhancement rather than replacement, diversification rather than standardization.

It is far from certain that democratic institutions can succeed in this task. Nietzsche's aristocratic model dismisses equality and mutual support, elevating exceptional individuals at the expense of the collective. The democratic model affirms equality and mutual support, yet aspires to preserve the space where excellence can thrive.

The tension reveals that collective cognitive evolution proceeds without guarantee of success. We could systematically develop human capacities across populations while preserving diversity and excellence. Or we could produce conformist mediocrity through our very attempts at universal capacity development. Or we could abandon democratic approaches and embrace aristocratic ones that celebrate excellence while abandoning most humans to their limitations.

The choice among these possibilities cannot be made on philosophical grounds alone. It requires empirical investigation of what actually happens when we attempt democratic cognitive evolution combined with ongoing vigilance against the dangers Nietzsche identified. We must remain alert to ways that systematization eliminates diversity, that therapeutic approaches pathologize difference, that technological augmentation produces uniformity, and that collective governance constrains individual creativity.

The Nietzschean perspective provides a necessary counterpoint to democratic optimism without resolving the fundamental tension between equality and excellence that any attempt at collective cognitive evolution must navigate.

The Future of Collective Becoming

Collective cognitive evolution reveals human development as an open-ended process that could continue indefinitely through conscious participation in cultural and technological innovation, building upon rather than replacing biological foundations.

Unlike biological species, which face inherent limitations determined by genetic constraints, humans can systematically transcend previous limitations through the modification of cultural and technological environments, shaping development without requiring genetic changes, a process that can take thousands of years to emerge through natural selection.

Yet this openness creates profound uncertainty about direction and the ultimate possibilities of human development. Conscious evolution enables trajectories that enhance human flourishing through the expansion of cognitive capacities, creative possibilities, and collaborative achievements, thereby transcending the achievements of previous generations.

However, conscious evolution also enables trajectories that eliminate human agency through technological substitution, social manipulation, and environmental destruction, thereby foreclosing developmental possibilities for future generations through shortsighted choices that serve immediate interests at the expense of long-term welfare.

We face choices between conscious democratic participation with wisdom about what enhances rather than diminishes human flourishing, or unconscious drift allowing collective development to be determined by commercial interests, technological momentum, short-term thinking, sacrificing long-term human welfare for immediate convenience and profit.

Those who understand these realities face a choice between passive spectatorship and active participation in the most significant transformation in history. Individual temporal scaffolding aggregates into collective patterns. Collective patterns shape individual possibilities. The recursion continues indefinitely, creating open-ended potential for human development, transcending any fixed endpoint, while remaining grounded in natural processes that science can investigate and humans can consciously navigate toward chosen rather than accidental futures.

Yet conscious navigation requires acknowledging that we lack maps for this territory. Previous cultural innovations emerged through unconscious variation and selection. We are the first generation attempting conscious collective self-modification based on a systematic understanding of what we are doing.

This unprecedented situation presents both opportunities and dangers. The opportunity lies in avoiding catastrophic errors through the foresight that previous generations lacked. The danger lies in overconfidence that our understanding suffices for the task. We know enough to recognize that we are reshaping human psychology. We do not know enough to predict all the consequences of our reshaping.

The appropriate stance combines ambition with humility. Ambition to consciously participate in human developmental trajectories rather than allowing unconscious drift. Humility in recognizing the limits of our understanding and the genuine possibility of catastrophic error.

This requires experimental approaches that test interventions cautiously, monitor outcomes carefully, and remain prepared to reverse course when evidence suggests our conscious modifications produce unintended harms. It requires preserving diversity so that errors in one cultural approach do not become species-wide catastrophes. It requires democratic participation, ensuring that decisions about human becoming reflect diverse perspectives rather than narrow interests.

Most importantly, it requires recognizing collective cognitive evolution as an ongoing achievement rather than a completed accomplishment. We cannot design optimal human development once and then implement it universally. We must continue to experiment, learn, and adapt as circumstances change and as we discover the unintended consequences of our previous interventions.

At the collective scale, this capacity creates possibilities for species-level self-transformation that could enhance or eliminate human agency depending on how consciously and democratically we navigate choices about technological development, cultural transmission, and institutional design shaping human psychology across generations.

We discover ourselves as simultaneously the inheritors of evolutionary processes operating across deep time and the architects of our species' future development. This dual nature creates both profound responsibility and genuine possibility. We are responsible for making choices about human developmental trajectories whose consequences will reverberate across centuries. We possess a genuine opportunity to consciously participate in our own evolution rather than remaining passive subjects of whatever selective pressures may operate.

Again, the question is not whether we will shape human cognitive development. We are already shaping it through every technological innovation, educational practice, media system, and cultural institution we create or maintain. The question is whether we will do so consciously and democratically with wisdom about what enhances rather than diminishes authentic human flourishing, or whether we will stumble forward, allowing collective development to be determined by the narrow interests of those who profit from current arrangements.

Natural Self-Creation

"What if the most liberating interpretation is the one that reveals self-improvement not as heroic transcendence of nature, but as nature's most sophisticated expression of itself?"

THE DEEPEST TENSION in human self-understanding has always been whether we are part of nature or apart from it.

A woman sits alone after another therapy session, confronting a question that hollows out everything she thought she had achieved. For three years, she worked systematically to break her pattern of choosing emotionally unavailable men. She mapped the pattern across relationships. She recognized the childhood dynamics that influenced her choices. She implemented multiple changes, including waiting periods before pursuing new attractions, consulting with friends who could spot warning signs she couldn't see through the fog of desire, and therapeutic work to understand how history shaped the present. She did everything the framework of temporal scaffolding prescribes.

And it worked. She now finds herself drawn to and choosing partners who possess emotional presence. Real change occurred through conscious effort sustained across time.

But late at night, a question arrives with surgical precision. Was any of this actually her doing?

She didn't choose the childhood that created these patterns. She didn't choose the intelligence enabling pattern recognition. She didn't choose the social circumstances providing therapy access. She didn't choose the neurological architecture enabling metacognitive observation. She didn't choose the culture that transmitted knowledge about systematic behavioral modification. Every single factor that made her "self-creation" possible was itself determined by causes she never controlled.

So what exactly did she create?

The river doesn't choose to carve the canyon. Wind doesn't choose to shape rock. Natural processes operating through deterministic mechanisms create elaborate structures without consciousness, without choice, and without any meaningful sense of creation. The river is not an author. The wind is not an architect. They are mechanisms through which nature organizes itself according to physical laws that permit no alternatives.

What makes the woman different? She observed the process. She participated consciously in mechanisms that modified her behavior. But observation isn't authorship. A camera observes without creating what it records. Participation isn't freedom. Gears participate in mechanisms without choosing their motion. The clock's second hand participates in timekeeping without possessing agency over temporal flow.

If everything about her self-modification operated through deterministic mechanisms—neural architectures shaped by evolution, cognitive capacities developed through fortunate circumstances, systematic methods learned from culture, motivation sustained by brain chemistry responding to environmental contingencies—then perhaps "self-creation" names nothing more than nature's most elaborate illusion. Consciousness taking credit for processes that would unfold identically in darkness.

This is not philosophical game-playing meant to undermine practical work. This is the crisis that the entire framework creates once you take it seriously. We have shown how agency operates through natural mechanisms. We have mapped neural systems. We have explained evolutionary history. We have demonstrated practical applications. We have grounded moral responsibility in psychological capacities. We have examined collective cognitive evolution.

We still do not know whether this amounts to genuine creation or merely a set of mechanical processes, with consciousness serving only as a witness to a story already authored by deterministic causation.

The libertarian avoided this problem through impossible magic. Choices spring uncaused from agents standing outside natural law, creating themselves through exemptions from causation that would make behavior random rather than rational. The solution proved incoherent. A choice uncaused by character, values, or reasoning would be arbitrary rather than free. It would be no more the agent's choice than a cosmic dice roll that happened to occur in their brain.

But at least libertarians preserved creation. However incoherent their metaphysics, they maintained that human development involves genuine authorship rather than merely witnessing natural processes unfold through us.

The hard determinist embraced the crisis with brutal honesty. No genuine creation exists. Mechanical processes generate everything, including the illusion that we create ourselves. We are sophisticated machines witnessing our own operation while mistaking observation for authorship. The sense of creating ourselves is a misunderstanding of consciousness in its role in causal processes that operate independently of conscious observation.

Accept this and stop pretending human existence involves genuine agency beyond what rocks possess in rolling downhill. Both follow natural laws with equal necessity. The difference is merely that human mechanisms are complex enough to generate the illusion of authorship.

Traditional compatibilism attempted to reconcile the difference through increasingly sophisticated analyses of what constitutes "acting from your own reasons" or "identifying with your desires." But if your reasons and desires themselves were determined by prior causes beyond your control. These have been thoroughly discussed already, including genetic endowments you didn't choose, developmental experiences that shaped you before you could consent, and cultural influences that programmed your values. What makes them genuinely yours rather than just nature's way of organizing itself through your particular neurological configuration?

The compatibilist argues that you act freely when your actions stem from your character rather than from external compulsion. But if your character itself was shaped entirely by factors beyond your control, how does this preserve genuine agency? You are the mechanism through which prior causes give rise to behavior. The mechanism is sophisticated, certainly. But sophisticated mechanisms remain mechanisms.

We must confront this directly. Either show why deterministic self-modification constitutes genuine creation despite operating through causation that permits no alternatives, or admit the entire framework collapses into an elaborate rationalization for mechanical determination dressed in agency's clothing.

The woman deserves an answer. So do we all.

The Therapeutic Evasion

Contemporary therapeutic culture offers an apparent resolution by denying that there was ever a genuine creation that required explanation. You are not creating a new self. You are restoring a damaged self, removing obstacles that prevented natural, healthy development from occurring.

Someone recovering from childhood trauma isn't building something new. They are uncovering the person they would have been in the absence of the trauma. The work involves excavation, not construction. Revealing what was always there beneath damage rather than creating what never existed before.

The therapist tells the woman that her destructive relationship patterns were never her authentic self. They were defenses erected against childhood wounds. Now, through therapeutic work, you are healing those wounds and returning to your authentic self that trauma had buried. This is restoration to the natural baseline, not creation of something new.

This eliminates the paradox by eliminating the concept of creation. Nature already created you through normal developmental processes. Trauma interfered with those processes. Therapy removes interference, allowing natural development to resume its proper course. No mysterious self-creation occurs; simply return to health, which represents your natural state.

The framework proves emotionally appealing. It eliminates shame by attributing problems to external factors rather than the essential self. Your destructive patterns weren't really you. They were damage done to you. Healing involves removing what never belonged rather than creating what you lacked. This sounds gentler, more forgiving, and less demanding than frameworks that emphasize genuine creation, requiring sustained conscious effort over time.

But observe what this framework actually accomplishes. It pathologizes all significant human development by treating change as restoration of health rather than genuine growth. Is someone systematically cultivating attention capacities beyond the normal human baseline? That's not enhancement. That's compensating for attention deficit. Is someone developing emotional regulation exceeding typical adult capacities? That's not growth beyond natural limits. That's healing emotional wounds that prevented normal development.

The framework cannot accommodate the possibility that you might develop capabilities that never existed in any natural baseline, that exceed what ordinary development produces, and that represent genuine novelty rather than the restoration of something that was always supposed to be there, waiting to emerge once obstacles were removed.

More fundamentally, what is this natural baseline that trauma supposedly disrupted? Human psychology varies enormously across individuals and contexts without any single template defining proper function. Different people develop distinct psychological architectures through various developmental pathways, all of which are equally natural in the sense that they follow from natural causal processes.

The person emerging from successful therapy doesn't return to some predetermined natural state that trauma prevented. They develop entirely new capacities that most people never develop, regardless of trauma history. They may develop sophisticated metacognitive awareness of psychological patterns, systematic approaches to emotional regulation, complex understanding of how personal history influences present behavior, or skillful deployment of environmental modification to support beneficial choices.

These represent genuine developments, not restorations. The therapeutic framework conceals this novelty while sidestepping the philosophical challenge of explaining how deterministic processes generate anything genuinely new that wasn't implicit in prior states.

The woman possesses capabilities she didn't possess before three years of conscious work. She can observe attraction arising without being controlled by it automatically. She can recognize pattern repetition before acting on it. She can implement systematic interventions that modify her behavioral trajectory. These capacities didn't exist in some natural baseline waiting to emerge once trauma was healed. They were built through sustained effort, deploying methods that the culture developed, and she learned and applied systematically.

This is creation, not restoration. Calling it restoration may seem like a convenient way to avoid the deeper question of whether deterministic creation can make sense. If every change is explained as a simple return to a natural baseline, then nothing genuinely new ever arises and nothing requires further explanation. The problem disappears only by denying the phenomenon itself.

Yet the denial cannot hold because the phenomenon persists. The woman recognizes that she now possesses capabilities she did not have before. She recognizes that these capabilities came into being through deliberate and sustained effort over time. She recognizes that they represent genuine development, rather than merely removing barriers that once hid capacities waiting to be uncovered. Her experience makes the reality of creation undeniable.

The therapeutic evasion fails not because of ill will but because of a basic confusion about what human development truly involves. By reducing every change to restoration, it strips away the very possibility of genuine growth, which is the possibility that makes human existence meaningful in the first place.

The Technological Fantasy

Perhaps natural human capacities prove insufficient for genuine self-creation. Yet technology might provide the powers we lack. Brain-computer interfaces could enable direct neural modification. Artificial intelligence might amplify cognitive capacities beyond biological limits. Genetic engineering could allow the redesign of psychological traits. Pharmaceutical interventions may enhance attention, memory, and emotional regulation. In this way, technological transcendence of biological limitations may break the deterministic chains that constrain natural agency.

This fantasy animates much contemporary thinking about human enhancement. Biological humans remain trapped by evolutionary heritage that shaped us for ancestral environments, the story goes. But technologically augmented humans could genuinely create themselves by transcending natural constraints. The enhanced human would possess capacities evolution never created, operating through mechanisms natural selection never shaped, enabling forms of self-modification impossible for merely biological consciousness.

The appeal proves obvious. If the problem is that natural human self-modification remains fully determined by prior causes, technological transcendence might provide genuine agency unavailable to purely biological systems. Add enough technological power and perhaps humans achieve the kind of self-creation that biological constraints prevent.

Yet this resolution fails more completely than therapeutic evasion because it rests on fundamental confusion about what technology is and how it relates to nature. Technology doesn't exempt anything from natural causation. Technological devices operate through natural laws just as biological systems do. Brain-computer interfaces function through electromagnetic principles. Artificial intelligence implements algorithms following mathematical necessity. Genetic modifications alter DNA according to biochemical rules. Pharmaceutical interventions modify neural chemistry through deterministic mechanisms.

Every technological intervention operates through deterministic natural processes. Adding technology to human cognitive systems doesn't solve the philosophical problem. It makes the system more complex while leaving the paradox unchanged.

The person whose brain connects to computer interfaces, enabling direct neural modification, faces exactly the same question the woman faces. Were the modifications genuinely created through conscious choice or mechanically determined by prior causes, including the decision to undergo enhancement itself? The technology changes what modifications are possible. It doesn't change whether modifications constitute genuine creation versus elaborate mechanical self-organization.

A more powerful machine remains a machine. Increasing computational capacity doesn't transform mechanism into agency. The enhanced human would possess greater power, but faces the same question about whether that power constitutes genuine self-creation or just more sophisticated deterministic processing.

Worse, the technological fantasy reveals profound confusion about what makes human agency valuable. Genuine self-creation doesn't require transcending biological limitations through technological augmentation. It requires conscious participation in developmental processes through capacities we already possess naturally.

The woman who broke her destructive relationship patterns did not require neural implants, genetic modification, or artificial intelligence augmentation. She relied on capacities already present within her natural neurological architecture. She observed her own patterns and worked to understand their origins through memory and reasoning. She designed systematic interventions using knowledge transmitted through her culture. She implemented these interventions with consistency, drawing on the motivational systems within her brain. These are natural human capacities, and they are remarkably precise because they arise from ordinary biological mechanisms, yet enable outcomes that seem to exceed mere biological mechanisms.

Waiting for technology to grant powers we supposedly lack misses what's remarkable about actual human self-modification, which is operating right now through temporal scaffolding and metacognitive awareness. The power we need we already possess. The question is whether that natural power constitutes genuine creation or elaborate illusion.

Technology cannot answer this question by adding more power. The question concerns not the quantity of power but the coherence of deterministic creation itself. No amount of technological enhancement resolves the question of whether self-creation makes sense in deterministic systems. It simply enhances the deterministic system's power while leaving the conceptual problem untouched.

The Mystical Escape

Perhaps consciousness itself provides the answer through emergent properties that somehow transcend deterministic mechanisms without violating natural law. Higher-level mental properties arise from lower-level physical properties while possessing genuine causal powers irreducible to physical processes. Self-creation becomes possible because conscious mental states possess emergent causal powers that affect physical brain states in ways not fully determined by prior physical causes.

The person engaging temporal scaffolding exercises genuine mental causation through emergent properties of consciousness that transcend while remaining grounded in deterministic physical processes. The woman's conscious recognition of her patterns genuinely causes behavioral change through emergent mental causation that cannot be reduced to purely physical neural mechanisms.

This sounds sophisticated, offering resolutions without requiring libertarian magic or accepting hard determinist elimination of agency. Emergence preserves naturalism while creating space for genuine mental causation that deterministic physical processes alone cannot provide.

Yet this resolution fails through vagueness masquerading as profundity. What exactly are these emergent causal powers consciousness supposedly possesses? How do they operate? How do they affect physical brain states without violating physical causal closure that science presupposes?

When pressed for details, emergentist accounts offer one of two responses, neither of which is satisfactory.

Strong emergence claims that higher-level mental properties possess genuinely novel causal powers unpredictable from and irreducible to lower-level physical properties. Consciousness operates through causal mechanisms that transcend physical explanation. Mental events genuinely affect physical events through powers that physics cannot capture.

But this appears to violate physical causal closure by allowing mental events to influence physical events through mechanisms transcending physical law. Every physical event has sufficient physical causes. If mental events possess additional causal powers beyond physical causes, where do those powers come from? How do they interface with physical causation without creating causal overdetermination where events have two independent sufficient causes?

Strong emergence sounds like dualism wearing the vocabulary of emergence as a disguise. It claims consciousness transcends physical causation while remaining somehow natural. But transcending physical causation through non-physical causal powers is exactly what dualism claims. Calling it an emergence rather than a separate substance doesn't resolve the conceptual problems.

Weak emergence claims merely that higher-level patterns prove difficult to predict from lower-level properties while remaining fully determined by them. The patterns are real and causally relevant, but don't involve genuinely novel causal powers. Weather patterns emerge from molecular interactions in this sense. The patterns are real and have causal effects. However, they operate entirely through underlying molecular mechanics, without additional causal powers that transcend physical laws.

Weak emergence avoids the problems with strong emergence but provides no basis for genuine self-creation. If mental properties are just complex patterns of physical properties operating through physical mechanisms, then consciousness adds nothing to causal processes beyond what physical mechanisms alone would produce. The woman's conscious recognition of patterns is just complex physical processing. Her behavioral change is entirely a result of physical neural mechanisms. Consciousness witnesses without authoring, observes without creating.

This returns us to the original problem. If mental causation reduces to physical causation operating deterministically, then genuine self-creation seems impossible regardless of how complex the physical mechanisms become.

Appeals to emergence typically function as philosophical stop signs marking places where explanation breaks down rather than actually explaining anything. When someone says consciousness "emerges" from brain activity and this emergence explains agency, they have renamed the mystery rather than solving it. How does emergence create genuine novelty in causal structure? What does consciousness add to deterministic physical processes? These questions remain unanswered because emergence vocabulary obscures rather than illuminates the mechanisms involved.

The woman needs more than vague gestures toward emergence. She needs to understand whether her conscious efforts at self-modification genuinely created new behavioral possibilities or merely witnessed mechanical processes that would have occurred anyway through unconscious neural mechanisms operating deterministically.

Emergence provides no answer. It names the phenomenon requiring explanation while pretending the naming constitutes explanation. We need to look elsewhere for a resolution.

What Recursion Creates

Something happens when systems observe themselves observing.

The woman feels attraction to someone who shows familiar warning signs. He is unavailable, emotionally distant, and likely to repeat the same harmful patterns she has experienced before. At the unconscious level, the attraction generates approach behavior automatically. The limbic system signals reward, the motivational systems direct attention toward the person, and the behavioral systems begin to initiate movement toward him. The causal chain runs directly from attraction to approach, leaving no obvious point of intervention.

This process unfolds through deterministic mechanisms shaped by evolution. The attraction emerges from neural patterns formed through her prior relationship history. The approach behaviors follow from motivational systems designed to pursue rewards. Everything takes place through natural causation, and the sequence allows no genuine alternatives.

Now add metacognitive observation. The woman notices attraction arising. "I am feeling attracted to this person." This noticing is itself a causal process. Prefrontal monitoring systems detect activation in limbic reward regions through neural connections transmitting information about current brain states. The information reaches consciousness, meaning it becomes available to working memory systems that can hold and manipulate representations.

But something crucial happens through this apparently simple information transfer. The explicit representation "I am experiencing attraction" creates a new node in the causal network that didn't exist before. The information now exists not just as implicit neural activation but as an explicit representation accessible to reasoning processes.

This explicit representation enables causal paths impossible without it. The woman can now ask: "Why am I attracted to this person?" The question triggers the retrieval of memories from past relationships. Pattern recognition compares current attraction to previous attractions. Evaluation systems assess similarities between this person's characteristics and known problematic patterns. Each of these processes follows deterministically from neural mechanisms. But they only get triggered because explicit representation enabled the question.

The pattern recognition reveals: "This person shares characteristics with past partners who were emotionally unavailable." This recognition is another deterministic causal process, in which association cortices detect similarities across episodic memories stored in hippocampal networks. But this causal process creates another new node in the network. The information "This matches a problematic pattern" now exists explicitly rather than remaining implicit in neural activation patterns.

This explicit recognition opens a further causal possibility that didn't exist before. The woman can choose not to act on attraction despite feeling it. This choice itself operates deterministically. Prefrontal systems, which implement cognitive control based on pattern recognition, inhibit approach behaviors that limbic systems continue to motivate. Inhibition occurs through neural mechanisms shaped by evolution and refined through practice. Nothing violates physical law. Everything follows from prior causes.

But something genuinely novel occurred. The behavioral possibility of not approaching despite attraction only became available through recursive observation, creating explicit representations that enabled new causal pathways. Without metacognitive monitoring, the causal chain runs directly from attraction to approach. With metacognitive monitoring, new intervention points emerge in the causal structure, allowing control systems to redirect behavior based on explicit pattern recognition.

The recursion extends further. The woman observes herself choosing not to approach. "I am noticing attraction but not acting on it." This creates another explicit representation. She can now recognize this as an instance of successful pattern modification. "I am changing my behavioral response to this type of attraction." Recognition enables further causal possibilities. She can reinforce the control strategy through positive evaluation. She can remember this success for future similar situations. She can share the strategy with others facing similar patterns.

Each level of recursive observation generates new information, enabling new causal pathways within the cognitive system. The information doesn't operate through mysterious non-physical causation. It operates through entirely physical neural mechanisms, transmitting information between regions operating at different levels of the processing hierarchy. But the hierarchical organization creates genuine novelty in causal structure.

This is what consciousness adds to deterministic causal processes: the possibility of recursive monitoring that creates exponentially expanding causal possibilities through entirely deterministic mechanisms operating within the laws of nature. Self-creation is genuine because the recursive architecture creates behavioral possibilities that wouldn't exist without conscious observation, even though everything operates through deterministic causation shaped by evolution and development.

The woman genuinely created new behavioral patterns. Not ex nihilo from nothing. Not through exemption from causation. But through recursive monitoring of existing patterns that created new causal possibilities by making implicit processes explicit and subject to conscious evaluation and modification.

The river cannot do this. No matter how complex the hydrological system becomes, it cannot observe itself flowing and modify its course based on observation. Rivers lack the recursive architecture that makes observation causally relevant. The observation changes nothing because rivers don't have hierarchical processing systems where higher levels monitor and regulate lower levels based on explicit representations of current states.

Human consciousness possesses such architecture. This makes all the difference between mechanical self-organization, which occurs through deterministic processes, and genuine self-creation, which also occurs through deterministic processes, enabling recursive participation in causal structure modification.

The difference is not supernatural intervention versus mechanical necessity. The difference lies in recursive monitoring, which creates new causal possibilities, versus non-recursive causation that follows fixed pathways. Both operate deterministically. But recursive systems create genuine novelty in causal structure through consciousness, making implicit processes explicit and subject to evaluation and modification.

Consider what this means in detail. Every time the woman practices recognizing attraction without automatically approaching, she strengthens neural connections between pattern recognition systems and behavioral inhibition systems. This strengthening occurs through entirely deterministic mechanisms called synaptic plasticity. Neurons that fire together wire together. The connections become more reliable through repeated activation.

However, what makes this creation more than a mere mechanism is that she consciously practices the pattern. She deliberately puts herself in situations where attraction might arise. She intentionally focuses on recognition rather than automatic response. She systematically evaluates her success and adjusts her strategies based on results. Each of these conscious choices triggers deterministic neural processes that modify her brain's causal architecture in specific directions.

The modification follows from conscious choices even though the choices themselves operate deterministically. This is recursive creation, with consciousness observing processes, evaluating them against values and goals, implementing modifications based on those evaluations, observing results, and refining approaches. Each step operates deterministically. Yet the overall process produces genuine novelty in behavioral possibilities by systematically modifying the causal architecture through which future choices will emerge.

The woman, three years later, possesses a different causal architecture than she possessed before. Her neural pathways connecting attraction recognition to behavioral choice operate differently. Her capacity for inhibiting automatic responses has strengthened through practice. Her pattern recognition across relationships has become more sophisticated through accumulated experience evaluated consciously. Her understanding of her own psychology has deepened through sustained metacognitive observation.

None of this required exemption from causation. All of it occurred through natural deterministic mechanisms. Yet all of it constitutes genuine creation because recursive observation enabled systematic modification of causal structure in directions that wouldn't occur through unconscious processes alone.

This resolves the paradox that opened the chapter. Self-creation proves coherent in deterministic systems when those systems possess recursive architectures enabling conscious participation in their own causal organization. The creation is genuine because recursion creates causal possibilities that didn't exist before conscious observation. The self is genuine because the recursive architecture operates as an integrated system rather than as a separate observer and observed. The determinism remains complete because everything operates through natural mechanisms shaped by evolution.

The resolution requires abandoning libertarian fantasies about exemption from causation while rejecting hard determinist elimination of genuine creation. What emerges is a naturalistic account of self-creation as a sophisticated expression of recursive natural processes rather than supernatural intervention or mechanical illusion.

The Nature of Natural Creation

Understanding self-creation as recursive participation in natural causal processes transforms what it means to be human without requiring supernatural exemptions or accepting mechanistic reduction.

We are not authors in the sense libertarians imagined, standing outside the causal order creating our characters from nothing through uncaused choices. Such authorship is impossible, incoherent, and not even desirable upon examination. The libertarian author would be arbitrary rather than rational, random rather than purposeful, disconnected from everything, making genuine agency valuable. A choice uncaused by character, values, reasoning, or any prior factors would be no more the agent's choice than a cosmic dice roll that happened to occur in their brain.

But neither are we mere mechanisms in the sense that hard determinists suggest, sophisticated machines that witness our operation without influencing outcomes. This fundamentally misunderstands what consciousness does in recursive systems. The observation is not epiphenomenal. The recursion creates causal possibilities that distinguish conscious from unconscious systems in ways that matter profoundly for agency.

What we are is something that traditional categories cannot capture: nature's capacity for recursive self-organization, which creates genuine novelty through conscious participation in causal processes. This represents an evolutionary achievement rather than a supernatural gift, but it creates something unprecedented in natural history.

When someone engages in temporal scaffolding to modify their behavior systematically, they participate consciously in causal processes that determine their future states. The participation matters not because it exempts them from causation but because recursive observation creates causal paths that wouldn't exist without it. They become co-authors of their own development, rather than sole authors, writing new chapters in a story whose earlier chapters they didn't write, but whose direction they can influence through a conscious understanding of narrative patterns.

This co-authorship with nature eliminates the impossible burden of ultimate self-creation that libertarian frameworks impose while preserving everything worth wanting in human agency. You don't need to have created yourself from nothing to take legitimate pride in who you've become through sustained effort. You don't need ultimate origination to bear genuine responsibility for choices that follow from capacities you've cultivated through conscious practice.

The naturalization transforms our relationship with necessity. Libertarians often treat necessity as the enemy of freedom, suggesting that anything causally determined cannot be truly free. This created permanent tension between science revealing causal determination and morality requiring freedom, forcing an impossible choice between scientific honesty and moral meaning.

But once we recognize freedom as conscious participation in causal processes rather than exemption from them, necessity becomes the ground of freedom rather than its negation. The reliable causal patterns that determinism describes make temporal scaffolding possible. Without causation operating reliably, present efforts cannot systematically influence future outcomes through predictable mechanisms. The very necessity libertarians feared proves essential for the only form of freedom worth wanting.

This idea resonates with Nietzsche's *amor fati*, or love of fate, but it grounds the concept in actual mechanisms rather than treating it as a call for passive acceptance. When you understand how present choices shape future character through causal processes that you can consciously guide, you come to love fate not as a mysterious decree but as a reliable structure that makes systematic self-development possible through active participation.

Someone who grasps this deeply experiences liberation rather than constraint in recognizing causal determination. The recognition doesn't eliminate agency but reveals how agency truly operates through natural mechanisms you can understand and deploy skillfully.

You become free not by exempting yourself from nature but by understanding nature well enough to participate consciously in its creative processes operating through you.

This is what Nietzsche meant by self-overcoming, but he could never fully articulate it because he lacked the cognitive science revealing how self-overcoming works. The will to power is not a mysterious metaphysical force transcending natural causation. It is the natural capacity for recursive self-organization that enables conscious participation in behavioral development through entirely deterministic mechanisms.

Nietzsche was right that self-overcoming represents life's fundamental drive. He was right that this drive operates through natural processes rather than supernatural intervention. He was right that genuine self-creation requires affirming necessity rather than seeking exemption from it. But he couldn't explain the mechanisms because the neuroscience revealing recursive architectures didn't exist in his time.

We can now see more clearly what Nietzsche intuited. Self-overcoming takes place through nature's capacity to participate consciously in its own development. A person who systematically cultivates capacities beyond present limitations engages in a form of self-overcoming that is both natural process and genuine creation. It is natural because it works through deterministic mechanisms shaped by evolution. It is creation because recursive monitoring introduces new causal possibilities that did not exist before conscious observation.

This creates genuine responsibility that goes deeper than libertarian accounts, despite operating through entirely deterministic mechanisms. You are responsible not because you created yourself ex nihilo but because you possess and can develop capacities for conscious participation in causal processes that shape your becoming. The responsibility grows with capacity, explaining graduated patterns that traditional frameworks struggle to accommodate.

Someone with minimal metacognitive awareness and limited environmental resources bears less responsibility than someone with sophisticated self-observation capacities and favorable circumstances enabling systematic scaffolding. Not because the first person possesses less libertarian freedom, which no one possesses, but because they possess less capacity for the kind of conscious causal participation that constitutes genuine agency.

Yet even minimal capacity creates some responsibility, because even basic conscious observation of behavioral patterns opens up causal possibilities that remain closed to unconscious systems. The responsibility scales with capacity rather than existing in binary present/absent states libertarians assume.

This explains why we appropriately reduce responsibility for actions flowing from severe trauma, mental illness, or developmental impairment. These conditions compromise recursive capacity, preventing the kind of conscious observation and systematic modification that grounds responsibility. The person retains consciousness but loses or never develops the recursive architecture enabling effective temporal scaffolding.

Someone whose trauma prevents metacognitive observation of their patterns, whose mental illness disrupts the neural connections between monitoring and regulatory systems, whose developmental impairment never allowed recursive capacities to develop, these people possess reduced responsibility because they possess reduced capacity for the conscious causal participation that creates genuine agency.

Understanding self-creation as recursive participation in causal processes preserves moral responsibility while remaining completely consistent with scientific understanding of behavior. No conflict arises between determinism and agency because agency is naturalized as a sophisticated deterministic process rather than an exemption from determinism.

Most profoundly, this framework reveals human existence as simultaneously humbling and exalting in ways neither traditional libertarianism nor hard determinism captured. Humbling because we are not gods creating ourselves from nothing, not supernatural authors standing above the natural order. We are natural systems operating through natural mechanisms, subject to natural laws, just like everything else in the universe.

But exalting because we represent nature's first achievement of recursive self-organization sophisticated enough to consciously participate in its own development. Billions of years of evolution produced unconscious processes of remarkable complexity. But only with human consciousness did nature become capable of observing and modifying its own operations through recursive architectures enabling genuine novelty despite complete causal determination.

We are not separate from nature, achieving something nature cannot. We are nature achieving something through us that nature couldn't achieve through unconscious processes alone. The achievement belongs to the universe's creative processes operating through the particular configuration of matter that constitutes human consciousness.

This eliminates alienation created by both libertarian and determinist frameworks. Libertarians locate genuine agency outside nature, creating permanent separation between human freedom and natural causation. Hard determinists eliminate agency by reducing humans to machines, creating a different separation between conscious experience and mechanical reality. Both frameworks render us strangers to nature, whether as supernatural exceptions to it or as mechanical products of it.

The naturalization of self-creation reveals us as fully natural beings whose remarkable capacities flow directly from our natural origins. We are not alienated from nature by consciousness but represent nature's highest achievement of conscious self-organization. Our freedom emerges through natural processes, and our creativity expresses nature's creative capacity, without requiring supernatural intervention.

The Recursive Unity

Individual self-creation and collective cognitive evolution represent one process operating at different scales through the same recursive mechanisms, enabling conscious participation in development.

When someone engages temporal scaffolding at the individual level, they deploy metacognitive awareness to observe behavioral patterns, identify factors maintaining problematic behaviors, design interventions modifying those factors, implement changes systematically, observe results, and refine approaches based on outcomes. This entire process operates through recursive monitoring, creating causal possibilities that wouldn't exist without conscious observation.

Collective cognitive evolution operates through an identical recursive structure at the species level. Humanity observes its own developmental patterns through historical analysis and scientific investigation. We identify the cultural and technological factors that shape collective psychology across generations. We design interventions at an institutional scale, modifying those factors. We implement changes through educational systems, legal frameworks, technological development, and media environments. We observe results through social science research. We refine approaches based on accumulated evidence.

The recursion at the collective level creates causal possibilities for human development that couldn't exist without species-level conscious observation. Just as individual metacognitive awareness enables behavioral possibilities that are impossible for unconscious animals, collective scientific and historical awareness enables developmental trajectories that are impossible for unconscious cultural evolution operating through blind variation and natural selection.

The same philosophical problem and resolution apply at both scales. How can collective self-direction constitute genuine creation rather than mechanical cultural evolution when everything operates through causal processes determined by prior states? The answer is the same: recursive observation creates genuine novelty in causal structure. Humanity consciously participating in its own evolution creates developmental possibilities that unconscious cultural variation and selection cannot produce, regardless of time available.

The two scales interact continuously through mechanisms that create feedback loops between individual and collective development. Individual innovations in temporal scaffolding spread through cultural transmission, becoming collective knowledge that enables more sophisticated individual practices. Collective institutional designs either support or undermine individual capacity development, shaping what becomes possible on a personal scale.

The woman who broke her destructive relationship patterns benefited from collective knowledge accumulated across generations. The therapeutic techniques she learned emerged from decades of clinical research investigating what helps people change. The metacognitive frameworks she deployed were developed through centuries of philosophical and psychological investigation into human consciousness. The social support that allowed her sustained effort depended on cultural values that stressed personal development and institutional structures that made therapy accessible.

Her individual self-creation occurred within collective contexts, providing the conceptual tools, practical methods, and social resources, making systematic behavioral modification possible. Remove the collective context, and her individual efforts would lack the cultural scaffolding enabling effective change.

Conversely, her individual innovation contributes to collective development. She developed specific techniques for recognizing and interrupting her patterns that might prove useful for others facing similar challenges. She learned what works in her circumstances, adding to the collective knowledge about behavioral modification across diverse situations. Her success demonstrates possibilities for change that others might doubt without concrete examples.

Neither individual nor collective development can proceed effectively without the other because they represent interdependent aspects of recursive natural processes rather than separate domains requiring choice between individual and collective priorities.

This integration eliminates false dichotomies fragmenting understanding. Nature versus culture dissolves into recognition that culture is how nature organized itself through linguistic and technological innovations, subsequently permitting new forms of collective information transmission. Cultural evolution is a form of biological evolution that continues through new mechanisms rather than transcending biological processes.

Individual versus social dissolves into recognition of recursive processes operating at multiple scales simultaneously. The individual developing sophisticated self-modification capacities does so through cultural knowledge transmitted socially. The society developing better institutional supports for individual capacity does so through individual innovations that spread collectively.

Freedom versus determinism dissolves into recognition that freedom is conscious participation in deterministic causal processes rather than exemption from them. The reliable causation libertarians feared proves essential for the only form of freedom worth wanting.

The naturalization provides a unified framework for understanding human existence from individual psychology to collective history as expressions of recursive natural processes enabling conscious self-organization. We don't need separate explanations for biological evolution, cultural development, individual agency, and collective progress. All reflect the same fundamental capacity for recursive organization.

This unity doesn't eliminate real tensions requiring careful navigation. Democratic versus aristocratic approaches to collective development create genuine conflicts that cannot be resolved philosophically but require empirical investigation and political choice. Individual autonomy versus collective welfare creates real dilemmas requiring careful balancing. Enhancement versus equality raises genuine questions about promoting human flourishing while respecting diversity and preventing the creation of new hierarchies.

But these genuine tensions differ from pseudoproblems created by false philosophical oppositions. The question is not whether we are free or determined but how to develop and deploy our actual capacities for conscious participation in causal processes. Not whether culture transcends nature, but how to organize cultural practices working with rather than against natural psychological mechanisms. Not whether individual or collective matters more, but how to create conditions where individual and collective development enhance rather than undermine each other.

The Transformation

The question that opened this work transforms entirely once we understand agency as a natural capacity for recursive self-organization through conscious participation in causal processes.

The question was never "Could we have chosen otherwise at the instant of decision?" That question generates pseudoproblems by assuming libertarian requirements for freedom that nothing could satisfy without incoherence. An uncaused choice would be random rather than rational, arbitrary rather than expressive of character and values, disconnected from everything making genuine agency valuable.

The question is "What if freedom were not the absence of chains, but the forging of better ones?" Or perhaps we can now reframe this as, "What capacities do we possess for systematically constructing the conditions under which decisions occur through conscious participation in causal processes shaping our development?"

This question lends itself to answers grounded in empirical investigation rather than metaphysical speculation. We possess metacognitive capacities for observing our own psychological processes through hierarchical neural architectures that evolved. We possess linguistic capacities for representing temporal patterns and constructing plans across extended horizons. We possess social capacities for cooperative transmission of knowledge about effective self-modification. We possess technological capacities for creating environments that either support or undermine individual development.

Each capacity can be systematically cultivated through practice and social support. Metacognitive awareness strengthens through meditation, contemplative practices, and therapeutic work, all of which teach systematic self-observation. Temporal reasoning improves through education, emphasizing planning skills, future orientation, and long-term thinking. Social cooperation benefits from institutional designs enabling effective collective action. Technological development can be directed toward augmenting rather than replacing human capacities through conscious choices about research priorities and design principles.

The transformed question reveals human agency as an ongoing achievement requiring sustained effort rather than a fixed property we either possess or lack. Agency develops through systematic cultivation of capacities existing as potential requiring appropriate conditions for actualization. The development never completes because circumstances change, new challenges arise, and capacities that sufficed previously become inadequate as complexity increases.

This creates both responsibility and possibility. Responsibility to consciously develop the capacities we possess in potential rather than remaining passive to whatever conditioning happens to occur. Possibility for continued enhancement beyond current limitations through systematic application of temporal scaffolding and collective institutional design.

The woman sitting alone after her therapy session can now answer the question that haunted her. Yes, she created herself through three years of conscious effort. Not ex nihilo from nothing. Not through exemption from causation. But through recursive participation in causal processes that shaped her development in directions that wouldn't have occurred through unconscious mechanisms alone.

Every factor enabling her self-creation was itself determined by prior causes beyond her initial control. But those prior causes created in her the capacity for recursive self-organization that enabled conscious participation in her own becoming. The participation created genuine novelty in her behavioral possibilities through mechanisms operating entirely within natural law.

She is both product and producer, created and creating, determined and determining, through recursive processes, distinguishing human consciousness from everything that came before in evolutionary history. Determination doesn't eliminate creation. The creation operates through determination by deploying recursive architectures that consciousness makes possible.

This is what it means to be human. We are not gods standing apart from nature, creating ourselves from nothing. We are not machines passively observing our own operation. We are recursive natural processes that enable conscious participation in our own development, generating genuine novelty while operating entirely through evolution-shaped causation.

The ghost in the machine dissolves into recognition that there never was a ghost requiring explanation. Only recursive natural processes sophisticated enough to create the illusion of supernatural agency by enabling conscious participation in development through mechanisms that traditional categories couldn't capture.

We are not ghosts inhabiting machines. We are machines that become conscious of their own operations and are capable of modifying those operations through recursive observation. We are nature's experiment in recursive self-organization, the universe's first instance of matter organized complexly enough that it can observe and modify its own organization through consciousness emerging from, yet transcending, the material processes that create it through recursion.

This naturalization eliminates mystery without eliminating meaning. Human existence becomes no less significant for being fully natural. Our agency becomes no less genuine for operating through deterministic mechanisms. Our creativity becomes no less remarkable for expressing nature's creative capacity rather than standing apart from it through supernatural intervention.

What proves most profound is recognizing that self-creation through temporal scaffolding represents not transcendence of our natural condition but its fullest expression. We become most fully ourselves not by escaping nature, but by consciously participating in the natural processes through which nature continues to create itself through us.

The capacity for such participation is itself natural, emerging through evolution that operates unconsciously over time. But the exercise of that capacity constitutes nature becoming conscious of its own creative potential and participating deliberately in its own continued elaboration through recursive processes to create genuine novelty.

This is the ghost in the machine reconsidered. It is not a supernatural exemption from causation, but rather a natural capacity for recursive self-organization that allows for conscious participation in becoming. Not an exemption from nature but nature's highest achievement in conscious self-creation operating through deterministic mechanisms that create genuine novelty through recursion, impossible for non-recursive systems regardless of their complexity.

We discover ourselves as simultaneously created and creating, determined and determining, products of evolutionary history and authors of developmental futures, natural systems achieving something unprecedented in natural history through capacities that are themselves products of that history operating through us.

The question that has tortured philosophy since its inception dissolves not through choosing one horn of an impossible dilemma, but by recognizing that the dilemma itself rests on confused assumptions about what nature permits and what consciousness achieves. Human freedom becomes real when we engage it. Human agency emerges genuinely through practice. Human creativity proves authentic in its exercise. All depend on natural capacities whose structure creates possibilities that must be actualized through practice, not merely understood in theory.

The recognition transforms everything about how we understand ourselves while changing nothing about what we are. We are nature's capacity for conscious self-transformation operating through recursive processes that create genuine novelty while remaining entirely natural. This is what we are. This is all we need to be. This is enough.

Further Reading and Selected Bibliography

The following list includes key thinkers and foundational texts discussed in this book, offering resources for readers who wish to explore these concepts in greater depth.

Primary Philosophical Sources

Aristotle. *Nicomachean Ethics*. Translated by Terence Irwin. 2nd ed. Indianapolis: Hackett Publishing, 1999. The foundational text for virtue ethics, discussing voluntary action, character development (*hexis*), the doctrine of the mean, and rational choice (*prohairesis*).

Aurelius, Marcus. *Meditations*. Translated by Gregory Hays. New York: Modern Library, 2002. A core text of Stoic philosophy, exemplifying the practice of aligning one's inner attitudes with a rational understanding of natural necessity and fate.

Descartes, René. *Discourse on Method and Meditations on First Philosophy*. Translated by Donald A. Cress. 4th ed. Indianapolis: Hackett Publishing, 1998. These works establish Cartesian dualism, the *cogito* argument, and a systematic method for rational inquiry that influenced modern philosophy.

Epictetus. *Discourses and Selected Writings*. Translated by Robert Dobbin. London: Penguin Classics, 2008. As a leading Stoic philosopher, his work details the distinction between what is "up to us" (our judgments and attitudes) and what is not, and outlines the disciplines of assent, action, and desire.

Nietzsche, Friedrich. *Beyond Good and Evil*. Translated by Walter Kaufmann. New York: Vintage Books, 1989.

———. *Thus Spoke Zarathustra*. Translated by Adrian Del Caro. Cambridge: Cambridge University Press, 2006. His concepts of the "will to power" and "self-overcoming" (*Übermensch*) provide a philosophical framework for understanding human development as a process of transcending limitations, though he rejected democratic and egalitarian values.

Spinoza, Baruch. *Ethics*. Translated by Edwin Curley. London: Penguin Classics, 1996. Presents a monistic and deterministic system that resolves the mind-body problem by treating thought and extension as attributes of a single substance (God or Nature). The work argues that true freedom comes from an intellectual understanding of necessity.

Contemporary Free Will & Moral Responsibility

Blackburn, Simon. *Ruling Passions: A Theory of Practical Reasoning*. Oxford: Oxford University Press, 1998. A leading proponent of quasi-realism, his theories explain how moral discourse can function as if it were describing objective facts while remaining fundamentally an expression of attitudes and commitments.

Chalmers, David J. *The Conscious Mind: In Search of a Fundamental Theory*. Oxford: Oxford University Press, 1996. Known for formulating the "hard problem of consciousness," which distinguishes the challenge of explaining subjective experience from the "easy problems" of explaining cognitive functions.

Fischer, John Martin, and **Mark Ravizza**. *Responsibility and Control: A Theory of Moral Responsibility*. Cambridge: Cambridge University Press, 1998. They develop a prominent compatibilist theory known as "guidance control," which argues that moral responsibility requires that an agent's actions issue from a "reasons-responsive" mechanism that they have taken ownership of through an appropriate history.

Frankfurt, Harry G. "Alternate Possibilities and Moral Responsibility." *Journal of Philosophy* 66, no. 23 (1969): 829–39.

———. "Freedom of the Will and the Concept of a Person." *Journal of Philosophy* 68, no. 1 (1971): 5–20. Frankfurt is a key figure in compatibilism, known for his hierarchical model of the will (identification with one's desires) and for his thought experiments ("Frankfurt cases") arguing that moral responsibility does not require the ability to do otherwise.

Gibbard, Allan. *Wise Choices, Apt Feelings: A Theory of Normative Judgment*. Cambridge, MA: Harvard University Press, 1990. A leading proponent of norm-expressivism, arguing that moral and normative judgments express the acceptance of systems of norms for feeling, action, and belief, which serve to coordinate social life.

Kane, Robert. *The Significance of Free Will*. Oxford: Oxford University Press, 1996. A leading contemporary defender of libertarian free will, Kane proposes a model centered on "self-forming actions" (SFAs) where quantum indeterminacy in the brain plays a role in decisions during moments of moral conflict.

Kim, Jaegwon. *Mind in a Physical World: An Essay on the Mind-Body Problem and Mental Causation.* Cambridge, MA: MIT Press, 1998. Famous for formulating the "causal exclusion argument," a major challenge for non-reductive physicalism that questions how mental events can have causal power if their underlying physical events already have complete physical causes.

Levy, Neil. *Hard Luck: How Luck Undermines Free Will and Moral Responsibility.* Oxford: Oxford University Press, 2011. A proponent of source incompatibilism, Levy argues that since we are not responsible for the psychological capacities (like empathy or self-regulation) that underpin our actions, we cannot be ultimately responsible for the actions themselves.

McKenna, Michael. *Conversation and Responsibility.* Oxford: Oxford University Press, 2012. A significant contributor to compatibilist theory and the free will debate, particularly regarding source incompatibilism and the conversational nature of responsibility practices.

Mele, Alfred R. *Free Will and Luck.* Oxford: Oxford University Press, 2006. Mele has written extensively on free will, action theory, and manipulation arguments. His work often clarifies and challenges existing positions, and he is known for developing sharp thought experiments that test the limits of compatibilist theories.

Nagel, Thomas. "Moral Luck." In *Mortal Questions*, 24–38. Cambridge: Cambridge University Press, 1979.

———. "What Is It Like to Be a Bat?" *Philosophical Review* 83, no. 4 (1974): 435–50. Nagel's work highlights the explanatory gap between subjective consciousness and objective science and explores the paradoxes of "moral luck," where responsibility is attributed to agents for outcomes beyond their control.

Nahmias, Eddy, and **Derrick Murray**, eds. *Is Free Will an Illusion? Confronting Challenges from the Modern Mind Sciences*. Oxford: Oxford University Press, 2023. A prominent experimental philosopher who has conducted studies on folk intuitions about free will, determinism, and moral responsibility, often finding that people's intuitions are more compatibilist than traditional philosophers have assumed.

Nichols, Shaun. *Sentimental Rules: On the Natural Foundations of Moral Judgment*. Oxford: Oxford University Press, 2004. A key figure in experimental philosophy, his cross-cultural and developmental research explores how folk concepts of free will and moral rules are shaped by cultural factors and evolved psychological mechanisms.

O'Connor, Timothy. *Persons and Causes: The Metaphysics of Free Will*. Oxford: Oxford University Press, 2000. A leading defender of agent-causal libertarianism, which posits that agents are enduring substances who can initiate new causal chains that are not determined by prior events.

Pereboom, Derk. *Living Without Free Will*. Cambridge: Cambridge University Press, 2001. A prominent advocate for hard incompatibilism, Pereboom uses "four-case arguments" to systematically argue that the kind of free will required for ultimate moral responsibility is incompatible with both determinism and indeterminism.

Strawson, P. F. "Freedom and Resentment." *Proceedings of the British Academy* 48 (1962): 1–25. A landmark essay that shifted the free will debate by arguing that our "reactive attitudes" (like resentment and gratitude) are a natural and indispensable part of human life, making the metaphysical truth of determinism largely irrelevant to the practice of holding one another responsible.

Waller, Bruce N. *Against Moral Responsibility*. Cambridge, MA: MIT Press, 2011. Waller argues against moral responsibility from a naturalistic perspective, contending that since no one is ultimately responsible for their character or psychological capacities, no one can deserve praise or blame.

Wolf, Susan. *Freedom Within Reason*. Oxford: Oxford University Press, 1990. Wolf offers a compatibilist view where freedom requires the ability to act in accordance with the "True and the Good"; that is, the ability to recognize and be guided by moral reasons.

Key Scientific Studies

Asch, Solomon E. "Opinions and Social Pressure." *Scientific American* 193, no. 5 (1955): 31–35. The Asch conformity experiments demonstrated how group pressure can lead individuals to give incorrect answers even when they know the correct one, highlighting the power of situational factors on behavior.

Darley, John M., and **C. Daniel Batson**. "'From Jerusalem to Jericho': A Study of Situational and Dispositional Variables in Helping Behavior." *Journal of Personality and Social Psychology* 27, no. 1 (1973): 100–108. This classic experiment with seminary students found that situational factors (like being in a hurry) were a better predictor of helping behavior than personal religious or moral commitments.

Milgram, Stanley. *Obedience to Authority: An Experimental View*. New York: Harper & Row, 1974. The Milgram experiments on obedience to authority showed that ordinary people are capable of inflicting severe harm on others when instructed to do so by an authority figure, emphasizing the influence of the situation over individual character.

Zimbardo, Philip G. *The Lucifer Effect: Understanding How Good People Turn Evil*. New York: Random House, 2007. The Stanford prison experiment illustrated how quickly individuals conform to assigned social roles (prisoner or guard), leading to extreme behaviors and demonstrating the profound impact of situational power dynamics.

INDEX

Acceptance-based approaches, 112
Addiction
  drug courts and, 260–268
  manipulation and, 228
  neural mechanisms, 344–345
  temporal scaffolding in recovery, 129–130
  unwilling vs. willing addict, 24–26
ADHD (Attention Deficit Hyperactivity Disorder), 269–275
Agency
  collective, 284–292, 358–362
  distributed, 237–247
  graduated levels of, 60–62
  natural capacity for, 351–357
  reactive vs. reflective, 60–61
Agricultural revolution, 298–300
Algorithm manipulation, 306–310
Amor fati, 353
Anterior cingulate cortex, 100, 183–185
Aristotle, 1, 65–71, 232
Artificial intelligence, 311–313
Asch conformity experiments, 18
Assessment, capacity-based, 255–259
Attachment patterns, 127–131
Attention regulation, 110–111
Authenticity, 228–231

Behavioral modification
  environmental design and, 114–115
  hierarchical interventions, 113–116
  resistance to, 150–155
Binary responsibility, collapse of, 251–254
Blackburn, Simon, 207
Brain development, 197–200
Brain-computer interfaces, 337–339

Causal exclusion argument, 44–48
Chalmers, David, 180
Character development, 68–71
Chimpanzee cognition, 132–134, 214
Chrysippus, 72, 75–76
Cognitive-behavioral therapy (CBT), 280–281
Cognitive decentering, 110–111
Collective responsibility, 237–247
Compatibilism
  Frankfurt's hierarchical model, 24–26
  identification criteria, 166–169
  manipulation arguments against, 29–36
  Strawson's reactive attitudes, 27–29
  traditional failures of, 22–36
  Wolf's reason-responsiveness, 26–27
Compulsive behavior, 276–280
Consciousness
  emergent properties of, 180–182, 340–343
  evolution of, 91–98
  hierarchical nature of, 176–179
  as recursive observation, 343–351

Constitutive luck, 235–237
Criminal justice, 260–268
Cultural evolution, 213–222, 295–304

Default mode network, 101, 185–188
Democracy, 305–310
Descartes, René, 77–83
Determinism, hard
  defeat of, 162–166
  Pereboom's arguments, 15–17
  self-refutation of, 19–20
  Waller's critique, 17–19
Developmental stages, 197–200
Dialectical behavior therapy (DBT), 281
Dignity-based systems, 219–220
Donne, John, 174
Dopamine, 189–192
Drug courts, 260–268

Educational systems
  capacity development in, 272–276
  graduated responsibility in, 269–276
  social-emotional learning, 273–275
  uniform assumptions in, 269–276
Elisabeth of Bohemia, Princess, 81
Emergence
  mystical escape via, 340–343
  strong vs. weak, 47–49, 341–342
Emotional regulation, 111–112
Emotions, evolved, 208–213
Environmental modification, 114–115, 153–154
Epictetus, 72–75
Error detection, 184–185
Evolution
  of consciousness, 91–98, 132–139
  cultural-cognitive coevolution, 295–304
  of metacognition, 134–139
  of moral emotions, 208–213
Executive control networks, 101–102
Experimental philosophy, 36–44
Expressivism, 203–247

Fischer, John Martin, 34–35, 231
Frankfurt, Harry, 24–26, 224–228
Frankfurt cases, 224–228
Free will (see also Libertarianism)
  as false dichotomy, 1–6
  historical burden of, 54–56

Gene-culture coevolution, 296–304
Genetic modification, 337
Gibbard, Allan, 206
Good Samaritan study, 18
Graduated responsibility
  framework for, 248–292
  in criminal justice, 260–268
  in education, 269–276
  in institutions, 249–259
  in therapy, 276–284
Guilt, evolutionary function of, 211–213

Hierarchical model of will, 24–26
Homunculus fallacy, 176–179
Honor-based systems, 218–219

Identity-level interventions, 115
Illusion of conscious will, 55
Impulse regulation, 256–257
Indigenous cultures, 38

Infinite regress, 173–176
Institutional design, 249–259
Interaction problem, 81–82
Interventionist causation, 51–54, 104–105

Kane, Robert, 9–11
Kim, Jaegwon, 44–48
Knobe, Joshua, 36–38

Language
  cognitive transformation via, 140–149
  recursive capacity of, 144–145
  temporal reference in, 141–142
Legal pluralism, 268–269
Levy, Neil, 32–33
Libertarianism
  agent-causal theories, 10
  impossibility of, 6–12
  Kane's self-forming actions, 9–11
  neuroscientific challenges to, 8–9
  O'Connor's substance dualism, 10
Literacy, cognitive effects of, 300–302
Luck, moral, 72–74, 233–237

Manipulation arguments, 29–36, 228–231
Marcus Aurelius, 72, 76–77
McKenna, Michael, 32
Meditation, 52–54, 105, 150–155
Mele, Alfred, 30–31
Mental causation
  evolutionary perspective on, 102–105
  hard problem of, 43–54
  interventionist approaches to, 51–54

Kim's exclusion argument, 44–48
  non-reductive physicalism and, 49–51
Mental time travel, 143–144, 185–188
Metacognition
  architecture of, 99–102
  development of, 106–113, 197–200
  evolution of, 91–98, 134–139
  expert levels of, 108–110
  three levels of, 106–108
Metacognitive compatibilism
  defined, 3–4
  foundation of, 63–90
  hierarchical structure of, 173–202
Milgram experiments, 18
Moral emotions, 208–213
Moral luck, 72–74, 233–237

Nagel, Thomas, 180, 235
Nahmias, Eddy, 39–40
Narrative self, 120–121
Neural networks, 99–102, 138–139
Neurochemistry, 189–196
Neuroplasticity, 122, 198–200
Neuroscience
  of decision-making, 8–9
  of self-observation, 99–102, 183–188
Nichols, Shaun, 36–38
Nietzsche, Friedrich, 317–322, 353–354
Non-reductive physicalism, 49–51
Norepinephrine, 195–196

O'Connor, Timothy, 10
Observer paradox, 116–119, 173–176

Pereboom, Derk, 15–17, 31–32

Pharmaceutical interventions, 193–194, 337
Plasticity, neural, 122, 198–200
Prefrontal cortex, 99–100, 138–139
Pride, moral, 213
Prohairesis, 70–71

Quantum indeterminacy, 9–11
Quasi-realism, 207

Ravizza, Mark, 34–35, 231
Reactive attitudes, 20, 27–29
Recursive control, 116–119
Recursive observation, 343–351, 358–362
Resentment, 212–213
Responsibility (see Graduated responsibility; Moral responsibility)
Restorative justice, 266–268
Resultant luck, 235–236

Salience network, 101
Scaffolding (see Temporal scaffolding)
Scientific method, 302–305
Self
    distributed model of, 121
    emergent hypothesis, 119–120
    narrative construction of, 120–121
    paradox of self-modifying, 119–122
Self-creation, natural, 327–367
Self-modification criterion, 222–237
Seminary study (Good Samaritan), 18
Serotonin, 193–195
Social accountability, 146–147
Social cognition, evolution of, 132–134

Social-emotional learning, 273–275
Socialization vs. manipulation, 167, 228–231
Socioeconomic factors, 284–289
Source incompatibilism, 32–33
Spinoza, Baruch, 83–90
Stanford prison experiment, 18
Stoicism, 72–77
Strawson, P.F., 20, 27–29

Technology
    and cognitive evolution, 308–316
    as false solution, 337–340
Temporal reasoning, 257
Temporal scaffolding
    defined, 3
    development of, 60–62
    in everyday life, 127–131
    mechanisms of, 126–131, 150–162
    neural basis of, 183–188
    recursive nature of, 116–119
Theory of mind, 134–136
Therapeutic approaches
    capacity-building in, 276–284
    evasion via restoration, 333–336
    expert-driven vs. collaborative, 282–284
    graduated responsibility in, 276–284
Thermostat analogy, 177–179
Trauma
    and capacity development, 168–169
    and responsibility, 221, 355–356

Ultimate origination, 5, 156–162
Universality of moral emotions, 208–211

Virtue ethics, 65–71

Waller, Bruce, 17–19
Weakness of will, 232–234
Will to power, 318, 354

Wolf, Susan, 26–27
Working memory, 139
Writing systems, cognitive effects of, 300–302

Zimbardo, Philip, 18

ABOUT THE AUTHOR

Joshua Robertson is an award-winning author of diverse titles, ranging from the bestselling Thrice Nine Legends Saga to compelling works of poetry, short fiction, and insightful non-fiction. His multifaceted career as an entrepreneur and life coach is further distinguished by a PhD in Philosophy and two decades of profound experience as a therapist, educator, and supervisor within behavioral health and child welfare systems. This unique fusion of creative storytelling, deep philosophical inquiry, and extensive real-world engagement offers readers a distinct and resonant voice across all his work. Joshua currently lives in North Carolina with his better half and his horde of goblins.

www.ingramcontent.com/pod-product-compliance
Lightning Source LLC
Chambersburg PA
CBHW070526090426
42735CB00013B/2875